INTERNATIONAL YEARBOOK COMMUNICATION DESIGN 2016/2017

[Edited by PETER ZEC]

VOL **1**

INTERNATIONAL YEARBOOK COMMUNICATION DESIGN 2016/2017

[Edited by PETER ZEC]

reddot award
communication design

VOL**1**

CONTENTS

Dear Readers,

We look back on a year full of tournaments and competitions. It was a sporting year, rounded off by the Olympic Games in Rio. There are some parallels between the Games and the Red Dot Award: the many different disciplines, the multicultural participants and, above all, the fact that each country's top ambassadors are present and the champions are crowned from their ranks.

However, there is one decisive methodological difference between the global sporting tournaments and our international design award. Evaluating design is much more complex than measuring speed or counting points. At the sporting events, individual athletes or teams compete against each other. Red Dot is interested in an individual assessment, with each of the entries evaluated one by one by the jury and tested for its respective design quality in the context of the market and the target groups.

The rationale behind this system is that it is rarely possible to compare individual communication design achievements. The website of an automobile manufacturer can be just as creative and user-friendly as that of an NGO, but the two are not comparable – particularly viewed against the standard of international communication design. From the trade fair stand of an IT company to that of a flower trader, from fruit packaging to wine packaging or a running app to a shopping app – there are endless directions, objectives and possibilities and therefore there is not only one best entry in each given category.

It is very fitting that Audi, the official vehicle supplier for the International Olympic Committee, is this year's winner of the special award "Red Dot: Brand of the Year", a title awarded since 2015. The company based in Ingolstadt can simply do no wrong at the moment when it comes to brand management. In this yearbook you will also read a lot about Serviceplan in particular: the largest partner-managed agency in Europe stands out with creative achievements that are superior not only in terms of quantity but also in terms of quality in virtually all areas of communication, from traditional advertising to digital creations or media. Serviceplan has been growing and flourishing for years now, also at an international level. The Red Dot jury was especially impressed by the results in 2016, awarding numerous Red Dots as well as four Red Dot: Best of the Best awards and one Red Dot: Grand Prix to Serviceplan, making the "House of Communication" the well-deserved winner of the honorary title "Red Dot: Agency of the Year 2016".

I hope that you will now enjoy reading about all the award winners in the Red Dot Award: Communication Design 2016!

Professor Dr. Peter Zec
Founder and CEO of Red Dot

RED DOT: AGENCY OF THE YEAR

SERVICEPLAN

Red Dot: Agency of the Year

Serviceplan was founded by Peter Haller and Rolf Stempel in Munich in 1970. Starting as an owner-managed communication agency, the company today operates as a partner-managed "House of Communication" that offers a full range of media services and brings together some 40 agencies under one roof. The groundwork for the current business model was laid as early as 1995, when the two managing directors turned Serviceplan into a holding company composed of a group of agencies. The model also prohibits that any of the partners' shares are sold to international agency networks. This change from an owner- to a partner-operated company proved to be a success. Today, about 40 companies working in creation and design, communication and brand management as well as media planning and marketing research are organised under the umbrella of the Serviceplan Group.

Florian Haller joined Serviceplan as manager of Unit 3 in 1996 and moved on to succeed his father in the company's management, becoming the CEO in 2002. Florian Haller promoted and set up the partner-led model and the concept of the "House of Communication" beyond the company's home base in Munich to other German cities, such as Hamburg, Frankfurt and Berlin. On a global level, Serviceplan has established its own agencies, affiliate partnerships and other strategic collaborations in cities like Amsterdam, Beijing, Bogotá, Brussels, Buenos Aires, Delhi, Dubai, Guayaquil, Hong Kong, Lima, London, Lyon, Madrid, Mexico City, Miami, Milan, Moscow, New York, Panama City, Paris, Quito, Rennes, Santiago de Chile, São Paulo, Seoul, Shanghai, Valencia, Vienna and Zurich. With more than 3,000 employees, the agency group is today represented in more than 35 major business locations and is the largest partner-managed and therefore independent agency group in Europe.

One of the partners is Alexander Schill, with whom we held the following interview. He joined Serviceplan in 2006, becoming CCO of the entire agency group only two years later. Though being anything but boastful and claiming to be "just an average guy", he is undoubtedly one of the most creative minds of the current agency and design scene. In 2016, he set up Serviceplan's "Creative Board", which is an independent team of experienced designers that oversees large-size budgets and clients across agencies, disciplines and countries. Together with Florian Haller, he is pursuing the goal of creating the first German international and independent agency group that operates worldwide.

Alexander Schill

WhatsGerman [Language-Learning App]
Red Dot: Best of the Best 2016

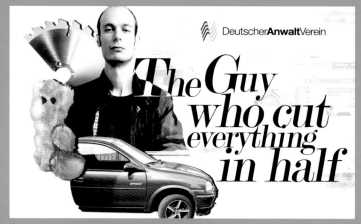

The Guy Who Cut Everything in Half [Digital Campaign]
Red Dot: Best of the Best 2016

Mr. Schill, the agency group Serviceplan likes to refer to itself as a "House of Communication". What idea do you associate with this term? And how is that different from a conventional advertising agency?

We don't even describe ourselves as an advertising agency any more. We are a house of communication that offers all services related to communication. Upon request, we also offer an all-round turnkey service. This might include the design and programming of a client's website, the development of a comprehensive media plan or the finding of strategic solutions to key business challenges.

What advantages does a "House of Communication" offer for the agency and its client?

Today, communication is infinitely more complex than it was only ten years ago. Whoever thinks they can do communication today with tools from back then won't be around for long. The issue today is to play a variety of chords in a coordinated and synchronised fashion. No one can get away with playing just one or three, as it was done in the 1980s. Today, as a client and contractee, you can either identify and network many individual smaller agencies, coordinate them on your own, and hope that they get on well together without too much rivalry and backbiting. Or else you can decide to commission a somewhat larger agency, meaning a house of communication in the broadest sense. In the latter case, you get all communication and media services from one source, seeing that all

processes are coordinated from the outset to synchronise and function smoothly. Both options are valid and there are good arguments for both of them. We opted for the second one.

What fascinates you personally about communication or advertising? Is the fascination today different than what it was ten or even 20 years ago?

If communication was still done the same way today than it was ten years ago, then I would no longer be in the game, that's for sure. What fascinates me about today's scene is that we can reach a huge number of people with a simple idea and pretty little media money. Using social media any run-of-the-mill admen can move things if they really want to. And change people's attitude towards a subject. It's fast and less complicated for us than for our chancellor, if you ask me.

Can you give an example?

Just think of works such as "Like a Girl" by Leo Burnett for Always. It's about equality and prejudice against girls. The alternative would be to launch actions, draft bills and so on. But a work of this kind can reach significantly more people around the world within only a few weeks than a new bill could accomplish in several years. Also, often ads of this type are thought up by a young team coming directly from university. The rules changed, I think that's awesome.

Eyes on Gigi [Digital Campaign]
Red Dot 2016

**Serviceplan's vision statement is "Building Best Brands".
What do you associate with this alliteration?**

We don't claim to be the most bustling creative hub, although we're
certainly an energetic network. So, we don't flaunt smashing hits,
nor do we aspire to impress with global campaigns that are adopted
across 50 markets at breakneck speed. We want to help our clients
build and maintain brands that are successful over the long term.

**Why is the difference between "Building Brands" and
"Building Best Brands" important for you?**

That seems relatively obvious to me. Anyone would rather be associated with having been involved in establishing a successful brand
than just any brand.

What distinguishes "Best Brands"?

In our assessments, we generally apply two criteria: the "share of
market" and the "share of soul". Only when both exist do we speak of
a "best brand". In other words, for a brand to be a best brand, it has
to have a high market share and be loved by people. It has to be considered to be important by them in their everyday life.

**How does brand building work, essentially? Is there a way of
summarising this phenomenon in a few simple words?**

For a brand to be a best brand, it has to be able to sustain itself over
the long term. And that's something that doesn't just happen like that,
contrary to what many people seem to think. There's a certain trend
in the business to reinvent a brand every three years; but that's hardly
anything that leads to a "best brand". In times when everything
changes fast, consistency is the key.

**The long-term effort to build a brand also requires creative
employees. And Serviceplan invests in or improves the "creative product", as it calls it. What is the core of this "creative
product"?**

Our service encompasses developing a strategy for a brand (brand
consulting); doing the digital programming, data analysis and all other
media types of services; building the creative concept, and ensuring
the systematic implementation of globally marketed products. Many of
these tasks inevitably require a high degree of creativity. Yet others,
equally important for the success of the brand, are merely about ensuring that things function the way they should. A good idea that is
put in the wrong media and therefore doesn't work, is not a good idea.

Saturn Shop Clock [App]
Red Dot 2016

How do you assess creative ideas? What do you look for in particular when you evaluate creative designs?

When evaluating an idea, the first thing I ask myself is whether I could see myself presenting it at an agency pitch to a new client. Would I be proud of it? Is it better than anything we've done before? Is there a story to be told? What makes this work special? Is it a showcase for the capabilities of our agency group?

Can the value of communication for the client even be measured at all?

It should be possible to evaluate the value of communication by its success. Poor communication can result in decreasing sales – just like good communication can, of course, lead to renown and raise popularity. All that can be measured, albeit only over time. What counts once more is the long-term success.

When looking at award-winning works of recent years, it is striking that creativity often comes hand in hand with good design and technology. Does Serviceplan make a point of using new technologies as a means to stand out from the competition?

The use of new technologies is always an easy way to capture consumers' attention and curiosity. And to spark curiosity, of course, what it's all about. For that reason, I strongly support the use of all

technological possibilities that are out there. Especially when they are new.

What impact do digital technologies have on ideas and the implementation of ideas? Do they function as a source of inspiration for "creatives"?

What's important is to understand that new technologies and new opportunities are not seen as an end in and of itself but as a starting point for developing an appropriate and relevant idea. If the technology isn't suitable, then, please, old school is better than any kind of technology posturing. In other words, I'm no fan of a chichi type of branding just to come across as innovative.

This year Serviceplan surprised the agency scene by introducing a "Creative Board". The board is composed of five creative people, each of whom carry the title Global Executive Creative Director and support the agency group and its directors independently, without a team, and without responsibility for budgets. What considerations have led to this decision?

The Creative Board is no hierarchy level, and no elite corps either. Essentially, it's simply a group of very experienced creative people who do what they actually love doing and what they're best at: promoting, supporting and driving high-quality creative work. Always firmly focused on only one brief and challenge at a time.

Sneak Preview [Digital Campaign]
Red Dot 2016

Iceberg Songs [Website]
Red Dot: Grand Prix 2016

Embrace the Unknown. [Short Film]
Red Dot 2016

The Daily Catch [Promotion]
Red Dot 2016

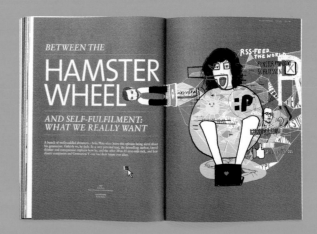
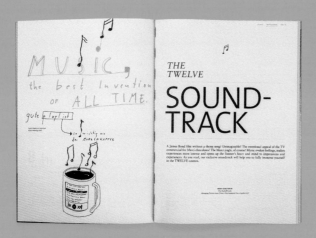

TWELVE – A Magazine by the Serviceplan Group
Red Dot 2016

To what extent could this model have a ripple effect on the agency scene or the business model of the advertising agency?

In Germany, the structure of agencies is unfortunately such that creatives, once they have reached a certain level, are forced to make the step to becoming a CCO, alongside all the administrative duties and red tape associated with that. This, in fact, moves the best creatives in Germany far away from the actual product. In other countries that is different. In England, for example, a highly experienced team consisting of executive creative directors may well focus on a single project for three months on end. That would be unthinkable in Germany.

What advantages does a Creative Board have?

The Creative Board is an investment in good design and finally in a better creative product. Our colleagues from our affiliate agencies worldwide do not necessarily have to ask for help. But there is the possibility. It's about offering support, and not about people's individual egos.

How can a Creative Board contribute to building a value for an agency and the client?

By allowing it to do its work without someone in the background mumbling about budgets, team structure, time frames, politics, etcetera. The Creative Board works without budget, team or client

responsibility. It strictly follows the creative idea. It doesn't take final decisions but just supports the responsible agency team in a single-minded way.

Which mid-term goal is Serviceplan pursuing, with a view, in particular, to this focus on creation?

Our goal is to become the first German agency group that is international, independent and operates worldwide. That is what we put all our effort into.

We hope that the award entitled Red Dot: Agency of the Year supports you and your agency group in reaching that goal!

I am absolutely thrilled about the award. Good design is not l'art pour l'art. Good design provides easy access to what we want to convey. Today, anything that's complicated has no chance of being consumed. No one has the time. It's as simple as that. Therefore, good design is the first step to success, always.

CORPORATE DESIGN

Red Dot: Grand Prix

The Real Time Brand

[Relaunch]

INEC, Ecuador's official government organisation for statistics, has the mission and the power to not only collect data, but also to distribute the information, making sure the entire country has access to it. The creative idea for the relaunch of its corporate design was to present the data reflecting the wellbeing of the population visually and in real time. A logo composed of five concentric circles was developed to represent the fields of literacy, access to clean drinking water, availability of decent housing, employment and job opportunities, and happiness. Each circle is a variable which is colour-coded in a colour of Ecuador's flag, according to the state of their evolution. Based on INEC's data, the logo updates automatically and constantly. Moreover, as variables change, the form of the logo transforms. In order to communicate the idea and to create interest among Ecuadorians, the logo idea was translated into a series of image posters, each representing a year or a month, displaying the data collected in that timeframe.

Statement by the jury

This corporate design relaunch displays a clever and simple idea of using and working with statistics. Not only does the design look strong, delivering a piece of insightful information that changes as the data change, the work also reflects an outstanding use of typography and the other parts of the identity that are consistently thought through from the outset.

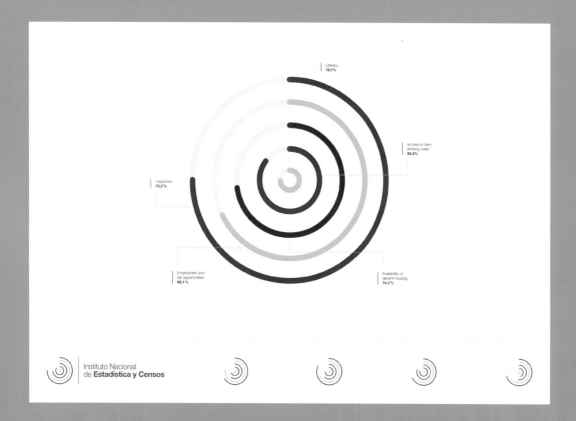

reddot award 2016
grand prix

Client
INEC, Quito

Design
Grey Germany / KW43 Branddesign,
Düsseldorf
Maruri Grey, Guayaquil

Chief Creative Officer
E. Maruri, Maruri Grey

General Management
F. Maruri, Maruri Grey

Executive Creative Direction
P. Morano, C. Cabrera, Maruri Grey

Client Service
S. Crespo, Maruri Grey

Associate Creative Direction
P. Pérez Cahueñas, Maruri Grey

Managing Director Creation
R. Goetz, KW43 Branddesign

Creative Direction
J. Adolph, KW43 Branddesign

Art Direction
G. Flores, P. Pérez Cahueñas, Maruri Grey

Copywriting
P. Pérez Cahueñas, Maruri Grey

Graphic Design
G. Flores, P. Pérez Cahueñas, Maruri Grey
T. Otto, T. Liedtke, KW43 Branddesign

Project Management
C. Bosshammer, KW43 Branddesign

Web Development
R. Dimate, Maruri Grey

App Development
S. García, Maruri Grey

Digital Creative
Á. Lechas, Maruri Grey

Production
F. Lizarzaburu, Maruri Grey

→ Designer portrait on page 498

Red Dot: Best of the Best

Hapag-Lloyd Cruises

[Relaunch]

Cruise operator Hapag-Lloyd Kreuzfahrten used the 125-year anniversary of its cruises to change its name and redesign its appearance in the cruise segment. "Hapag-Lloyd Kreuzfahrten" was changed to "Hapag-Lloyd Cruises", not only to create a tangible separation between the luxury cruises and container shipping segments, and to no longer have them sail under the same flag and brand logo. This also allowed lending the luxury cruise segment a more refined appearance. The new corporate design features reduction to a minimum and the new Brown corporate typeface, a finely crafted sans-serif font reminiscent of advertising graphics and the heyday of luxury cruises. Corresponding to the adapted colour code, the orange was remixed to achieve a sunset mood, making it serve no longer as a mere signal colour, and the brand colour of blue was enhanced by opting for the depth of "ocean blue". As part of this evolutionary re-design, the icon was also modernised and the founding year, 1891, was integrated in order to strengthen the company's market position in this premium segment.

Statement by the jury
The redesign of Hapag-Lloyd Cruises shows the great evolution of the brand, bringing up an unseen touch of visual appearance to this segment. The simple and strong use of the colour palette, a clear typography and a contemporary execution of the old established style are truly eye-catching and not only call the attention of a younger audience to the brand but also invite them to consider taking a cruise.

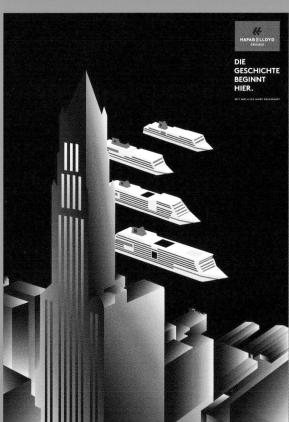

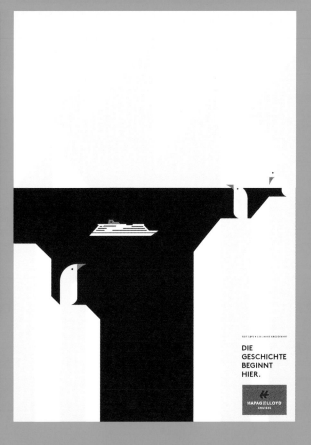

Client
Hapag-Lloyd Cruises GmbH, Hamburg

Design
MUTABOR Design GmbH, Hamburg

Art Direction
Paul Neulinger

Project Management
Stephanie Krieger

Graphic Design
Barbara Madl, Carolin Stiller,
Simon Büßem

Art Buying
Anika Fregin

→ Designer portrait on page 513

Red Dot: Best of the Best

Deutsche Stimmklinik – The Voiceprint

[Corporate Signet]

The corporate design for Deutsche Stimmklinik in Hamburg was inspired by the idea of human fingerprints. Since the human voice is equally unique and individual, it can be transformed, by means of an especially developed matrix, into the visual form of a voiceprint. Each patient's voice undergoes a quantitative sound analysis that captures it in a multidimensional voice profile. The resulting spectral order is then divided into frequency partitions and distributed across diverse spectral lines, transforming the distribution into a graphic code that allows the visual identification of various voiceprints and thus of each single patient. The corresponding brand image is aimed at establishing a link between medicine and design: it visualises the human voice in an abstract form, such as that of the founder and initiator of the clinic in the logo, and conveys the message in a clear and highly concise form.

Statement by the jury
The uniqueness of the voice, which all individuals possess analogous to their fingerprints, is translated by this design work into a stylistically outstanding logo. It is a mark of concision that a clinic takes such an approach for a visible identity to be made out of a highly specific acoustic procedure. In addition, the aesthetics in simple black and white is strong, clean and, above all, clever.

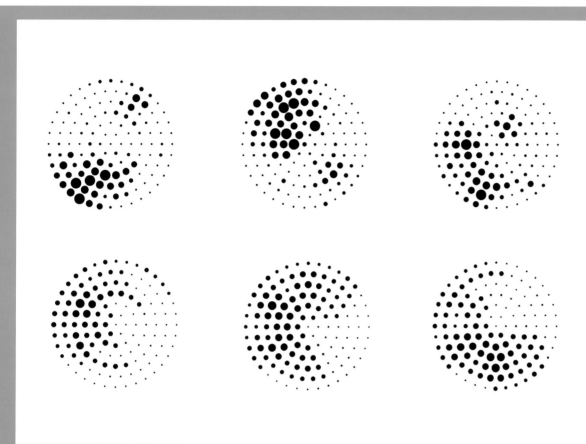

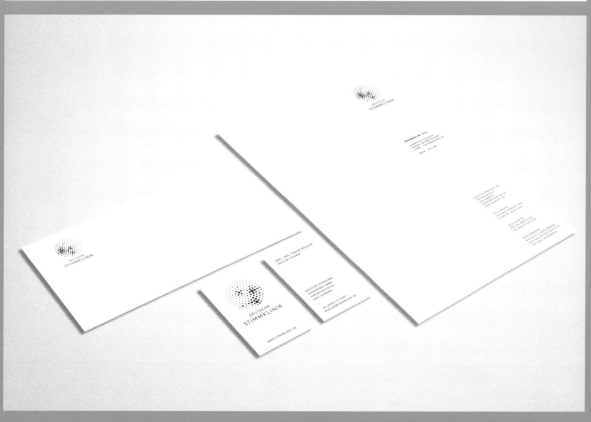

Client
Deutsche Stimmklinik
Management GmbH, Hamburg

Design
MUTABOR Design GmbH, Hamburg

Creative Direction
Sven Ritterhoff

Art Direction
Patricia Kleeberg

Project Management
Edda Schäfer

Graphic Design
Evangelos Pentazopoulos, Dimitri Wiss

→ Designer portrait on page 512

Les Trois Rois

[Relaunch]

Client
Les Trois Rois, Basel

Design
Wirz Corporate AG, Zurich

Account Management
Michel Reichmuth, Bianca Costa

Artwork
Christina Widmann, Daria Baumgartner

After a comprehensive relaunch, the visual identity of the Basel Grand Hotel Les Trois Rois stands out from the usual image of the superior hotel category. The brand slogan "Rich in history, young at heart" aims to highlight its blend of tradition and esprit. This combination is reflected in the minimalist graphical style of the brand design. Unusual colour combinations and staff portraits that surprise attract attention. As a central theme, the corporate design consistently runs through the website, hotel and seasonal brochures, advertising media, various giveaways for guests, the team's clothing and the sophisticated looking stationery.

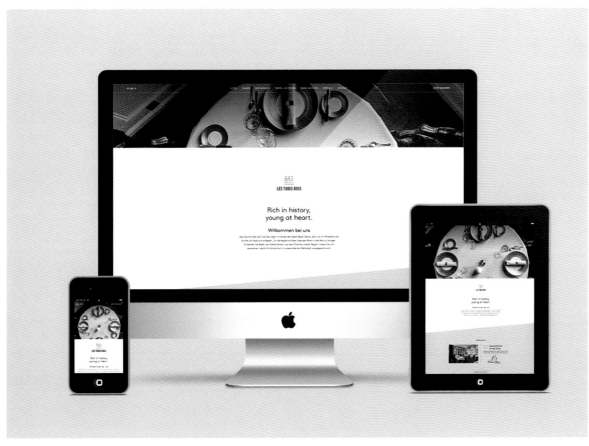

Mobile Kochkunst (MOKO)

[Corporate Identity]

Client
Mobile Kochkunst, Nuremberg

Design
FYFF GmbH, Nuremberg

Photography
Kathrin Koschitzki, Nuremberg

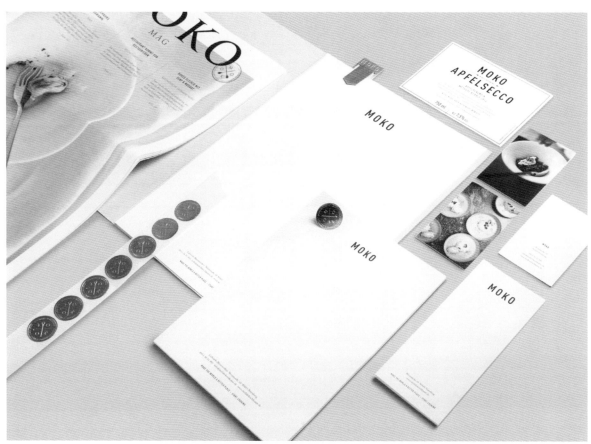

The new corporate design of Gabriele Hussenether's culinary school and event location highlights sophisticated quality standards. The overall impression plays an important role in successfully attracting companies and private individuals who would like to host their events at this place. This thought served as the basis for the unobtrusive high-quality MOKO corporate design. The application is consistent across all areas: from outdoor advertising to notepads and labels, and from premium cookery course folders with brass clips to business stationery. In addition to the minimalist word mark, a signet is used, as a golden sticker or in printed form, to visualise an uncompromising commitment to quality.

einsunternull
Restaurant

[Corporate Identity]

With the aim of developing a corporate design that breaks with the usual standards, a strikingly original visual appearance was created for the Berlin based underground restaurant "einsunternull". In its minimalist and authentic form, the new look precisely conveys the culinary essence of the restaurant. Following this, the unusual imagery, design language and colour palette reflect the high-contrast world of Berlin gourmets. The slogan "Free your taste" sends a clear and unmistakeable message of a visionary cuisine. Furthermore, its appealing words have a fascinating quality.

Client
einsunternull – Ebert Fine Dining GmbH, Berlin

Design
cyclos design GmbH, Münster

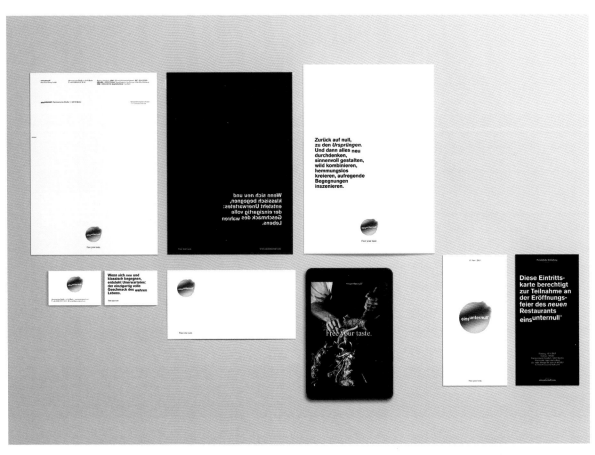

Bangkok Recipe

[Corporate Identity]

The concept behind the corporate identity of Bangkok Recipe, a new Thai restaurant in Sydney, was based on utilising the core elements of the city of Bangkok and translating them into various experiences with regards to food and environment. Besides being referred to as residing place of angels, Bangkok is also known as a street food paradise. The logo visualises the concept of the restaurant by giving traditional Thailand-specific illustrations a new, contemporary look. The imagery is supplemented by additional sketchy motifs. The bright yellow house colour creates a strong contrast to the black and white imagery.

Client
Bangkok Recipe, Randwick,
New South Wales

Design
Adhock Studio Co., Ltd., Bangkok

Illustration
Koranan Chuenpichai

→ Designer portrait on page 483

Foodtruck
"Zum grünen Wagen"

[Corporate Design]

The name "Zum grünen Wagen" refers
to the look of a food truck and the
quality of its food. A trained cook and
gastronomer tours the Rhine-Main area
to combine the good old times and the
cuisine of today's modern world with a
sense of adventure and creativity. The
corporate design communicates all this.
The classic impression with its modern
elements establishes a unique flair. The
applied love of detail shows the appreciation for the products and is part of
the playful use of design, illustrations
and language – just in line with the fine
food of the green truck itself.

Client
Zum grünen Wagen, Lisa Dressler und
Philipp Fuhge GbR, Frankfurt / Main

Design
SchleeGleixner GmbH, Aschaffenburg

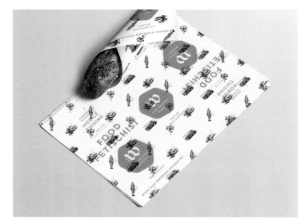

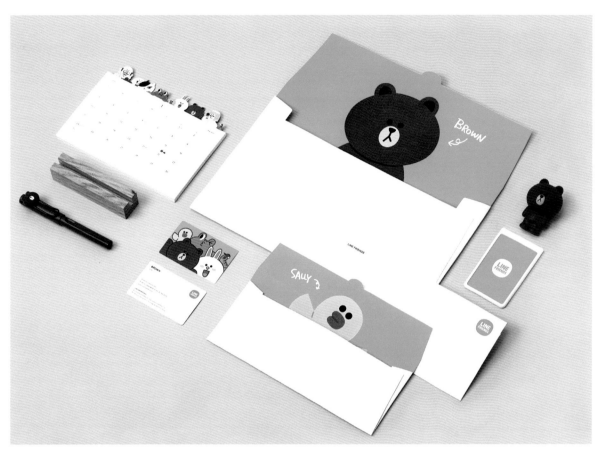

LINE FRIENDS

[Corporate Identity]

Starting as Character Emoticon for a mobile messaging app, Line Friends became an independent company. In order to further establish its professional image, a new corporate identity was developed. By utilising basic logos, colours, fonts and hundreds of source characters made for emoticons, possibilities for expression and expansion have been left open as much as possible. From business cards, employee ID cards and signage to interior design, everything was created to display the wit and individuality of the company's identity. The nine different types of business cards create a friendly atmosphere.

Client
LINE FRIENDS Corporation, Seoul

Design
LINE FRIENDS Corporation, Seoul

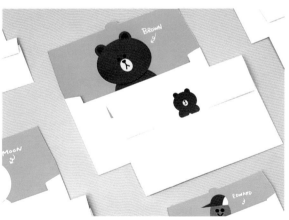

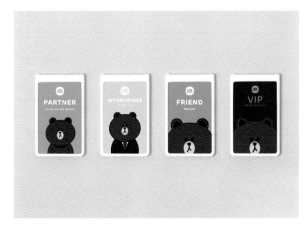

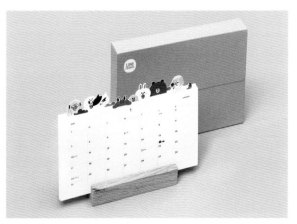

Gold–Smidt Assembly

[Corporate Concept, Visual Identity]

Gold-Smidt Assembly is a pop-up art gallery and consulting service company based in Copenhagen that curates and exhibits contemporary fine art at changing locations across Europe. Bolstering the narrative of the gallery, the visual identity is based on the concept of collecting and assembling. Contrasting colours, textures and materials are arranged in layered compositions that serve as a basis for layout, signage and display. Designed to accommodate and support shifting artistic themes, the system is dynamic and the visual expression ever-changing.

Client
Gold–Smidt Assembly, Copenhagen

Design
Re-public, Copenhagen

Art Direction
Romeo Vidner

Graphic Design
Thomas Bræstrup

Strategic Planning
Morten Windelev

Photography
Romeo Vidner
Courtesy of Chatsworth House Trust,
Bakewell

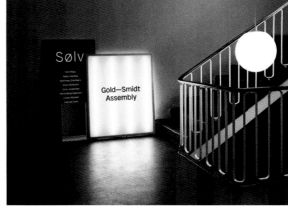

MUSÉE
UNTER
LINDEN

Le nouvel
Unterlinden
12.12.15

Unterlinden Museum Colmar

[Corporate Design]

Musée Unterlinden, a former Antonine convent dating from 1245, houses the famous Issenheim Altarpiece. Thanks to an extension, a large number of modern and contemporary masterpieces, which had previously been in storage, are now part of the exhibition. Therefore the new corporate design connects the 11th century with the 21st, Matthias Grünewald with Jeff Wall, and communication with signage – all this by means of a new logo, typography, striking design elements, and its imagery as well as its colour scheme. The communication concept of the exhibition puts this province of eastern France on the cultural map of Europe and points at the enormous quality of the past and present culture of the Rhineland.

Client
Musée Unterlinden Colmar

Design
New Identity Ltd., Basel

Creative Direction
Christian Bannholzer, Heiko J. Klemme

Art Direction
Max Nestor, Hélène Schnaitmann

Graphic Design
Helen Bartenschlager, Ramon Classen, Heike Hilterscheid, Barbara Mayer, Robert Wesseler

Exhibition "Aussichten"

[Corporate Design]

"Aussichten" (vistas) was a large art exhibition with 29 selected artists in an outdoor setting that stayed in place for an entire year. KOKONEO developed the corporate design of the exhibition, including the catalogues, the invitation cards and the posters. The logo is only shown in two dimensions, as a cut form, and hints at the steepness of the terrain. It is a fragment of the first letter of the exhibition title and symbolises the fact that the exhibition site was located on a hill. The catalogue cover was printed in three indicative Pantone neon combinations which reflect the seasonal changes during the time of the exhibition.

Client
Exhibition "Aussichten", Sissach

Design
KOKONEO GmbH, Sissach

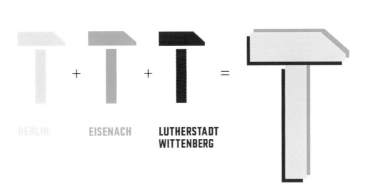

BERLIN   EISENACH   LUTHERSTADT WITTENBERG

Hammer! Die volle Wucht der Reformation
Hammer! The full power of the Reformation

[Corporate Design]

2017 marks 500 years since Martin Luther is said to have nailed his thesis to the door of Wittenberg's castle church. For this anniversary, three museums set up exhibitions on "Reformation". To target a wide audience, an eye-catching umbrella brand was created using a bold key visual – the hammer. It refers to the historic event, furthermore "Hammer!" translates into "awesome". The brand bundles all marketing activities and still allows the museums to communicate their own motifs.

Client
Staatliche Geschäftsstelle „Luther 2017", Wittenberg

Design
kleiner und bold GmbH, Berlin

Creative Direction
Tammo F. Bruns

Design Direction
Robert A. Schaefer

Graphic Design
Annika Beste, Marcel Hillebrand, Michaela Patzner

Project Management
Nicolas Glagow

Positive Film Festival

[Corporate Identity]

The idea of the corporate identity for the Ukrainian "Positive Film Festival" is based on the most memorable characters in the world of cinema. The main design elements are small, funny cartoon characters, all created in the same unique style. Their smiles are supposed to bring joy and positive emotions to a wide audience. The corporate identity is immersed in an atmosphere of happiness. A world of pleasant colours gives the corporate design the desired sense of ease, while the dynamic lines of the motifs symbolise joy in life.

Client
Positive Film Festival, Kyiv

Design
Saatchi & Saatchi Ukraine, Kyiv

Creative Direction
Kosta Schneider

Graphic Design
Mykola Kovalenko, Alexander Litvin

Account Management
Marina Valeyeva

ISAS

[Corporate Design]

In view of international competition it is crucial for ISAS to be perceived by students as a modern institute with progressive ideas. Its ageing corporate design therefore has undergone a complete overhaul. The new logo visualises the analytical process itself. At the same time, it represents the institute's interdisciplinary character. Used with a wide range of media – from the responsive website to the extensive list of templates for business stationery and reporting, as well as a digital information hub for visitors – the new corporate identity enables ISAS to present itself as innovative and a driving force in its field.

Client
Leibniz-Institut für Analytische Wissenschaften – ISAS – e.V., Dortmund

Design
labor b designbüro, Dortmund

Photography
Hannes Woidich, Dortmund

Film Production
Kobayashi Film, Bochum

Brand in Context

[Corporate Identity]

Client
VIA University College, Risskov

Design
1508, Copenhagen

Graphic Design
Tore Rosbo, Stina Nordquist

Copywriting
Jonas Haugaard

Programming
Dennis Bille Krogh

Project Management
Line Rix

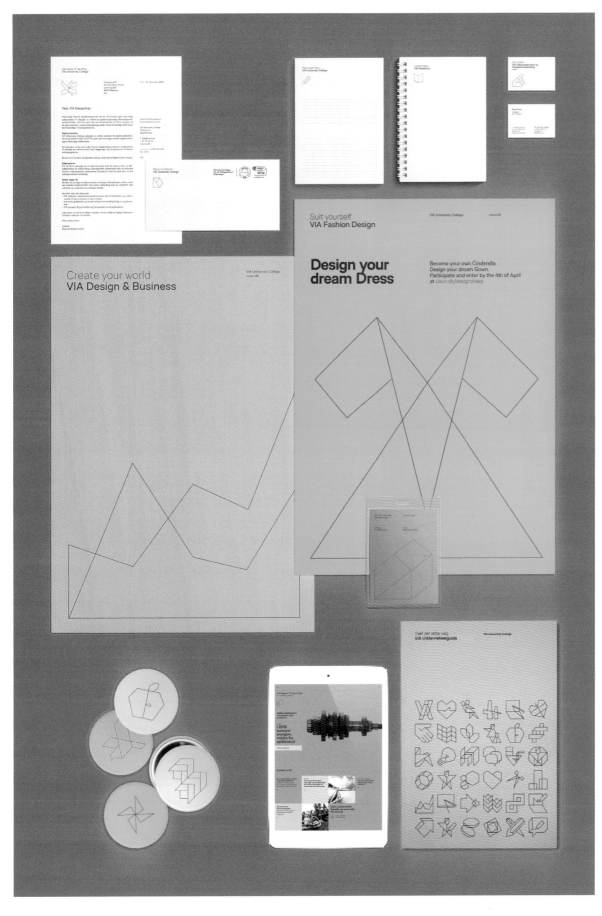

VIA University College was established in 2008 as a merger between various teaching centres and is now the largest Danish university college, with eight different campuses in Jutland. During its relatively brief time of existence, VIA had managed to achieve a high level of brand awareness among their primary target groups. A survey, however, showed that there was a general dislike towards the organisation. Therefore the main objective was to create a clear image that would make VIA the first university college that comes to mind as an engaging and appealing organisation. The new corporate design does not feature a pictorial logo. Instead, it combines a word mark with the name of the respective institute. Another 110 context-supported icons are used referring to individual subject areas.

**engineering.
tomorrow. together.**
[Corporate Design]

Client
thyssenkrupp AG, Essen

Design
thjnk / loved, Hamburg

Managing Director
Peter Matz

Account Director
Jonathan Sven Amelung, Philipp Stamer

Creative Direction
Maik Beimdieck

Art Direction
Imke Jurok, Patrick Freund

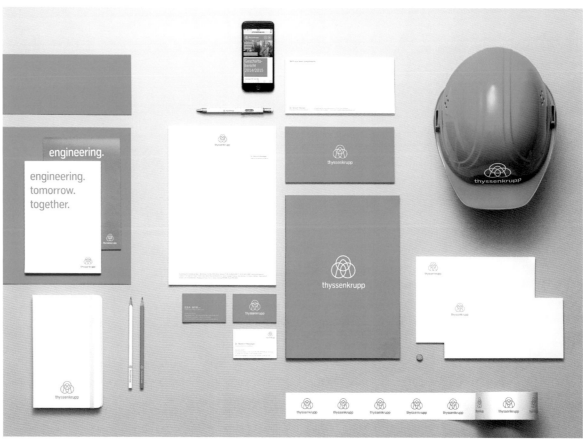

In the repositioning of the companies Thyssen and Krupp as a diversified industrial group, a new corporate design was developed that reflects the unity of both companies visually with a fresh look that communicates the brand in a visionary way. The design will serve as an ambassador in external and provide identity in internal communication. In particular, the new look is supposed to demonstrate coherence and strength. The logo uses historic signets, the Krupp rings and Thyssen curve, melding them into a contemporary symbol of unity and innovative strength.

Schlossgut Lüll

[Corporate Design]

Schlossgut Lüll is a winery in Rheinhessen, Germany. Passing down the business from one generation to the next, the sales strategy has changed from bulk-wine sales to estate bottling and marketing of their own product. Through this change, a new design was developed, representing the winery's new direction. The striking logo not only visualises a wine bottle, but also the "Lüll" brand name. A matching wine label was created using the same visual elements. The remaining corporate design is based on the five black stripes of the brand name and opens up a new "world" of design.

Client
Schlossgut Lüll, Wachenheim

Design
Stanislaw Lewicki, Vienna
Jonas Weber, Vienna

Animation
Stefan Krische, Vienna

Text
Florian Schmidt, Berlin

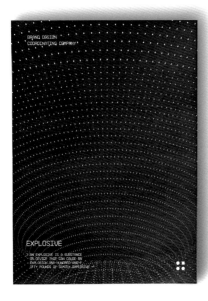
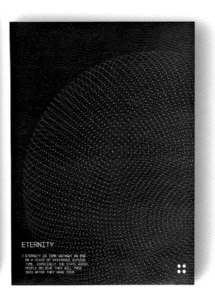

Eightyfive

[Corporate Identity]

Eightyfive is a design initiative, established in Seoul in 2016, with a creative focus on digital pixels. The branding philosophy of Eightyfive is based on the meaning of numbers. The number "eight" represents the infinity of space, while "five" stands for the elements wood, fire, earth, metal and water, which make up the universe. The minimalist logo was designed with this meaning in mind and utilises the negative space of the number 85. A square in the upper right symbolises pixels, which are the elements of the digital world, while the rest are dots, referring to the elements which compose the real world.

Client
Eightyfive, Seoul

Design
Eightyfive, Seoul

SP Cream Cards

[Corporate Guidelines]

These SP Cards were created with the aim of communicating the current corporate guidelines to the agency's staff. Each of the 43 cards shows an individually designed motif on the front, which creates a diverse overall image in combination with the other cards. The back of each card features a text related to a specific guideline. Their layout consistently follows the agency's corporate design. By contrast, the motifs on the front were designed by a team of creative professionals without any design brief in just one day, making the process a team building and employer branding exercise in one go.

Client
Schindler Parent GmbH, Meersburg

Design
Schindler Parent GmbH, Meersburg

Editorial Work
Dr. Constance Hotz, Christoph Siwek,
David Bumiller, Michael Nipp,
Sebastian Sona

Artwork
Annika Förderer, Flavia Monti,
Hannah Schienle, Janine Kühner,
Jessica Laub, Mareike Aßfahl,
Billy Contreras, Johannes Kretz,
Jörg Bluhm, Michael Barthelme,
Sebastian Fuhr, Thilo Riedesser

Pre-Press
Bernhard Spieß

Project Management
Sebastian Schnell

Printing
Christine Schöler,
Schöler Druck & Medien,
Immenstadt im Allgäu

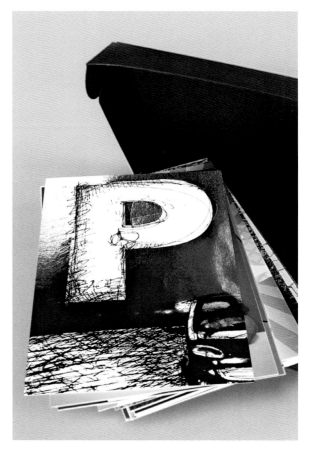

Boris Blase ...
igus corporate design
!new! 2016 manual

[Corporate Design Guide]

In addition to clear basics, the igus design manual shows how the current corporate design of the company is to be implemented across the world. For the creation of this third edition, which was published in 2016, the entire design was reassessed, in part significantly revised, updated and reworked in a contemporary style. The manual, which is available in 25 countries, comprises the visual design of print ads, trade fairs, catalogues, mailings, websites, bags, signs, packaging and clothing. Clear examples of application convey the reduced design concept.

Client
igus GmbH, Cologne

Design
igus agentur, Cologne

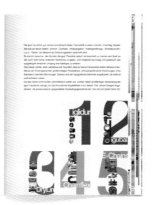

White Christmas

[Corporate Promotion]

Instead of creating another impressive designer Christmas card, Fargo decided to let the well-known Christmas melody White Christmas draw itself. An individually developed device transfers the sound structure of the 7-inch vinyl single via a 0.1 mm ink-pen onto rotating premium fine paper. No manual influence distracts from the beauty of the spiral. The unique Christmas gift represents the corporate design as well as the design philosophy of the studio. The documenting movie has been viewed and shared more than half a million times on social media and several design platforms worldwide.

Client
Fargo Design GmbH, Hamburg

Design
Fargo Design GmbH, Hamburg

Creative Direction
Lorenz Dietrich

Art Direction
Friedemann Ledendecker

Concept
Lorenz Dietrich, Dominic Nagel

Typography
Julian Zimmerling

Film Direction
Tim Koenecke

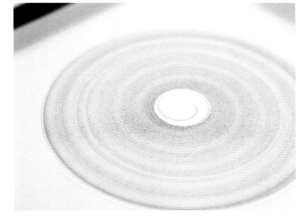

Telling Tales
[Corporate Promotion]

Telling Tales is the name of LZF's communication campaign for 2016, which illuminates a collection of stories about the Spanish lamp manufacturer. Its corporate design is based on three ideas that make this catalogue different from previous ones: the images were to be set at night, providing an opportunity to showcase the lamps when lit; the focus was to shift from interior spaces to the human beings that inhabit them; and the catalogue was supposed to move away from traditional formats, becoming a work of artistic creation. The first stories refer to the works of the painter Edward Hopper and the film Rear Window by Alfred Hitchcock.

Client
LZF Lamps, Luziferlamps, S.L.,
Chiva, Valencia

Design
LZF Lamps, Luziferlamps, S.L.,
Chiva, Valencia

Creative Direction
Marivi Calvo

Art Direction
Masquespacio Studio, Valencia
LZF Lamps, Luziferlamps, S.L.

Text
Grassa Toro

Project Management
Ester Colomina

Photography
Maria Mira
Cualiti

Artwork
Riki Blanco

BRAND DESIGN

Red Dot: Best of the Best

Moscow Identity

[Brand Identity]

The brand identity for the semi-annual meeting of the Global Local Branding Alliance (GLBA) in Moscow started with a question: How can this city, its mood and authenticity be explained to a foreigner only staying in Moscow for two days? The answer was: With the city itself! The identity is based on three main pillars. Firstly, there is the radial design of the city as it grows in rings, such as the boulevard ring, the garden ring, and a third ring with the Kremlin and Saint Basil's Cathedral at the centre. Secondly, there is the city's authenticity based on certain patterns typical of several of Moscow's iconic places and sights. Thirdly, there is the positive mood which is shared by people who encounter the design. These ideas resulted in a rich and vibrant visual idiom, realised across a wide range of digital and analogue media, including the programme, the brand book, the spatial design and flags, all featuring a plethora of colourful and creative visuals that rendered the identity not only remarkably versatile but also tangible in the form of lollies, bags or bicycles.

Statement by the jury

This brand identity captures the colourful architecture of the Russian capital in beautiful illustrations. It cleverly uses objects such as skirts and umbrellas, shown from above, to underline the circular design of the city. With its playful patterns, the gorgeous colour screen and visual style, the identity achieves a remarkable and likeable aesthetic.

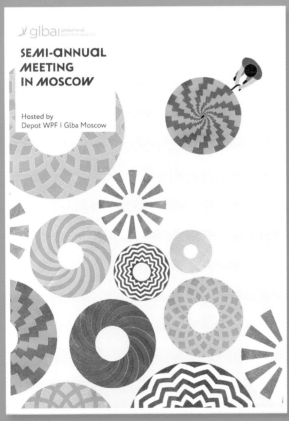

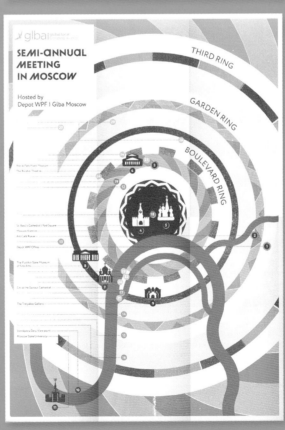

Client
GLBA, Berlin

Design
Depot WPF, Moscow

Creative Direction
Alexandr Zagorsky, Alexey Andreev

Art Direction
Tatiana Mikolaevskaya

Copywriting
Fara Kuchkarov

Account Management
Ekaterina Lavrova

→ Designer portraits on page 495, 496

Red Dot: Best of the Best

Shopping List

[Brand Design]

This brand design of a private label was created based on the simplest and most iconic metaphor of shopping, the shopping list, as such lists help people remember what they need to buy. The design is kept as plain and clear as possible and needs no decorative elements except for the font, which looks handwritten. All the labels of the different food packagings feature several words typically found on shopping lists. Only the word for the product that is inside the box or bottle is not crossed out. This is enough to inform customers sufficiently what is included in the packaging. The typography comes in slightly different colours only to highlight the individual products, but otherwise makes the products unambiguously recognisable as one brand. The idea was born of the realisation that today's consumers are rather busy and do not want to waste time on examining thousands of logos, colours and images when buying just basic foods. The brand aimed at a design where nothing diverts the attention of the customer – making shopping as easy as following a shopping list.

Statement by the jury

In this project, the concept of a shopping list serving as a brand design delivers a very delightful and charming realisation. The design of the product labels is simple and straightforward, only needs a minimum of resources, and attracts attention with its innovative look no matter where it is displayed. In addition, it also gives consumers the chance to buy what they may forget otherwise.

Client
Ambar, Moscow

Design
Depot WPF, Moscow

Creative Direction
Alexandr Zagorsky

Art Direction
Tatiana Mikolaevskaya

Copywriting
Ekaterina Lavrova, Fara Kuchkarov

→ Designer portraits on page 495, 496

I·SEOUL·U

[Brand Identity]

Client
Seoul Metropolitan Government, Seoul

Design
CDR associates, Seoul

Project Management
Alex Kim, CDR associates
Hanggi Park, Metabranding

Graphic Design
Dohyung Kim, Changseung Park,
Hyeyoung Jung, Boreum Han, Miso Kim

I·SEOUL·U
너와 나의 서울

Representing Seoul, the capital of South Korea, I·SEOUL·U is a new citizen-driven city brand. The development, beginning with its naming and design, was based on many different ideas and was approached using a concept of collaboration between citizens and marketing experts. The brand logo visualises Seoul as a soulful city, where people enjoy an affluent, relaxed lifestyle full of passion. In its bilingualism, the word mark emphasises the international orientation of the metropolis. Using a phonetic abbreviation for the addressee – U representing the word "you" – a contemporary identity has been created, which also successfully appeals to younger target groups.

Marquise Minhocão

[Brand Identity]

Minhocão is the popular name for the Costa e Silva, built in the centre of São Paulo in 1971. This elevated road was an attempt to solve the city's chaotic traffic situation, but it only made things worse. In order to attract investors to revitalise and resolve the misuse of the area beneath the Minhocão, a new brand identity was created: Marquise Minhocão. The creative idea is inspired by the possibilities of the architectural project – to look at the area underneath the elevated road and to make it more colourful. The brand design visualised a new perspective for the city based on the city's wide range of colours.

Client
São Paulo City Hall, São Paulo

Design
Interbrand, São Paulo
Tryptique Architecture, São Paulo

Creative Direction
Sérgio Cury, Felipe Valério,
Beto Almeida, Interbrand
Carolina Bueno, Tryptique Architecture
Guil Blanche, Movimento 90, São Paulo

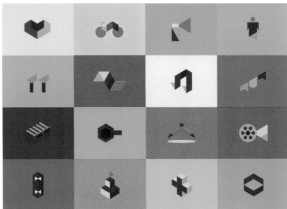

VAUNCE

[Brand Identity]

VAUNCE Trampoline Park is a playground and cultural space in the city which has five core values: health, joy, freedom, satisfaction and culture. It required a distinctive design language based on these values to consistently display its identity. The graphic brand identity combines a diagonal line of 45 degrees with images of people jumping on a trampoline. These elements help users experience the brand identity throughout all design applications including the logo and the typography. The design, which is applied to all components at various marketing interfaces, provides a consistent brand image.

Client
VAUNCE, Seoul

Project Management
Yeojin Kim, Martin Berry

Design
Plus X, Seoul

BX Team
Myungsup Shin, Junhyuck Chun, Dajung Hyeon, Taesu Im, Minkyung Kim

Skansen

[Brand Identity]

At the end of 2015, Skansen, an open-air museum in the centre of Stockholm, launched its new brand platform and visual identity. The traditional Swedish collection represents the past and the present, fantasy and facts, animals and culture, traditions and trends. The brand design consists of a logo, a brand pattern, typography, a colour palette and imagery, and can be used on everything from Skansen's own products to clothing, communication materials, tickets, stationery and signs. Its natural colours and picturesque motifs create a harmonious overall impression.

Client
Skansen, Stockholm

Design
Silver, Stockholm

Creative Direction
Jacob Bergström

Graphic Design
Sofia Frank Öberg, Tobias Rehnvall

Production
Sabine Price

SAMMLUNG SAMMLUNG
THE NEUE NEUE
DESIGN DIE DIE
MUSEUM

Die Neue Sammlung

[Brand Concept, Brand Identity]

This new corporate identity confidently reflects the Museum's international significance and its new programme. The slight change in name, from "Die Neue Sammlung - The International Design Museum" to "Die Neue Sammlung - The Design Museum", stands for concentration and focus. Since a part of the wording is English, the adjective "international" is dispensable. The uniqueness of the logo has been achieved using a surprising visual solution: the German part of the logo is rotated by 180 degrees. And together with the English part, a compact word mark comes into existence, the capital letters of which highlight the significance of the museum.

Client
Die Neue Sammlung –
The Design Museum, Munich

Director
Angelika Nollert

Design
Bureau Mirko Borsche, Munich

Co-Creation! Camp

[Brand Identity]

Japan faces unprecedented social issues
such as a low birthrate, an ageing
population and the depopulation of the
region. This is the background of the
logo design and branding for the event
"Co-Creation! Camp", in which people
talk about local revitalisation for the
future. The target group are the people
involved in the Japanese tourism industry. The various colours of the brand
design symbolise individual wishes. The
imagery emphasises networking as well
as diverse future perspectives. The event
produced many ideas and resulted in
more than 100 projects.

Client
Recruit Lifestyle Co., Ltd., Tokyo

Production
Ai Sanda

Design
Recruit Communications Co., Ltd., Tokyo
Number8 Creative Inc., Tokyo

Creative Direction
Takahiro Nagahama

Art Direction
Kei Sato

Design Team
Haruma Yonekawa, Ryo Shimomura,
Moe Uchimura, Yasuhiro Tamura,
Daisuke Yano

Typography
Junko Igarashi, TAKI Corporation, Tokyo

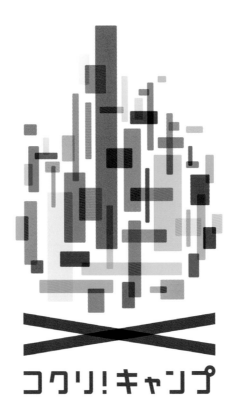

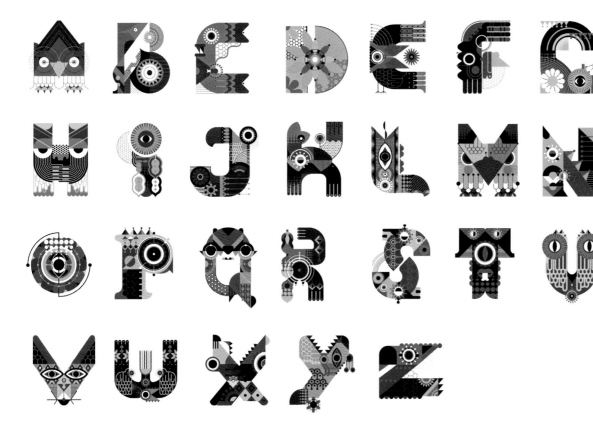

Seoul Zoo

[Brand Identity]

This new brand design is the result of the attempt to visualise the graphic identity of Seoul Zoo in a pictorial alphabet. The design identifies the location using graphic letters in order to establish Seoul Zoo's identity as a unique brand. The graphic motifs are illustrations of basic shapes and characteristics of animals and plants. Additionally, the design adopts drawing styles which employ the look of Chinese characters in order to finally create a unique alphabet. Trying to harmonise Eastern and Western characteristics, Egyptian art styles were borrowed, such as a mix of front and side views.

Client
Seoul Grand Park, Gwacheon City, Gyeonggi Province

Design
Jeongkee Park, Sewoong Kim, Minjung Kim, Joonwoo Park, Seoul

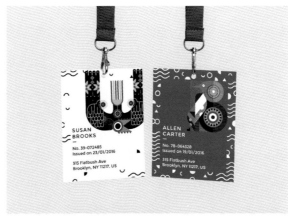

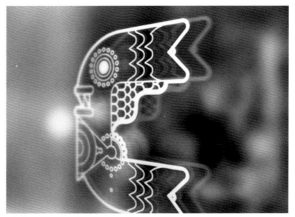

phoenolux – Scheufelen's Premium Packaging Board

[Brand Promotion]

This promotion box was created as part of a brand development project for the German paper factory Papierfabrik Scheufelen, an innovative tool which combines all their expertise and competence in the art of paper- and board-making. The bright white premium cardboard box features graphically impressive applications, which are supposed to target potential customers in the packaging market. The brand design of the outer packaging conveys a sophisticated look and has a pleasant feel, while the conically shaped tube packaging with its creative design applications provides a visually appealing addition to the special edition.

Client
Papierfabrik Scheufelen GmbH + Co. KG, Lenningen

Design
Strichpunkt Design, Stuttgart/Berlin

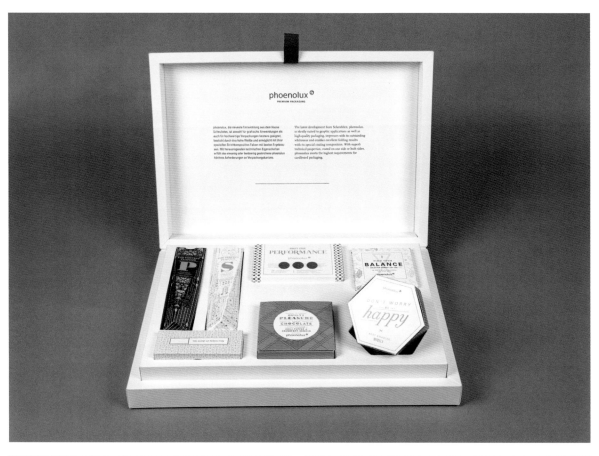

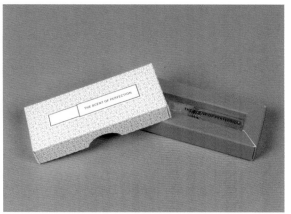

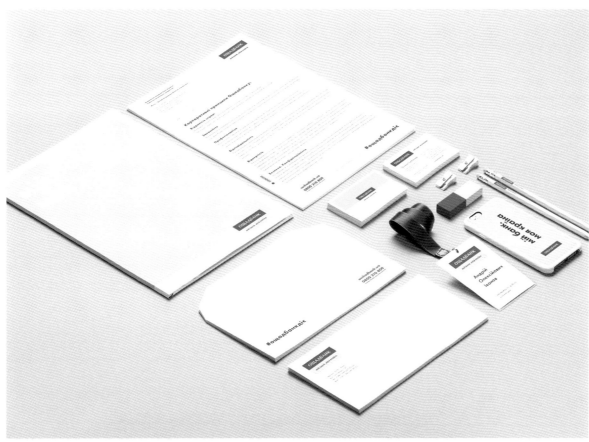

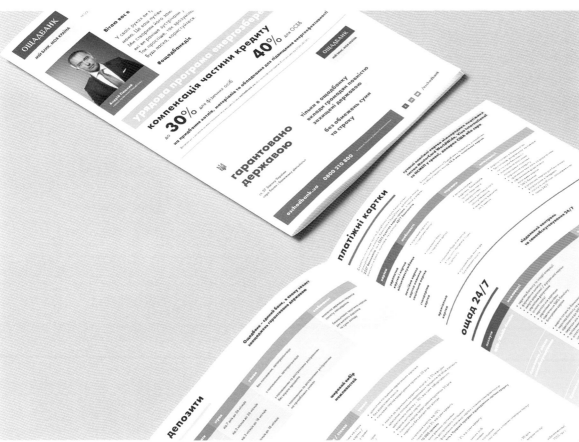

Oschadbank

[Relaunch]

Oschadbank is the Ukrainian State Savings Bank, employing 35,000 staff and providing 100 per cent state-insured savings. The bank implemented cutting-edge technologies and opened innovative branches, which made a rebranding necessary. The repositioning of the brand is based on the slogan "My bank. My country." The visual identity was intentionally reduced to a word mark. In addition, the colour palette, ranging from bright yellow to traditional deep green, conveys a contemporary identity and is reminiscent of the Ukrainian national flag.

Client
Oschadbank,
State Savings Bank of Ukraine, Kyiv

Design
FEDORIV, Kyiv

Strategic Vision
Andriy Fedoriv

Design Concept
Vitaliy Parfilev

Team Lead
Arkadij Pasechnik

Screenwriting / Copywriting
Olya Paholok

Motion Design
Yura Homovsky

Interactive Art Direction
Yuri Lence

Project Management
Olesya Motorna

Morioka Shoten
Bookstore

[Brand Design]

Morioka Shoten is a tiny bookstore in
Tokyo. As its slogan "A Single Room with
a Single Book" describes, the bookshop
sells only one book; more precisely, multiple copies of a single title that changes
weekly, with a small, book-inspired art
exhibition on the walls. Its minimalist
attitude and well-curated shows attract
visitors from across the globe. The
branding director created a logo stating
the address and the slogan to express
the importance of a physical venue
in the era of digital reading. The brand
design is characterised by effective
colour contrasts.

Client
Morioka Shoten, Tokyo

Design
takram design engineering, Tokyo

Creative Direction
Yoshiyuki Morioka, Morioka Shoten
Kotaro Watanabe,
takram design engineering
Tomoya Yoshida, AZ Holdings, Tokyo

Art Direction
Kotaro Yamaguchi,
takram design engineering

Investor
Toyama Masamichi, Smiles Co., Ltd., Tokyo

Divan.ru

[Brand Identity]

Divan.ru is a new online discount furniture store specialising in sofas. Launched in August 2015, the store chooses a simple and memorable name. The logo comes in different versions, with each one showing a sofa from the current range instead of the word "divan". By adding the price and the name of the sofa at the bottom of all corporate identity elements, customers can find and buy each sofa online for the indicated price. Therefore, the brand design functions as a display window, an advertisement and a sofa index as well as a web address.

Client
Divan.ru, online furniture store, Moscow

Design
Suprematika, Moscow

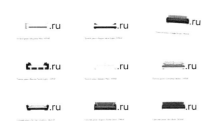

Askul

[Brand Identity]

Askul, a Japanese office supplies retailer founded in 1963, sells everything from paper, pens and batteries to chairs, tools and tea, as well as thousands of other items through their website and cata-logue. As part of a new brand identity, a design system was introduced that is striking in its stylish simplicity. Each item has been reduced to its bare essen-tials. Adding design to more than 200 everyday products has boosted brand equity, but also simplified and bright-ened offices across Japan.

Client
Askul Corporation, Tokyo

Design
Stockholm Design Lab, Stockholm

L'EAUNDRY Fragrance Laundry Detergent

[Brand Design]

L'EAUNDRY is a luxury fragrance laundry detergent, launched in 2014. Due to its success, the range was extended to include other scented products in 2016 and it was decided to give the brand its own visual identity, which spans from products to stationery. The visual identity is based on the shape of the bottle, including its black cap, which created the first visual representation of the brand. The result is a consistent, strong and unique visual brand identity.

Client
T.D.G. Vertriebs GmbH & Co. KG, Hamburg

Design
KOREFE, Hamburg
Kolle Rebbe GmbH, Hamburg

Chief Creative Officer
Stefan Kolle

Creative Direction/Product Design
Christian Doering

Project Management
Jana Bier

Text
Lorenz Ritter

Photography
Imke Jansen

Retouch Artist
Tommy Szewczuk

Production
Martin Lühe

→ Designer portrait on page 507

Seoul Public Bike

[Brand Identity]

Client
Seoul Metropolitan Government, Seoul

Design
CRAFIK, Seoul

Creative Direction
Jae Hee Joh

Graphic Design
Seung Won Yoo, Hyun Ju Kim

Strategic Planning
Seung Won Yoo

BASIC SYSTEM

BASIC SYMBOL

BIKE SIGN

SPECIAL PATTERN

SERVICE CENTER

PLACE & LANDMARK

HANGANG RIVER

SEOUL FOREST

DDP

KWANGHWAMUN

SPONSORSHIP

CORPORATE LOGO

COFFEE SHOP

DONUT STORE

CHARACTER PRODUCT

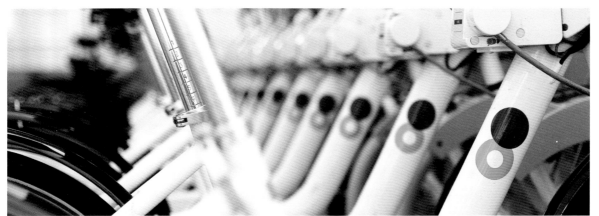

Seoul Public Bike is an unmanned rental system which can be used anywhere, anytime and by anyone, and which is run by the City of Seoul. In order to revitalise the public bike service and secure operational cost via sponsorship, a flexible brand identity was created. The logo with its two circles was applied to the bicycle design while the graphic elements create a unified identity. The basic design elements are a combination of white and green, communicating a clean and eco-friendly image. The graphics on the bicycles can easily be changed to match sponsors' advertising requirements.

700bike

[Brand Identity, Key Visual]

700bike is an information platform, which vividly illustrates brands and trends of the new generation of bicycles. It also aspires to bring new perspectives to cyclists. The figure 700 was turned into the time concept "7:00", because in Chinese the pronunciation of "seven o'clock" is phonetically similar to the meaning of origin or starting point. Based on this, the logotype implies that 700bike is the start of a new bicycle culture in China. Representing the beginning of a new story about bicycles, the logo combines the colon with the time association.

Client
700bike (Beijing) Technology Development Co., Ltd., Beijing

Design
Dongdao Creative Branding Group, Beijing

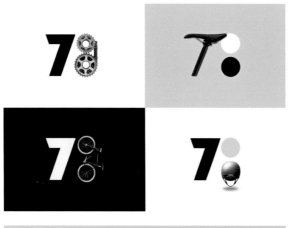

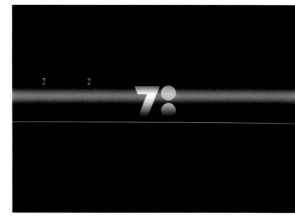

AND GO.

[Brand Concept]

The task was to create a unique identity for the launch of a new low-budget brand in the industry sector of toilet facility solutions. An unusual name, which includes the brand promise and quickly communicates its unique selling proposition, was developed. In order to establish a strong image, the bold word mark characterises the suitable corporate design, which authentically communicates its claim: "EASY. EFFICIENT. AND GO". The comprehensive identity concept includes the name, a modular claim-system, pictorial language, layout, and illustrative style.

Client
AND GO., Dreieich

Design
hauser lacour kommunikationsgestaltung gmbh, Frankfurt/Main

Creative Direction
Kristina Schmidt

Art Direction
Felix Kopp, Roxana Raschidi, Hannah Rindfleisch

Strategy
Georg Bertsch

Text
Michael Häußler

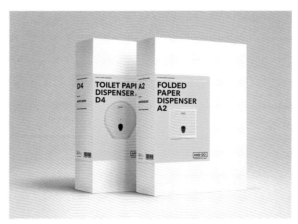

Osteo Poly Clinic

[Brand Identity, Visual Identity]

The Osteo Poly Clinic is a clinic special-ising in osteopathic treatment. In order to explain what osteopathy is and how it works, the circle within the logo is supposed to be a symbol of a human being in perfect condition. A broken circle is a visual symbol for health prob-lems and the aim is to get back to the perfect circle, which stands for recovery. All elements of the visual identity work in connection with the logo. If any part of the circle moves to the left, so do the other elements. The brand design is characterised by its black and white contrast and works in all media: from stationery and printed material to doc-tors' uniforms and the interior of the clinic.

Client
Osteo Poly Clinic, Moscow

Design
Ermolaev Bureau, Moscow

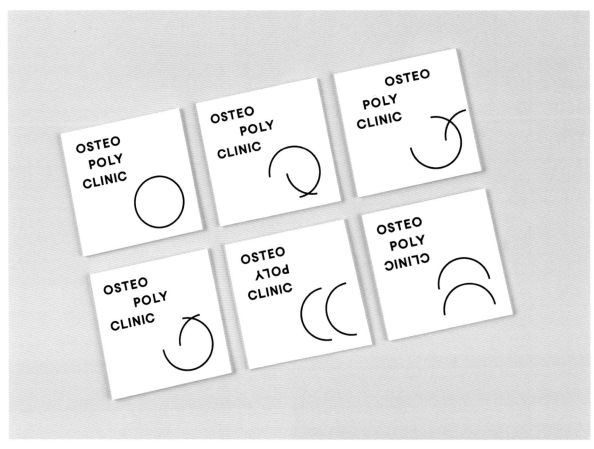

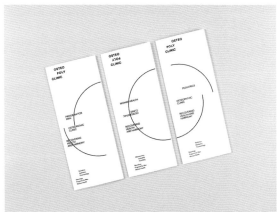

BespinGlobal

[Brand Identity]

The most important thematic aspect for BespinGlobal's branding development is the concept of a "dynamically generated cloud symbol" that responds uniquely to variable conditions and environments. Rather than a single symbol for a cloud, this dynamic element of the brand identity serves as both a visual and a symbolic anchor for a flexible, ever-changing service environment. Furthermore, the invisible process of a bit of data being transferred to the cloud is expressed visually by using a single dot and a bold, solid arrow. This creates a sense of credibility and stability by emphasising the brand's core competence in expert cloud management platforms and services.

Client
BespinGlobal, Seoul

Design
Daylight Design, San Francisco

Team Lead
Daniel Kim

Design Direction
June-Hyeong Lee

Code Design
David Lee

Photography
Young-Soo Kim

Deutsche Börse
Photography
Foundation

[Brand Design, Brand Identity]

Client
Deutsche Börse Photography Foundation
gGmbH, Frankfurt/Main

Design
hauser lacour kommunikationsgestaltung
gmbh, Frankfurt/Main

Creative Direction
Laurent Lacour, Kristina Schmidt

Art Direction
Mirjam Platz

Programming
Florian Reußenzehn

As a nonprofit limited liability company, the work of the Deutsche Börse Photography Foundation is focused on collecting, exhibiting and promoting photographic art. The letters, derived from the foundation's name, form the key visual, complementing the logo as a striking and yet contained frame for each photography. It is an essential function of the flexible design concept to focus on the artworks in order to let them speak for themselves. They are presented in full format with suitable white space in all media. Alongside the classic print material, the web presence is essential.

Danish Design Award: Celebrating Design

[Brand Identity, Visual Identity]

The visual identity for Danish Design Award captures both tradition and innovation in a recognisable font. This unique typography is based on the functionalistic aesthetics of Danish design pioneer Knud V. Engelhardt. It consists of uppercase letters which have been designed in three weights to highlight the solemn award ceremony. Together with the simple black and white graphic style, the typeface gives this award a strong voice to promote the power of design. It has been applied to everything from website to posters and promotional materials as well as the trophy itself, which is made of ash wood with its surface covered with gold leaf.

Client
Dansk Design Center, Copenhagen
Design Denmark, Copenhagen

Design
Kontrapunkt Group A/S, Copenhagen

Creative Direction
Kim Meyer Andersen, Bo Linnemann

Graphic Design
Rasmus Lund Mathisen,
Rasmus Hylgaard Schønning,
Britt Engelhardt Gundersen,
Nille Halding

Project Management
Esther Barfred

→ Designer portrait on page 506

DANISH DESIGN AWARD **CELEBRATES** THE **DIFFERENCE** DESIGN MAKES – EVEN **BEYOND** OUR **IMAGINATION.** THE **AWARD** COVERS 11 CATEGORIES FROM **BUSINESS** DESIGN AND **SERVICE** DESIGN TO **EXPERIENCE** DESIGN, **BROADENING** OUR **CONCEPT OF DESIGN** AND HOW DESIGN MAKES OUR **LIVES BETTER,** HEALTHIER AND HAPPIER. DANISH DESIGN AWARD WANTED A **VISUAL IDENTITY** THAT MATCHED THE **HIGH QUALITY** OF THE PROJECTS **NOMINATED.** AND MORE IMPORTANTLY, A VISUAL IDENTITY THAT **SUPPORTS** THE OVERALL MESSAGE: **DESIGN MAKES A DIFFERENCE.** WE STARTED BY **LOOKING BACK.** DANISH DESIGN HAS A LONG, PROUD TRADITION FOR **HUMANISTIC** AND **DEMOCRATIC** DESIGN. ESPECIALLY THE **EARLY MODERNIST** AND DANISH DESIGN **PIONEER KNUD V. ENGELHARDT'S** TYPOGRAPHIC WORK BECAME **KEY** IN OUR SEARCH FOR **INSPIRATION.** SO WE DECIDED TO DESIGN A **NEW TYPOGRAPHY** THAT WE CALLED **"DANISH",** BASED ON ENGELHARDT'S **FUNCTIONALISTIC AESTHETICS.** THEN WE LOOKED **FORWARD.** WE WORKED WITH **TIGHT** AND **"CHUNKY"** TYPEFACE COMPOSITIONS AND **BLACK** AND **WHITE** GRAPHICS TO GIVE IT A **CONTEMPORARY** TOUCH AND NOT GET TOO **NOSTALGIC.** THE RESULT IS A VISUAL IDENTITY THAT **CAPTURES** THE **COMBINATION** OF **TRADITION** AND **INNOVATION** IN A **RECOGNIZABLE** FONT. **TOGETHER** WITH THE **TIGHT** AND **SIMPLE** GRAPHICAL UNIVERSE THE TYPEFACE GIVES DANISH DESIGN AWARD A **STRONG VOICE** TO PROMOTE THE **POWER OF DESIGN.**

Selfish Club

[Brand Design]

Selfish Club is a fishing club in the country which additionally offers high quality food and accommodation. The club has been positioned as a prestigious haven for a male community. The target was to design a logo that included a visual communication system as well as to develop the further promotion of the club. The logo, two crossed metal fishhooks, conveys an impression of strength to represent the project's main idea of a strong community. Calm dark colours resemble water surfaces and fish scales. Light colours of a sandy shore and wood were added to the palette for natural contrast.

Client
Igor Diakonov, Selfish Club, Kiylov

Design
Ginger Brand, Kyiv

Creative Direction
Sergiy Minyuk

Graphic Design
Sergiy Minyuk, Anastasiia Sotsenko

3D Production
Yuri Meshalkin

Project Management
Eugenia Dneprova

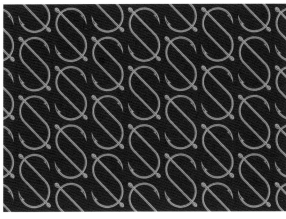

HATO Restaurants

[Brand Design]

Client
Good Restaurants Company AG, Zurich

Design
allink AG, Zurich

Creative Direction
David Zangger

Graphic Design
Davide Rossetto, Martina Kellenberger

Interior Design
Sandro E. Büeler, Atelier Estimo AG, Zurich

Project Management
Dr. Wolf Wagschal,
WW Worldwide Hospitality GmbH, Zurich

→ Designer portrait on page 484

The HATO restaurant has devoted itself to fine Asian cuisine, offering its guests in Zurich and St. Moritz exotic creations of the highest quality. An opulent looking brand design, including the naming and a unique visual language, was developed on the basis of straight lines in order to market the restaurant. The overall impression is characterised by a playful use of the individual design elements. The red logo resembles a wax seal, the delicate lines of which are continued in the motif design. The brand design has not only been attractively implemented in the stationery, but also in the design of the interior and of the house sake label.

Marché Mövenpick

[Brand Identity]

Client
Marché International, Kemptthal

Design
Process, Zurich

Creative Direction
Fabian Bertschinger

Strategic Planning
Martin Fawer, Elmar Müller

Graphic Design
Séverine Telley, Sandra Scheffknecht

Account Management
Julia Wieler

With new culinary creations, its own brand communications and a stand-alone corporate identity, the relaunch of Marché Mövenpick was created for the target group of an urban population. Its brand design is all about enjoyment and sophistication. The new logo is minimalist and refined, and comes in a fresh and light green. Drawn by the Swedish artist Klas Herbert, the illustrations, which are strong iconic elements of recognition, highlight the company's values and give the brand a playful urban touch. The atmosphere of the images highlights the freshness of the food and the warmth of the restaurant.

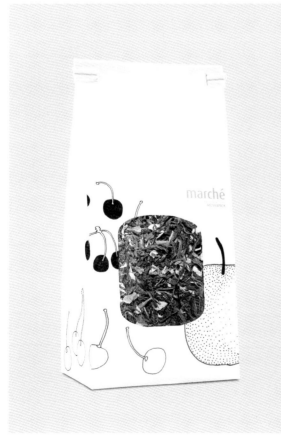

HaiDiLao Family

[Brand Design]

With its 22 years of experience, HaiDiLao Hot Pot, one of the biggest catering brands in mainland China, sets standards in the industry and is well-known for its excellent services. In order to stand out from other competitors and to emphasise its advantages, a new brand design, visualising the new slogan "Service is Kung Fu", was launched. In the Chinese language Kung Fu has two meanings. Besides fighting skills it also refers to a good basis, which requires time and patience to establish. Derived from its house specials, a series of vivid Kung Fu mascots, wearing the HaiDiLao uniform, were created to bring this idea to life.

Client
HaiDiLao, Beijing

Design
HaiDiLao, Brand Management
Department, Beijing

Creative Direction
Bamboo Huan

Design Direction
Camidi Liu

Graphic Design
Danyan Zhao

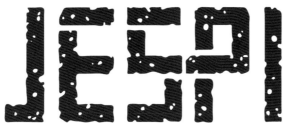

JESPI

[Brand Identity]

Jespi, a local craft beer brand from the Jeju Province Development Corporation, exemplifies the "spirit of Jeju". The brand name was created by combining the words Jeju and spirit. The harmonious colours are indicative of the island's natural beauty and match the five main ingredients of the beer. Additionally, they also represent the emotional value of the island's landscape. The different motifs inside the logo symbolise, for example, a quiet night with the moon rising over Mount Halla. The logotype was inspired by the texture of basalt, a symbol of the volcanic rock found around the island of Jeju.

Client
Jeju Province Development Co., Jeju City

Design
designfever, Seoul

Art Direction
Donghyun Choi

Graphic Design
Sanghun Lee, Minkyung Lee

Project Management
Binna Kim

OMIBERRY

[Brand Design]

This South Korean brand stands for the collective philosophy of three generations: harvesting fruit from clean land. In order to modernise and globalise the fruit's image, a word mark was created by combining the words "Omija" and berry. The design concept adds value to all elements, such as the bottle and the label, through a traditional but contemporary look. The illustration of the fruit is the key element that conveys authenticity and naturalness, while the systematic combination of Korean and English typography expresses modernity. The brand design can be flexibly applied with other products.

Client
Hyojongwon, Gyeonggi Province

Design
S/O PROJECT Studio #2, Seoul

Creative Direction
Hyun Cho,
Korea National University of Arts, Seoul

Art Direction
Jihye Lee, S/O PROJECT Studio #2

Illustration
Eunhye Lee, Seoul

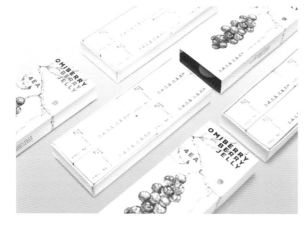

| Chinese Characters | Chinese Window | Test Tube | Magnifier | Herbs |

City Herbs

[Brand Identity, Brand Design]

City Herbs is a new brand established by a professional biotechnology research team which has launched a line of products containing the essences of hundreds of herbs. The idea of the logo design was inspired by the Chinese character "FU", which is also part of the brand name. This character is surrounded by a circle which looks like a classic round Chinese window and symbolises the opening of a window to the human body. On closer inspection, customers will discover interesting details in the logo such as the images of a test tube, a magnifying glass and genetic codes. The dominant colours of black and light green represent the brand spirit, which is based on extracting the essences from all herbs and aims at nourishing the individual.

Client
FECO Biotechnology Co., Ltd., Taipei City

Design
Fengworks Design Office, Taipei City

Creative Direction
Mark Wei-Tang Feng

Art Direction
Akasha Wan-Ling Tseng

Graphic Design
Akasha Wan-Ling Tseng,
Mark Wei-Tang Feng

Strategic Planning
Amy Ting-Yin Cheng

Text
Eric Yong-Chuan Chen,
Fay Shih-Ke Huang

One 2 Tea House

[Brand Design]

Client
One 2 Tea House, Tainan City

Design
Zi Huai Shen, Kun Shan University /
SUMP DESIGN, Tainan City

→ Designer portrait on page 524

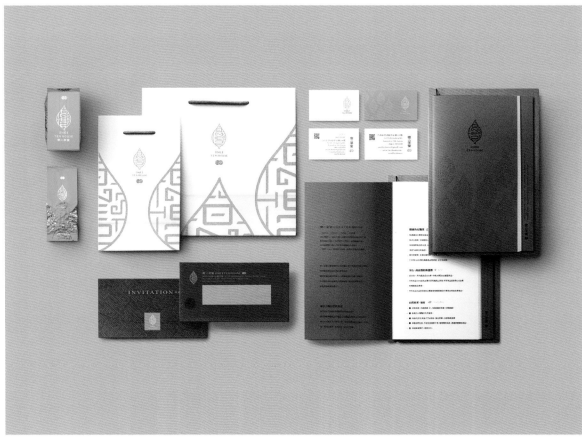

One 2 is a tea house brand located in Taiwan. Its brand design was basically created following the core values of two generations. The logo is inspired by the tea making process as well as the typical Taiwanese window frame of the old tea houses. All in all, the result is elegant and with a modern touch for the target group of young people. The green colour stands for the organic aspect of history and is combined with a warm grey, representing minimalism and modernism. The brand design has been consistently applied to packaging, advertising media and stationery.

Circuit Lab

[Brand Identity]

Circuit Lab is a start-up company that produces and distributes handcrafted coffee. The brand design, in product-related colours, conveys high-quality standards and increases the appeal to its target audience. The distinctive logo is derived from the expression of drip brewing. The contour map of the series is the key design element for the packaging of this coffee. Its delicate lines create a strong symbolic power and a remarkable effect.

Client
Circuit Lab, Taoyuan City

Design
Wan-Ju Shen, Taoyuan City

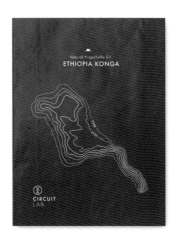

Sarmae Farm

[Brand Design]

The upmarket look of the brand design of these ginseng products from South Korea conveys high quality standards and uses storytelling to establish the brand's image. The story of the Sarmae farm tells about the company's founder, who went back to his home town, leaving behind his life in the city. His promise to grow ginseng using natural farming practices was motivated by the mission of keeping the environment clean. With the ginseng roots being clearly visible on the product packaging, the design concept delivers the entire farming experience to the customers and highlights the value of natural farming.

Client
Doolbob, Social Enterprise, Seoul

Design
the ZIDDA, Seoul

Creative Direction
Youjin Lee

Strategic Planning
Seulki Oh

Graphic Design
Youjin Lee, Seulki Oh, Younog Kim

H&

[Brand Design]

The concept of this brand focuses on healthy food alternatives for individuals who are gluten intolerant and would nevertheless like to eat biscuits. The "h" in the logo stands for home-made and healthy. The sugar-free biscuits made from brown rice are shown in a minimalist look on the packaging. The font as well as the bright colours convey the character of a natural brand. The entire design visualises reliability and emphasises the fact that these foods do not contain any artificial ingredients.

Client
Tsan Yu Yen Food Co., Ltd., Taichung City

Design
SCHEMA, Inc., Tokyo

Creative Direction
Ko Lin, SCHEMA, Inc., Taipei

Botong Dosirak

[Brand Identity]

The Botong box lunch concept emphasises the idea of serving delicious takeaway food from different countries. Representing the box lunch, the black square gives the logo a distinctive frame. The Korean, English and Chinese characters within the square symbolise the international character of the brand. In contrast to the white packaging, the logo looks particularly upmarket and high-quality. On uniforms, print-outs and online media, the brand design creates an attractive visual identity, which is to entice customers into focusing on the quality of the dishes.

Client
Simple Project & Co, Seoul

Design
Simple Project & Co,
Brand Marketing & Design Team, Seoul

Creative Direction / Art Direction
Hyunjin Lee

Graphic Design
Hyunjin Lee, Hyewon Lee

Photography
Sangjae Lee

Baskin Robbins Korea

[Brand Identity]

This new identity design of
Baskin Robbins was created by the
well known designer and architect
Alessandro Mendini. It was a relaunch
that was an opportunity to, once
again, highlight the brand's concept of
ice cream by using the beauty of curves.
Mendini's designs always strive to see
the world through the eyes of children
and this philosophy is directly reflected
in the branding. Bold colours and unique
characters characterise a distinctive
product world, the versatile motifs of
which appeal to the target group and
encourage collecting.

Client
BR Korea Co., Ltd., Seoul

Concept
Alessandro Mendini,
Atelier Mendini, Milan

Design
SPC Design Center, Seoul

Project Management
Hee Soo Hur

Creative Direction
Joong Gyu Kang

Graphic Design
Eugenia Rhee, Eun Young Bae,
So Yeon Yu

BAE

[Brand Design, Key Visual]

BAE is the name of an innovative brand providing products for children under the age of ten. Although the logo consists of just two rings, it contains profound connotations. Through a combination of graphics and an expanded use of the logo's components, visual content is presented in a minimalist form. The refreshingly plain colours represent the innocence and sunny disposition of children. A rich and varied visual expansion injects vigour into the brand and expresses a simple yet deep love for children, thus greatly enhancing the connotations of the brand.

Client
Hongyi Invest Company, Shanghai

Design
Rong, Shanghai

Artwork
Ruan Houfu

→ Designer portrait on page 521

Love

Growth

Exploring

Creativity

Exclamation Mark

Initial B

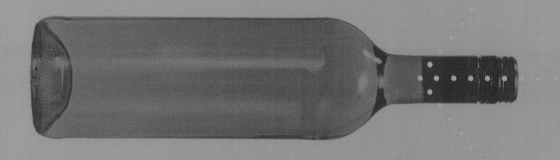

PACKAGING DESIGN

Red Dot: Grand Prix

Ageing Wine Bottle

[Beverage Packaging]

The excellent wines by Knipser Winery age for years in barrels and bottles. Time is the most important factor to their quality and flavour. In order to adequately commemorate the wine year of 2012 with clients and collectors, a unique packaging was created for a limited edition Cuvée XR, which was supposed to be bottled in 2015 after three years of ripening in barrels. The idea for the design was to create not only an innovative bottle label, but also an entire bottle that would turn the message of the wine into a visual and tactile experience. Therefore, a special seamless copper jacket, wrapping the bottle, was created to make the ageing process inside the bottle visible on the outside. This conveys the notion that the longer the wine ripens in the bottle, the more the copper jacket "ripens" too, visualising the ripening process by changing its surface colour. The bottle thus turns into a unique, individual and, above all, natural design item, changing with and marked by time. In addition, it reflects the corporate message reading "True greatness comes with age".

Statement by the jury

Equipping the bottle of this limited wine edition with a copper jacket stands out as a brilliant idea. Without the need for words, this directly reflects the most important factor for wines, namely time to ripen and developing the best flavour. It is this very process, which takes place inside the bottle, that the packaging design makes visible on the outside – thus lending the object an outer appearance that is as unique as the adventure of experiencing the flavour of this natural product.

reddot award 2016
grand prix

Client
Weingut Knipser, Laumersheim

Design
KOREFE, Hamburg
Kolle Rebbe GmbH, Hamburg

Chief Creative Officer
Stefan Kolle

Executive Creative Direction
Rolf Leger

Art Direction
Ursula Ritter

Text
Lorenz Ritter

Packaging Design
Patrick Schröder

Production
Martin Lühe

Red Dot: Best of the Best

Litos Valentina Passalacqua

[Beverage Packaging]

The vines in the Valentina Passalacqua Winery are grown on white stone soil. The wine is called "Litos", derived from the Latin word for "stone", in reference to the soil conditions of the land located in Apricena, in the region of Apulia, Italy. The wine, the fruits of which are a result of organic farming methods, is a completely natural product and expresses the characteristics of the rock layers in the soil. Serving as an inspiration, this "rock layering" was supposed to be reflected in the label with its three different types of natural paper in distinct shades of white, lending the label an original and sophisticated appeal. The unique concentric overlapping of the three labels was achieved through a specific automated production process and resulted in the creation of a three-layered, self-adhesive label made of different types of paper, which are attached to one another. This approach guarantees a production of labels that are not only identical but also minimalist in design, which immediately catches the eye.

Statement by the jury
The label design of the Litos wine is truly outstanding. The idea of three layers of different papers, on the one hand, tangibly illustrates the natural multilayered soil on which the delicate vines grow. On the other hand, the idea implements a previously unseen approach that further-more reflects the high quality of the wine in an elegant and striking way.

Client
Valentina Passalacqua, Apricena (Foggia)

Design
Spazio Di Paolo, Spoltore (Pescara)

Art Direction
Mario Di Paolo

→ Designer portrait on page 526

Red Dot: Best of the Best

Jägermeister COOLPACK

[Beverage Packaging]

Jägermeister's complex flavours taste best at minus 18 degrees centigrade or lower. However, consumers often overlook the "Serve Ice Cold" note on the back label, and, instead, store and even drink Jägermeister at room temperature, resulting in a subpar taste experience. Moreover, the bottle needs to be cooled intensively in the freezer to reach that perfect serving temperature. Instead of opting for a usual advertising campaign, which would tell consumers about the benefits of serving Jägermeister at such low temperatures, the problem was tackled at the most immediate point of contact: the bottle itself. Therefore, an entirely new COOLPACK Edition was developed by combining the classic 0.25-litre Jägermeister bottle with the iconic shape of typical coolpacks. The packaging thus turns into the message, promoting the idea of "best used ice cold" all by itself. The innovative design, which uses the same kind of molten glass that is used for the original Jägermeister bottle, is distinctive and unique, boasting a literally cool shape, the message of which is intuitively understood by consumers worldwide.

Statement by the jury
The new packaging design for Jägermeister pulls off an ingenious coup: in order to inform the young target group about the ideal serving temperature, the bottle was given the form and appearance of a classic coolpack. The packaging thus does not only serve to convey a message; it can also be used as a coolpack.

Client
Mast-Jägermeister, Wolfenbüttel

Design
Cheil Germany GmbH, Schwalbach

Chief Creative Officer
Roland Rudolf

Executive Creative Direction
Jörn Welle

Design Direction
Daniel Gumbert

Design Team
Martin Wenzlawiak, Stephan Merkle,
Ron Stasch, Sean-Andino Konrad

Client Service Director
Frank Neuhaus

→ Designer portrait on page 493

Red Dot: Best of the Best

BAANCHA

[Packaging]

BAANCHA is a new brand specialised in instant tea which comes in five traditional and popular Thai fruit flavours, offering a genuine taste of Thailand, their country of origin. The products have a natural taste and aim at making consumers feel as if they were drinking straight from the fruit, evoking the notion of a natural and healthy beverage. The packaging captures this concept by creating a stunning visual of a half-sliced piece of fruit that is made to resemble a teacup. The five different fruits, among them coconut mango and cantaloupe, immediately appeal to the senses of consumers. Set against a plain black background, each of the bright-coloured fruits radiates its own self-sufficient appeal. The intention was to make the design stand out from other brands on supermarket shelves. These first five products are the beginning of a more extensive range of flavours to come.

Statement by the jury
The design of the BAANCHA tea packaging excites with wonderful graphics. To cut the fruits of the individual flavours in half and represent the lower part as a teacup is a highly original and appropriate idea. It makes consumers understand the product immediately. In addition, the matte black of the packaging lends the simple instant tea a natural premium appearance.

Client
BCT BAANCHA

Design
Adhock Studio Co., Ltd., Bangkok

Graphic Design
Kasidist Sokantat

→ Designer portrait on page 483

Red Dot: Best of the Best

Coco Easy

[Beverage Packaging]

Promoting the benefits of eating coconut, Coco Easy was created to communicate the taste experience and the premium quality of this fresh fruit product. The concept of the packaging focuses on conveying the notion of freshness in a simple and easy way. A coconut is a natural product, with each coconut having a distinctive shape and size as well as continuing to breathe and ripen even after harvest. Consequently, there were high demands on the packaging material, as it had to present the product in an attractive way and, at the same time, provide adequate functionality. The highly breathable and waterproof plastic seal bag not only protects the coconut, but also allows consumers to check the freshness of the fruit through the transparent window. Furthermore, the kraft paper on the outside creates the texture and key message "Simple, Natural, Fresh" in order to highlight the philosophy behind the product directly on the packaging. Natural colours and an unobtrusive typeface further underline the notion of high quality and freshness.

Statement by the jury

This design concept solves the task of developing a packaging for fresh coconuts through a consequent extension of the fruit. A clever opening, for inserting a straw, was added to the shell itself, while a breathable and waterproof plastic seal bag protects the coconut and gives consumers a view and proof of the fruit's quality. This communicates the brand message of offering a real natural product both properly and pleasantly.

Client
Coco Life International Ltd. (Hong Kong),
Taiwan Branch, Taipei City

Design
Vetica Group AG, Taiwan Branch,
Taipei City

Head of Department
Jillian Cheng

Art Direction
Hisa Lee

Graphic Design
Kimi Huang

Strategic Planning
Yoji Yang

→ Designer portrait on page 531

Red Dot: Best of the Best

Chu Cheng

[Food Packaging]

In China, Chu Shijian is a legend – and his fruit and fruit boxes, showing the portrait of the "King of Oranges", are widely known. After a turbulent business life, including imprisonment, he started up a new business after his release, at the age of 74. Cultivating oranges on 130 hectares of former wasteland, his new business had an annual sales volume of several hundred million after ten years. Because of all the positive energy his entrepreneurship carries, these oranges are famed as "inspirational oranges" so that no better persuasive expression could be found for the packaging design than Chu Shijian himself. Therefore, the logo on the cardboard fruit boxes shows the woodcut of his head, wearing the typical hat of a farmer, next to the company name as a reference to both the famous figure behind the fruit imperium and the natural origin of the fruits. The creatively designed boxes elevate the fruits automatically when unpacked with a simple pull for easy access. On top of that, every single orange comes wrapped in a well thought-out protective cover.

Statement by the jury

This packaging was developed for both transporting and selling. It convinces with its nice and simple two-coloured prints and graphic design as well as with an outstandingly clever functionality, highlighting the fruits by means of an easy mechanism. Made of plain cardboard, this packaging presents the oranges on the market shelves as if each of them were a piece of jewellery.

Client
Yunnan Shijian Fruit Co., Ltd.

Design
TigerPan Packaging Design Lab.,
Shenzhen

Art Direction
Tiger Pan

→ Designer portrait on page 530

Red Dot: Best of the Best

Kaavi Porcini

[Food Packaging]

What does a packaging design for a regional food product need to look like to be positioned on the international market, while taking into account different cultural and visual nuances, and targeting both home-cooks and star chefs? This was the challenge for the design concept of these jars for high-quality wild mushrooms, handpicked from the Finnish forests at Kaavi. In order to ensure that the design stands out in the category of comparable premium products and breaks with the traditional design of premium packages, the concept aimed at introducing a bold and fresh element, yet retaining a touch of craftsmanship and premium feel. While each of the four different species – Porcini, Chanterelle, Funnel Chanterelle and Black Chanterelle – and its authentic quality is reflected and immediately recognisable on the label, glass jars were chosen as containers as they best save the aroma. The purist aesthetic and clear design of the label features a white subfont with a graphic illustration of the actual product, which is accompanied by abstract colour blots, each representing one of the species.

Statement by the jury
The label and packaging design of this wild Finnish gourmet product convinces with a very clear and original approach. Presenting the mushrooms in a jar not only conveys their naturalness, which consumers can thus recognise immediately, but also delivers the perfect solution to keeping the aromas. Moreover, the simple and charming illustrations on the label give the concept an artistic touch.

Client
Kaavin Herkkutattitehdas Ltd., Helsinki

Design
Aune Creative Oy, Helsinki

Creative Direction
Helena Masalin

→ Designer portrait on page 486

Red Dot: Best of the Best

Zhangren Workshop
[Food Packaging]

Rice candy from Zhangren Workshop is a well-known Chinese specialty from Dujiangyan, in the province of Sichuan. Since the product is often imitated, this design concept aimed at following a new approach by creating a package that is inspired by nearby Mount Qingcheng. Called Mount Zhangren in ancient times, this mountain is considered the birthplace of Taoism and features a historic monastery which has always been visited by scholars and monks, not least for seclusion and meditation. It is also said, and this is the core of the brand story, that the very first rice candies were made here and served here to followers. Therefore, the bag, which is inspired by the look of a typical rice bag, shows the illustrated image of a monk. Its distinctive feature is that the bag's opening is sealed with a rope, corresponding to the bun hairstyle of the shown Taoist monk, whereby the packaging creates a visual bridge to its contents.

Statement by the jury
The packaging design for this traditional Chinese product interprets the contents in a modern way, with an outstanding illustration. Having the Taoist's hair, respectively his bun, as the closure, which is wrapped round with a strong rope, is not only a great and innovative idea, but also gives the product a strong visual appearance. As a result, a recognisable and well thought-out brand design was developed.

Client
Sichuan Guge Dynasty Brand Design
Consultant Co., Ltd., Chengdu

Design
Sichuan Guge Dynasty Brand Design
Consultant Co., Ltd., Chengdu

Art Direction
Xia Ke

Graphic Design
Shan Chunhao, Jiang Peng

→ Designer portrait on page 499

Red Dot: Best of the Best

innisfree My Cushion

[Cosmetics Packaging]

innisfree, a cosmetics brand only using organic ingredients, developed a special product called My Cushion that allows customers to create their own cosmetic cushions. The series offers a selection of 100 different cushion cases and beauty tools featuring different patterns, including polka dots, stripes and many others, and 12 colours that are inspired by the landscape of Jeju Island. Pastel tones and vivid colours may be chosen to attain the pattern of one's choice and liking. The new case is remarkably light in weight and 22.5 mm thick. Furthermore, it is angled towards the bottom, presenting a slim and compact shape, and is packed in a simple box of paper, which also has a modest and natural appearance. All 100 types of cushion cases have a matte finish and exude a feeling of warmth and softness as well as they, despite their different surfaces, have a uniform look. Thus, the brand identity creates a high recognition value while, at the same time, the packaging design fulfils the demands for individuality.

Statement by the jury

Many stylish variations from which consumers can choose, a beautiful graphic design as well as an intuitive opening mechanism: these are the striking qualities of this eye-catching product packaging design for the cosmetics brand innisfree. The pleasant and immediately recognisable visual appearance convinces with its consumer-oriented concept.

Client
innisfree Corporation, Seoul

Design
innisfree Design Team, Seoul
purunimage, Seoul

Creative Direction
Mi-Young Park, innisfree

Art Direction/Product Design
Sunny Na, innisfree

Graphic Design
Sunny Na, innisfree
Min-Sook Kang, purunimage

Head of Marketing
So-Hee Park, Yi-Soo Bea, innisfree

→ Designer portrait on page 503

Red Dot: Best of the Best

Urban Breeze
[Cosmetics Packaging]

Urban Breeze is a unisex fragrance line that was created to reflect natural elements of the earth, such as stones and wood, in a modern design. Targeted at both men and women, the design of the containers was developed from a plain rectangular shape. The simplicity of this shape was then harmonised with a touch of real-wood-like material for the bottom and for the original cap, which, in addition, shows the organic form of a stone to evoke a sense of nature when using the products. Basic black was chosen as the main colour for the containers in order to give them an air of dignity, while the soft-toned accent colour makes each product of the line stand out in terms of its own identity. Following a distinctive design concept, the box communicates continuation in creating fragrance containers for one and the same brand. The strictly formal design idiom is complemented by clear typography, turning this packaging into a consistently crafted design work.

Statement by the jury
Thanks to its packaging design, the Urban Breeze fragrance line has emerged as a very beautiful and minimalist cosmetic series. Featuring clear rectangular and square shapes, combined with the organic form of a stone as well as natural materials and colours, the packaging lends the product an appearance that conveys premium quality and elegance.

Client
The SAEM International Co., Ltd., Seoul

Design
The SAEM International Co., Ltd., Seoul

→ Designer portrait on page 529

Red Dot: Best of the Best

L'EAUNDRY
Fragrance Laundry Detergent

[Packaging]

The key product by L'EAUNDRY, a brand for scented luxury products, is a fragrance laundry detergent of premium quality, which was relaunched in 2016 with new scents. In order to make the product work in its segment and justify the high price, it was necessary to bring a sense of glamour and luxury into the unsexy world of washing detergents. Therefore, the packaging design is based on the shape and style of classic perfume bottles. The huge and difficult challenge of finding a way to lend PVC an exclusive first-class appearance resulted in a new design that makes the bottle look like an oversized one-litre perfume flacon. The reduced and thus clear, elegant shape of the packaging underlines the premium appearance of the prod- uct and piques consumer curiosity. The labels boast a textile surface feel and come in different colour schemes so that customers can easily distinguish between different scents. Created in collaboration with a perfume expert, the scents were particularly developed to be long lasting on the washed textiles.

Statement by the jury
Creating a packaging design for a laundry detergent that has the appearance of a luxury per- fume flacon is an unusual idea. In a clever manner, the hardly exciting market segment of detergents thus not only sees an innovative shift in direction, the product by L'EAUNDRY also boasts an aesthetic that turns it into an appealing eye-catcher within a premium price segment.

Client
T.D.G. Vertriebs GmbH & Co. KG,
Hamburg

Design
KOREFE, Hamburg
Kolle Rebbe GmbH, Hamburg

Chief Creative Officer
Stefan Kolle

Creative Direction/Product Design
Christian Doering

Project Management
Jana Bier

Text
Lorenz Ritter

Photography
Imke Jansen

Retouch Artist
Tommy Szewczuk

Production
Martin Lühe

→ Designer portrait on page 507

Red Dot: Best of the Best

Lenovo Yoga Series

[Packaging]

For the future Lenovo Yoga series, consisting of a smartphone, a tablet and a notebook, in both standard and premium product categories, a new family package design was created. Overall emphasis on the earth-tone paper material and sparse printing lend the design a simple and bold as well as intimate and authentic appeal. While the brown paper is used for the standard category to highlight its eco-friendliness, the darker soft paper is used for the premium category to highlight quality and high value. The Lenovo "tag" logo is a representation of the essence of the new Lenovo brand visual identity. The packaging was designed to be as thin as possible so that it is optimally space-saving, easy to transport and aesthetically contemporary. When opening the box, the lifting structure will slightly raise the product, making it look inviting and as if coming towards the user. Integrated into the fully stringent design concept, this detail adds a nice element of surprise.

Statement by the jury

The packaging concept for the Lenovo Yoga series captivates with a spectacularly minimalistic and aesthetic graphic design. Thus, the set of different products shows a coherent overall appearance, complemented by a well thought-out material use and implementation. Furthermore, the beautiful single boxes are equipped with functional features that perform very well.

Client
Lenovo (Beijing) Ltd., Beijing

Design
Lenovo (Beijing) Ltd., Beijing

→ Designer portrait on page 509

AKIU Wine

[Beverage Packaging]

Akiu Wine is a small Japanese vineyard surrounded by mountains. Inspired by Mt. Daitodake, the vineyard's prominent terroir and classical Japanese lattice design, this packaging concept combines tradition with modernity in redesigning the brand. The pattern selected expresses Akiu's seasons, which match each type of wine, but also the expansion inspired by the owner's wish to increase international brand awareness. To emphasise the wine's complex flavours and the craftsmanship behind it, the label uses hot stamping on textured paper, fostering a unique and colourful look.

Client
Raisin de Akiu, Miyagi

Design
Dentsu Inc., Tokyo

Creative Direction
Tomohiro Nozawa

Graphic Design
Shunichi Sato

Librottiglia

[Beverage Packaging]

Librottiglia, the evocative name of this wine range, comes from the union of two Italian words: "libro" (book) and "bottiglia" (bottle). Its label is reimagined as a mini-book presenting one of three different short stories, illustrated with an intriguing cover image and attached to the bottle with a fine cord. The cord converts the opening and closing of the book into a ritual and strengthens the coordinated identity of the range. The textured paper and the special print finishes enhance the tactile aspect of the experience. Finally, the 375 ml bottle was chosen to express the concept of the project: a short story to read while enjoying two glasses of wine.

Client
Matteo Correggia, Canale d'Alba (Cuneo)

Design
Reverse Innovation, Milan/Amsterdam

Art Direction/Concept
Mirco Onesti

Graphic Design
Michela De Nicolis

Coordination
Paula Acosta

Photography
Francesco Zanet, Milan
Studio Effe, Milan

Author
Patrizia Laquidara, Danilo Zanelli,
Regina Nadaes Marques

Theopetra

[Beverage Packaging]

This packaging design was created for
wines from organically grown grapes in
the family vineyards of the Theopetra
Estate. The vineyards of the estate extend around the prehistoric cave of
Theopetra at the foothills of the Meteora
Rocks. The imagery artfully highlights
the mystery of Meteora: red blotches of
colour, which are reminiscent of fingerprints, adorn the label and make it easy
to choose between several types of
wine. The four different key visuals also
create a characteristic and distinctive
overall image on the white cardboard
packaging.

Client
Tsililis Winery, Athens

Design
k2design, Athens

Creative Direction
Yiannis Kouroudis

Consentido

[Beverage Packaging]

Consentido is a wine line from a vine-yard cooperative in southeastern Spain offering five wines made from just one grape. To depict all influences such as climate, technical requirements and soil properties in an artistic manner, the individual labels show a coherent collage, combining sophisticated colours and hot foil stamping with illustrations. Icons taken from weather maps and fragments of photographs provide an experience of the wine-growing region, aesthetically demonstrating the manifold factors which make up the taste of the wine in the end. Short poetic texts on the back label, set in puristic typography, continue the story.

Client
Bodegas La Púrisima, Yecla, Murcia

Design
Ruska, Martin, Associates GmbH, Berlin

Art Direction/Creative Direction
Francisca Martin

Graphic Design
Paula Cano, Joao Colaco

Illustration
Paula Cano

Amber Wine

[Beverage Packaging]

Originating from Shandong during the
Dawenkou culture period six thousand
years ago, Hua Diao wine is a repre-
sentative of the long history of wine
culture in China. Due to its long storage
and brewing process, the wine is very
similar to amber in its golden colour.
The black packaging intends to show
the cultural nature of the wine as a gift
while enhancing its select qualities. With
its innovative structure, the packaging
design likens the wine to a gem. The
exquisite traditional Chinese knot rein-
forces the brand's cultural significance
and enriches the overall image.

Client
Fengfan Farm Products, Jintan

Design
Rong, Shanghai

→ Designer portrait on page 521

Yunnan Red

[Beverage Packaging]

Yunnan is one of the most charming and exotic places in China. It is home to 25 ethnic groups and thus the largest population of Chinese ethnic minorities. Both the box and the wine bottle are decorated with the silver headwear that is a fashion accessory typically worn at major festivals. The inside of the black box is dotted with hand-drawn bird patterns, which embody unique regional characteristics and the natural environment. The packaging design is an impressive work of oriental art. Moreover, it blends in with luxury brand equity and corporate culture as well.

Client

Yunnan Red Wine Co., Ltd., Kunming City

Design

Shenzhen Lingyun
Creative Packaging Design Co., Ltd.,
Shenzhen

The Skoupil Winery

[Beverage Packaging]

The Skoupil Winery is a family vineyard
in southern Moravia in the Czech
Republic. The yellow diagonal in the logo
was inspired by the diagonal on the flag
of the village where this wine-growing
estate and its vineyards are located. The
basis of the wine-label design for the
terroir range is a hand-drawn map of
the village of Velké Bílovice. The monochrome map is supplemented by individual vineyard trails and attractive
small details. The label of each specific
wine has a map with highlights in colour to show exactly where the grapes
were grown.

Client
Vinařství Petr Skoupil, Velké Bílovice

Design
Pergamen, Trnava

Creative Direction
Juraj Demovič

Graphic Design
Juraj Demovič, Lívia Lörinczová

Photography
Jakub Dvořák

Illustration
Veronika Klimová

Piquentum

[Beverage Packaging]

In order to show the vintage of this natural wine, this label takes a creative approach to providing information about the weather conditions during the year of harvest, and thus about the natural conditions in which the wine matured. In cooperation with the Croatian Meteorological Service, data on weather conditions in vineyard regions were collected. Circles, as standard meteorological rain symbols, show the amount of rainfall in a particular month. The aggregation of circles with different sizes, which are embossed into the label, create a characteristic overall image. Each label (2013, 2014, 2015) indicates what the year was like, making it possible to compare the different vintages easily.

Client
Vinski podrum Buzet

Winemaker
Dimitri Brečević

Design
STUDIO SONDA, Vižinada

Creative Direction
Jelena Fiškuš, Sean Poropat

3D Shaping
Eugen Slavik

Old Hands

[Beverage Packaging]

This wine named Old Hands is dedicated
to the pioneers of the biological vini-
culture of Bodegas La Purisima. The challenge was to create a label design that
conveys exactly this homage to the ef-
forts of the vintners. Thus, two illustrations of the vineyards and fields were
created, where the palm of an old hand
can be discerned only at second glance.
Just like plowed furrows in the soil,
hands are a testimony of time which is
carved line by line, each line a story.
The gold details on the label reflect the
high quality of the product and the appreciation of nature.

Client
Bodegas La Púrisima, Yecla, Murcia

Design
Ruska, Martin, Associates GmbH, Berlin

Creative Direction/Art Direction
Francisca Martin, Roman Ruska

Graphic Design
Roman Ruska, Joao Colaco,
Laurie Millotte

Illustration
Joao Colaco, Jacobo Labella

Xiraz!

[Beverage Packaging]

The design concept of this wine label follows the guiding principle "prohibitively good" in order to communicate the renown of the vintner Xavier Vignon and the high quality of his wines. Unconventional imagery puts the initial letter of his first name into focus. In combination with the name of a red wine, this creates the product name "XIRAZ!". With a red X in the background, the label is eye-catching and reminiscent of a prohibition sign. Three background colour variants, which form a visual unit together with the key visual, make the wine selection easier and create a distinctive overall appearance.

Client
Wine in Black GmbH, Berlin

Design
Ruska, Martin, Associates GmbH, Berlin

Creative Direction/Art Direction
Roman Ruska

Graphic Design
Roman Ruska, Irvan Syaffrudin

Winehunters

[Beverage Packaging]

The name of the vineyard Winehunters is based on the aim of its six owners to capture taste trends with their special wines. Analogous to the subject of hunting, a target became the key element of the packaging design. The names of the wines are likewise inspired by the subject of hunting. The Pinot Noir, which is a great accompaniment to red meat, is called "Der Jäger" (The Hunter) and the white Pinot Gris as a good companion to fish has been named "Der Fischer" (The Fisherman). Each grape variety is represented by an intuitively understandable coat of arms on the label, which as a cropped key visual provides a clear view of the wine.

Client
Winehunters,
Neustadt an der Weinstraße

Design
Peter Schmidt Group, Hamburg

Design Direction
Dennis Dominguez

Design Team
Aurelio Escuredo, Juliana Fischer

Production
Tobias Gagelmann

D'Alessandro

[Beverage Packaging]

The design of these wine labels visually incorporates an aspect of the vineyard's history, namely that a noble ancestor was a horse breeder. As a symbol of both strength and elegance, the paper cut of a horse functions as a reference to the origin and quality of the wine. The typographic technique and the grace of the motifs are rendered by the sobriety of the labels. The consistent implementation in three different variants helps to distinguish the three grape varieties, vividly emphasising the character of the wine.

Client
Azienda Agricola Francesco D'Alessandro, Ortona (Chieti)

Design
Spazio Di Paolo, Spoltore (Pescara)

Art Direction
Mario Di Paolo

→ Designer portrait on page 526

Slow Village

[Beverage Packaging]

Slow Village is a brand of fermented wine produced in the traditional Korean way. The packaging design focuses on conveying the special features of the products by displaying the shape of the raw ingredients of the wine. The zigzags on the label symbolise the fermentation of fruit. The image of traditional wine was interpreted and expressed in simple, contemporary imagery. In terms of colour strategy, the refreshing taste of the wine and its modern image were emphasised through the use of different colours, matching each type of fruit.

Client
nextbrand. Co., Ltd., Seoul

Design
nextbrand. Co. Ltd., Seoul

Zhu Gu Huan

[Beverage Packaging]

This gift packaging for Cereal Wine reinterprets traditional imagery and employs a crested ibis as the key visual in order to emphasise the ecological quality of the product. Sophisticated graphic techniques give the product a premium look. The black-and-white contrasting, which consistently characterises all packaging elements, is a distinctive feature. A sophisticated outer package was created for this gift set with two different wines, which are easy to distinguish due to their colour design. The bottles feature a print that covers the entire glass surface and come in a small cardboard box, two of which are combined in each outer box.

Client
Shenzhen Baixinglong Creative Packaging Co., Ltd., Shenzhen

Design
Shenzhen Baixinglong Creative Packaging Co., Ltd., Shenzhen

Fresh Bamboo Wine

[Beverage Packaging]

In western China there are vast areas that are mountainous and rich in lakes, known for their special climate. The natural unpolluted environment provides excellent growing conditions for fresh bamboo wine. Therefore, the designer incorporated freehand brushwork of the growing environment into the packaging design. The mountain silhouettes express the high quality of this fresh bamboo wine and the product concept of a close connection with nature. The bottle was fired with porcelain and has a ceramic coating, the contours and green colour of which evoke associations with bamboo.

Client
Bamboo Wine Co., Ltd., Jiangxi

Design
Shenzhen Yuto Packaging
Technology Co., Ltd., Shenzhen

Art Direction
Chen Ying Song

Graphic Design
Wan Yue Ding

→ Designer portraits on page 535, 536

KOI Japanese Sake

[Beverage Packaging]

This packaging design for Sake, called "KOI", has chosen the most famous Japanese ornamental koi fish as a key visual. Its typical red pattern is printed directly onto the white bottle, which resembles the shape of a koi, using a Japanese brushstroke technique. By cutting the shape of the fish silhouette out of the box, the image of a koi is visually emphasised. The colour contrast in combination with the gold-hued accents creates a luxury impression and achieves a high degree of differentiation from competing products at the point of sale. The beauty of the design encourages reuse of the bottle as a decorative object.

Client
Imayotsukasa Sake Brewery Co. Ltd., Niigata

Design
BULLET Inc., Tokyo

Art Direction
Aya Codama, BULLET Inc.

Typography
Kasetsu, Tokyo

Project Management
Masayuki Habuki,
Wakyo Shouten Co. Ltd., Tokyo
Yosuke Tanaka,
Imayotsukasa Sake Brewery Co. Ltd.

Printing
Tatsuhiro Yamagishi,
Yamaharu Glass Co. Ltd., Tokyo
Shunsuke Kayama,
Taiyo Printing Co. Ltd., Tokyo

→ Designer portrait on page 492

He Wine

[Beverage Packaging]

The dragon boat festival, a traditional Chinese festival, is celebrated on 5 May in the Chinese lunar calendar each year to memorialise the patriotic poet Qu Yuan, who drowned himself in the Miluo River on that day. In order to target the young generation born after the 1980s and 1990s, this packaging design shows an original hand-drawn illustration of a harmonious memorial scene – riding a fish to celebrate, Qu Yuan is eating rice dumplings and drinking this He Wine. With bright colours, the motif conveys a joyful mood. Moreover, the overall packaging style is contemporary with strong visual impact and distinction.

Client
Shenzhen Baixinglong Creative Packaging Co., Ltd., Shenzhen

Design
Shenzhen Baixinglong Creative Packaging Co., Ltd., Shenzhen

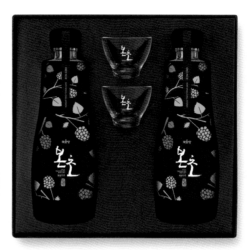

Bon Cho

[Beverage Packaging]

Kooksoondang, a leading producer of traditional Korean liquors, has launched Bon Cho as a mass luxury product for traditional holidays only. Aside from the label design on the bottle, which depicts a rich and full flavour as well as scent, the packaging design illustrates the dispersion of the flavour and scent against a clean white background. The black on the sides and bottom keeps the eye focused on the message on top, thereby completing the stylish and up-market quality of the Boncho gift sets. Thus, a new interpretation of the stereo-typical image of traditional liquor has been achieved in a contemporary way.

Client
Kooksoondang Brewery Co., Ltd., Seoul

Design
Kooksoondang Brewery Co., Ltd., Seoul

Executive Creative Direction
Young-Ho Suk

Graphic Design
Sung-Gu Hwang

Lao Tzu Liquor

[Beverage Packaging]

Full of oriental aesthetics and Zen inspiration, the packaging design of the Lao Tzu Liquor makes a strong visual impact. The packaging shows a contemporary interpretation of the traditional craft of making black pottery. Lao Tzu was the founder of Taoism, therefore the design employs the most symbolic image of Taoism and black pottery to interpret the essence of this philosophy. All packaging materials are sourced from the product's original location. The elegantly shaped bottle comes in artistic cardboard packing. The overall impression piques the customers' buying interest and highlights the value of the gift.

Client
Lao Tzu Liquor Co., Ltd., Anhui

Design
Shenzhen Yuto Packaging
Technology Co., Ltd., Shenzhen

Art Direction/Graphic Design
Chen Ying Song

→ Designer portrait on page 535

BEMBEL-WITH-CARE

[Beverage Packaging]

In line with a surprising product concept, this gift box contains drink cans with "Apfelwein" (German dry cider) in four flavours in a trendy design. The eye-catching packaging design clearly stands out in this more conservative, traditional market segment and is aimed at a young target audience. The so-called "care package" is made of strong, premium-grade black cardboard. The outer packaging and contents form a harmonious unit, with colour contrasts used effectively. All in all, the gift box clearly embodies the brand identity.

Client
BEMBEL-WITH-CARE GmbH & Co. KG, Mannheim

Design
BEMBEL-WITH-CARE GmbH & Co. KG, Mannheim

→ Designer portrait on page 491

Dr. P. Lacebo Drops

[Beverage Packaging]

Pseudo-medical preparations have been
developed, designed and manufactured
in-house as humorous gift articles under
the label "Dr. P. Lacebo" since 2011. The
packaging design for a new product
series consisting of five fine brandies
imitates the look and feel of a medicine
bottle. The labels humorously and ironically indicate different areas of application and promote, for instance, rasp-
berry brandy as an anti-senility tonic.
The monochrome design is a successful
contemporary and original interpretation of traditional pharmacy labels.

Client
Dr. P. Lacebo, Westhausen

Design
abraxas design – Büro für Gestaltung,
Westhausen

Creative Direction/Art Direction
Riccarda Mueller, Patricia Doleschel,
Christine Doleschel

Concept/Text
Riccarda Mueller

Dr. P. Lacebo Elixirs

[Beverage Packaging]

These liquors – ironically marketed as miracle elixirs – are an original gift idea. Under the label "Dr. P. Lacebo", a packaging design with an iconic look was developed to attract a great deal of attention to these elixirs. The name of the brand already hints at the ironic character of the gift items, which offers five label variations in order to match the individual gifting occasion. The "Work Life Balance" elixir, a Williams Christ pear brandy, for instance, is suitable for stressed people.

Client
Dr. P. Lacebo, Westhausen

Design
abraxas design – Büro für Gestaltung, Westhausen

Creative Direction/Art Direction
Riccarda Mueller, Patricia Doleschel, Christine Doleschel

Concept/Text
Riccarda Mueller

64° Reykjavík Distillery –
Three Icelandic Liqueurs

[Beverage Packaging]

This packaging design showcases the unique product qualities of these three Icelandic liqueurs. The label is charac-terised by the three-by-three letter com-bination reflecting three kinds of indi-genous Icelandic fruit or plant: blueberry, rhubarb and crowberry. Three is also the number of ingredients in each bottle: wild grown fruit, sugar and alcohol. The label's colours are derived from the natural hues of the fruits, underlining the source of the wild ingredients. The logo gives a clear description of the origin of the contents, both in words and symbols, with Reykjavik being lo-cated near latitude 64 degrees north.

Client
Reykjavik Distillery ehf, Reykjavik

Design
Reykjavik Distillery ehf, Reykjavik

Creative Direction
Judith Orlishausen, Snorri Jonsson

Graphic Design
Mathias Gödert, Kristin Beier

Wealth & Honor

[Beverage Packaging]

The Johnnie Walker Blue special edition was launched on the Korean market to celebrate the New Year of 2016. It includes Korean characters and mother-of-pearl inlays in the design, making it a special gift and collectible. Its bottle, which is inlaid with the symbols of wealth and prosperity, such as peony, deer and peacock, is a work of art. Each side of the brand's square signature bottle bears the letters of the Korean translation of "Wealth and Honor". When the four bottles are put together in a line, it turns into a complete motif displaying these two words.

Client
Johnnie Walker House Seoul

Head of Marketing
Hyuk Soo (James) Lee, Hye Ja Kim, Ji Sun Park, Diageo, Seoul

Design
Indirain, Seoul

Project Management
Jung Hwa Lee, Indirain

Art Direction
Ji Yeon Chang, Jing Dong Cui, Indirain

Artwork
Ji Yoon Kim, Seoul

Istanblue Vodka

[Beverage Packaging]

Istanblue is a vodka brand with a name
that refers to the soul of the city of
Istanbul. To express the unique spirit of
the metropolis, the Bosporus is represented by an indentation in the glass,
which is unusual in beverage bottles.
Both shores of the Bosporus are illustrated in serigraph printing, which
depicts the culture and lifestyle of the
Asian and European parts of the city.
To create a young, dynamic look, the
graphics resemble graffiti style. The main
packaging material is glass. Minimum
waste is being considered here, which is
important in such high-quantity mass
productions.

Client
Mey Icki Sanayi ve Ticaret A.S.,
Istanbul

Design
Shotopop, London
Tasarim Ussu Ltd., Istanbul

Graphic Design
Shotopop

Bottle Design
Tasarim Ussu Ltd.

Smirnoff
Peppermint Twist

[Beverage Packaging]

In time for the winter season, this packaging design for Smirnoff Peppermint Twist, a seasonal peppermint-flavoured vodka sold in a limited edition, was created for the US market. Inspired by the colours and peppermint flavour associated with the festive winter season, the entire bottle was wrapped in striking red-and-white stripes with an added twist of cool peppermint green. The white scented ink has a frost-like textured finish, which adds to the tactility of the bottle. The overall result is a design that cleverly evokes the vodka's cool peppermint taste with a premium look and flavourful appeal.

Client
Diageo, Norwalk, Connecticut

Design
Design Bridge, London

Creative Direction
Asa Cook

Graphic Design
Sam Cutler, Rebecca Clarke, Gavin Daniels

Account Management
Laura Strusiewicz, Susanne Wild

28 DRINKS

[Beverage Packaging]

The colourful packaging design of these drink cans is classically elegant and markedly subtle. The reduction to a few striking design elements ensures that 28 Drinks blend harmoniously into their surroundings. Specifically designed for the restaurant market, the cans cut a fine figure next to any bottle of spirits. Their specific colours – such as yellow for tonic water, petrol blue for bitter lemon, green for ginger ale, or red for pink grapefruit – also make certain that, even in dark bars, no one picks up the wrong product. Functionality and time-less design thus combine in a harmoni-ous way.

Client
Splendid Drinks AG, Senningerberg

Design
Werbeagentur Zweipunktnull GmbH, Föhren

Graphic Design
Uli Deus, Achim Bach, Reiner Rempis

Komju

[Beverage Packaging]

Komju is an alcoholic drink with a taste of citron and lemon. It mainly targets women in their late twenties and early thirties, who enjoy soft alcoholic drinks in the company of their friends. Metallic silver and green hues characterise the premium look of the bottle. Also, the vertical oval shapes are used in a distinctive way to convey various taste concepts. In order to avoid creating a visual impression that is too strong due to the dominant green colour scheme, curved serifs have been applied to the font. Furthermore, the dot in the "j" is emphasised with a pink circle to add a contrasting accent.

Client
Kooksoondang Brewery Co., Ltd., Seoul

Design
Kooksoondang Brewery Co., Ltd., Seoul

Art Direction
Youngho Suk

Artwork
Gini Kwak

Hopfmeister
Microbrewery

[Beverage Packaging]

Hopfmeister beers are a mix of Bavarian heritage and a humorous approach to design and storytelling. Ingredients and craftsmanship are taken seriously, whereas the Hopfmeister brand and its concept created by a group of designers are amusing. The label design comprises a series of different versions, which, according to each individual beer type, illustrate a unique taste experience and show a mix of vintage and modern elements with patterns made of steel engravings, and a typography combining letterpress and classic styles. The names of the beers, in particular, create an appealing quality, while the colour coding along with matching illustrations tells funny stories.

Client
Hopfmeister, Munich

Design
Gallo Design, Munich

Art Direction
Marc Gallo

Mazelprost

[Beverage Packaging]

In 2015, Israel and Germany celebrated the 50th anniversary of their diplomatic relations. Inspired by the ideal of true friendship, an innovative hummus beer called Mazelprost was created. The brand name combines two specialities for which the countries are famous, hummus and beer, but also the Hebrew expression "Mazel Tov!" and the German word "Prost!". Its transparent label, seal and colour scheme reflect current trends within the craft beer segment to give Mazelprost a contemporary image. In December 2015, Mazelprost was added to the collection of the Jewish Museum in Berlin.

Client

Botschaft des Staates Israel, Berlin

Design

Peter Schmidt Group, Hamburg
BBDO Berlin
BBDO Tel Aviv

Coors Light

[Beverage Packaging]

This citrus variant was released as the brand's light beer during the summer season. Its packaging was designed to appeal to the specific target market of Hispanic millennials. The solution combines the new Coors Light visual identity elements, including the iconic Rocky Mountain range and a silver and red colour palette, and also introduces citrus flavour cues. The elegant use of citrus wedges to form the epic mountains of the Rockies provides differentiation from the core range, while also communicating the refreshing flavour. The citrus hues of the wedges are offset against the cool silver background, adding impact to the store shelf.

Client
MillerCoors, Chicago

Design
Turner Duckworth, London/San Francisco

Head of Design
David Turner, Bruce Duckworth

Creative Direction
Mark Waters

Design Direction
David Thompson

Graphic Design
David Thompson, Matt Lurcock,
John Randall, Stuart Madden,
Adam Cartwright, Jennie Spiller,
Miles Marshall, Mathilde Solanet

Production
James Norris, Will Rawlings

Account Management
Fay Bandoula, Kate Elkins

ID Jons

[Beverage Packaging]

Alexander is a well-known beer blogger in Russia. More recently he became a brewer with the brand name ID Jons. Inspired by the name, this packaging design focuses on the topic of identification. The design adds humour by placing identikit portraits of persons who resemble famous people on the labels. This imagery is a fairly revolutionary solution for the label, even in the craft beer category, but it allows this beer to stand out and attract new experience hunters. The key visuals are supplemented by style names relating to the characters of the different beer types.

Client
ID Jons, Moscow

Design
Svoe Mnenie, Moscow

Creative Direction
Andrey Kugaevskikh

Art Direction
Yaroslav Zheleznyakov

Illustration
Antonina Shvets

Pepsi Prestige Bottle

[Beverage Packaging]

With the introduction of the sleek aluminium Pepsi Prestige bottle, the Pepsi experience is enhanced across the range, including Pepsi, Pepsi MAX and Diet Pepsi. Its shape reflects the Pepsi heritage by taking its inspiration from earlier classic glass designs in their most recognisable and simplified form. The smooth aluminium finish is cool to the touch, communicating the refreshment of the product inside. Subtle graphic patterns and vibrant colours capture the eye and differentiate between the variants. The clean shape allows for countless designs to be incorporated into future versions of the Prestige bottle.

Client
PepsiCo, Purchase, New York

Design
PepsiCo Design & Innovation Center, New York

Pepsi HomeMade

[Packaging]

Pepsi and SodaStream have teamed up to give consumers the customisable experience of a freshly made soda to meet their changing needs. With the introduction of Pepsi HomeMade, they can transform water into a personalised version of their favourite soda brands, Pepsi and Sierra Mist. Alongside capsules, the packaging design for Pepsi HomeMade comprises branded bottles, in which the self-mixed beverage can be served and consumed. The clear colour coding of the outer packaging makes the caps easy to distinguish, while the geometric patterns visually emphasise the colour contrasts.

Client
PepsiCo, Purchase, New York

Design
PepsiCo Design & Innovation Center, New York

Nongfu Spring Mineral Water for Infants

[Beverage Packaging]

Nongfu Spring is a natural mineral water suitable for mixing with baby formula. The packaging design was specifically developed to meet the needs of young parents. To accommodate different hand sizes, the design allows the bottle to be comfortably held in two ways, from the front and the back. The one-litre capacity covers the full-day requirements of under-two-year-old babies. The label design communicates the purity of the source, conveying a sense of growth and nurturing through the use of an icon that depicts water, forest and birds.

Client
Nongfu Spring Co., Ltd., Hangzhou

Design
Hangzhou Hotdesign Co., Ltd., Hangzhou

Project Management
Hu Yu

Nongfu Spring
Mineral Water for Kids

[Beverage Packaging]

This new mineral water from Nongfu Spring with its leak-free cap targets the youth market. Even when the cap is open, water cannot leak out if the bottle falls over. Thanks to the slim silhouette of the bottle, teenagers can use it with one hand. The imaginative, unique label design conveys a sense of the natural world of the water source. A set of inspiring illustrations were commissioned to reflect the four seasons, bringing to life the wild species that inhabit the nature reserve where the mineral water is sourced.

Client
Nongfu Spring Co., Ltd., Hangzhou

Design
Hangzhou Hotdesign Co., Ltd.,
Hangzhou
Horse, Peterborough

Art Direction
Dong Lei

Project Management
Hu Yu

Kirin Natural Mineral Water

[Beverage Packaging]

Kirin Natural Mineral Water is a bottled water product sold only via an e-commerce website. Since the water is delivered, customers do not have to carry any water crates. Thirty 310 ml bottles with six different designs are assorted in one crate. To blend in with various kinds of interiors, the bottles featuring a blue print show motifs of water in nature. Only one side of the bottle displays the product name printed in a small font, so that the patterns on the back are seen through the refraction of the mineral water. The patterns look different depending on the angle and the movement of the water.

Client
Kirin Beverage Company, Limited,
Tokyo

Head of Marketing
Masahiro Chiba

Design
SAGA Inc., Tokyo
DENTSU Inc., Tokyo

Creative Direction
Tatsuya Hamajima, DENTSU Inc.
Kota Sagae, SAGA Inc.

Art Direction
Kota Sagae, SAGA Inc.
Yukie Tamura, DENTSU Inc.

Graphic Design
Kota Sagae, SAGA Inc.

UNI-WATER

[Beverage Packaging]

UNI-WATER is a drinking-water brand
with an innovative and fashionable
theme. The core idea behind the product
is to become a medium to express individuality and personal taste. The packaging design is based on seven colours
(red, orange, yellow, green, blue, indigo
and purple) and a combination of
52 letters plus seven symbols. With
a total of 59 variations, the consumers
may combine bottles to form words or
sentences to their liking. The crystal-like
hexagonal bottle also further emphasises the purity of the drinking water. All
in all, the product creates an overall
visual impact and a distinct personal
experience.

Client
Uni-President, Tainan City

Design
Styleplus Design, Taipei City

Creative Direction
Tsen Wang, Rong-Hong Wang

→ Designer portrait on page 528

ICA Rescued Fruit

[Beverage Packaging]

Approximately a third of all fruit grown
around the world will not be eaten, just
because it is too mature or has been
bruised. Instead of wasting the fruit that
couldn't be sold, Sweden's grocery retailer ICA decided to take advantage of
the situation. The result is three different
fruit juices, made from "rescued" fruit
that otherwise would have been thrown
away. The packaging design communicates both the good taste of the juice
and the sustainable idea behind it. In
order to heighten awareness at the point
of sale, twelve of the small bottles are
arranged in a cardboard box. Their light
colours and emotionally appealing imagery emphasise the product promise.

Client
ICA, Solna

Design
Silver, Stockholm

Creative Direction
Jacob Bergström

Graphic Design
Magda Lipka Falck

Project Management
Ida Stagles

Bünting Tee Matcha Pur & Matcha Mix

[Packaging]

Matcha is a stone-ground Japanese green tea, which was launched on the German market in a convenient portion stick. Its independent, reduced packaging design clearly stands out and attracts interest. At the same time, the text printed on the packaging explains the novel product. The round container, which is new for this market, underpins the product's special character, creating a high-quality feel. Furthermore, the compact packaging form aims to enable further positioning at the point of sale. It also can be used as a drink to go, for example at petrol stations.

Client
J. Bünting Teehandelshaus
GmbH & Comp., Leer

Product Management
Christina Terwey

Design
KAAPKE GmbH, Emstek

Art Direction
David Willen, Dirk Milzarek

Account Management
Judith Kurz

meingenuss.de
Tea Range

[Packaging]

True to the motto "It's T(ea)-time", each
tea by the delicacies label Mein Genuss
is associated with the letter T in an
individualised typeface. The different
versions of the letter T for the 20 kinds
of tea appear punched out, so the tea in
the glass jar fills the outline. The letter
as a key visual is also placed on the lid
label, which doubles as a freshness seal.
The glass product packaging provides a
clear view of each tea mix, thus conveying the tea's high quality. In addition,
the premium cork stopper emphasises
the value of this natural product.

Client
Mein Genuss GmbH, Landsberg am Lech

Design
Clormann Design GmbH, Penzing

Creative Direction
Michaela Vargas Coronado

Ankerkraut Tea Range

[Packaging]

This range of tea packaging was developed for the Hamburg-based Geschmacksmanufaktur Ankerkraut (flavour manufactory). The jars feature labels on both the front and the lid. The label design uses illustrations that combine the maritime world of the brand with the world of tea. Each of the seven different types of tea tells a little story: a sailor peeks out of a teapot, a crab enjoys a cup of tee, or a teapot sets sail and is grabbed by a gigantic octopus. To further support the serial character, a colour code was assigned to the tea range.

Client
Ankerkraut GmbH, Jesteburg

Design
Clormann Design GmbH, Penzing

Creative Direction
Michaela Vargas Coronado

Tea Quiero

[Packaging]

Tea Quiero is the tea brand developed for Spain's premium coffee manufacturer Catunambú. Blended with organic, ethically sourced ingredients from Fair Trade farmers in Sri Lanka, the brand name was created from the Spanish declaration of love, "Te quiero". The identity and packaging designs are inspired by Andalusian tiles found in coffee shops and tea houses in southern Spain and all eight flavours are named after areas within the region. Each individual pack features a story of the tea and the place of origin, with the aim of engaging and enlightening the customer.

Client
Catunambú, Hengelo

Design
Exit Communicatie, Weert

Creative Direction
Matthew Phillips

Art Direction
Anieke Schrader

Graphic Design
Sarah de Bruijn, Frank Jacobs,
Rick Sonnemans

Account Management
Luuk de Kunder

Tea Talent

[Packaging]

Tea Talent is an EU-certified brand of organic tea launched in Taiwan. In an attempt to emphasise the branding spirit of environmental protection, a packaging concept was developed that is self-explanatory and highlights the identifiable content. The minimalist box consists of recycled materials. The teapot-shaped coaster was inspired by the form of the Yixing Zisha teapot, and its reusability is a response to environmental protection. It was combined with vibrant glass beads as a stylish utensil for consumers to collect. The ornate gold logo of the manufacturer not only deepens the consumers' impression but also reminds them to remain loyal to the brand.

Client
Shinshen Tranding, Ltd, Taipei City

Design
K.E.A. Design Consultants, Inc., Taipei City

Blossom with Grace – Jasmine Tea Bag Collection

[Packaging]

Huatan Township in Taiwan was the major production area of jasmine in the 1960s. Today, the crop area has declined from 180 to 20 hectares. In order to renew this local industry, an alliance of farmers launched the brand Jasmine Huatan and developed jasmine-related products. This packaging design for tea scented with jasmine presents the traditional Ruyao and Chinese painting pattern of jasmine, illustrating the fresh and graceful character of the product. The high-contrast combination with the upmarket red gift box fosters an appealing overall impression.

Client
Farmers' Association of Huatan, Changhua County

Design
PH7 Creative Lab, Taichung City

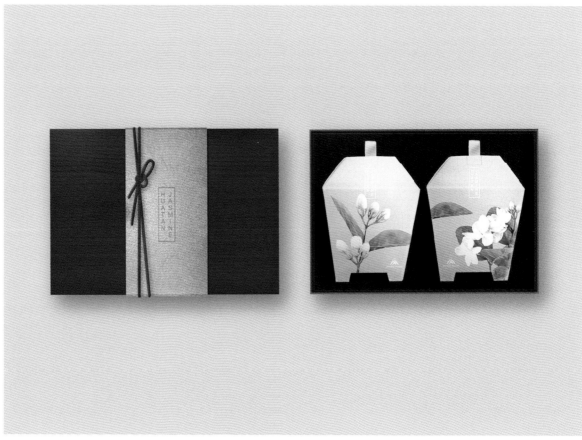

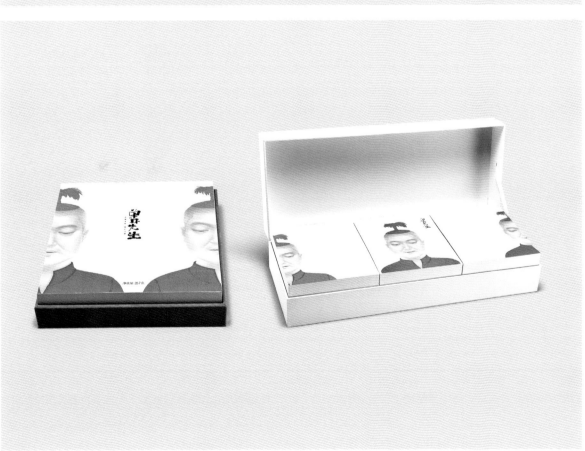

Chuxin – Masterpiece Danzhu
[Packaging]

The image used in this packaging design for the tea brand Danzhu shows the figure of a Chinese Chan master and his hairstyle, combined with the pictographic depiction of a tea tree, giving it a Zen quality. The design employs painting and other expressive techniques, while materials including paper flannelette are used to create the texture of tea, bringing to life the original experience of tea culture. The techniques include hot stamping, black stamping and light oiling to appropriately reflect the brand value.

Client
Sichuan Guge Dynasty Brand Design Consultant Co., Ltd., Chengdu

Design
Sichuan Guge Dynasty Brand Design Consultant Co., Ltd., Chengdu

Graphic Design
Shan Chunhao, Pan Xian, Fu Yan

→ Designer portrait on page 499

Paretto

[Packaging]

Client
Soyuz Coffee Roasting, Moscow

Design
Skybox Design Agency, Amsterdam

→ Designer portrait on page 525

The Paretto brand targets sophisticated, educated Russians. The task of this packaging concept is based on the product promise of subtle coffee nuances and the highest quality. By creating a high-end feel for the brand, a specific visual language was created. In addition, mystical coloured shapes were chosen to represent each blend. The basic colour of black in combination with detailed pictograms fosters a unique design language to strengthen the brand image. This has resulted in distinctive packaging, which effectively increases market share.

oz. – Big Flavour in Little Pots

[Food Packaging]

True to the brand motto "Big flavour in small jars", the packaging design of the oz. brand follows an original product concept. Selected spices, filled into individual small jars, are combined to form harmonious spice sets. The space-saving jars create order in the spice cupboard, while also making the seasoning of dishes easier. The stackable and connectable jars have a volume of one ounce. Due to the small size of the jars, there are no out-of-date spices to be thrown away.

Client
zurgams Kommunikationsagentur GmbH, Dornbirn

Design
zurgams Kommunikationsagentur GmbH, Dornbirn

Art Direction
Thomas Gschossmann

Text
Ono Mothwurf, Jörg Ströhle

kariott Eau de Sel

[Food Packaging]

kariott Eau de Sel is a product series of innovative food perfumes. The handmade liquid salt essences and their packaging create an exclusive visual identity. The packaging design uses the classic aesthetics of perfume flacons and reflects the uniqueness of the fine mist spray distributing a delicate smell. The glass bottle shows the transparency and clearness of the product, while the only colour image on each label reflects the essences, which take more than three months to produce. The boutique manufactory is free of any machines since labelling, packaging and filling are carried out by hand.

Client
kariott, Remagen

Design
kariott, Remagen

Creative Direction
Sandra Loy, Dr. Richard Loy

Production
Sandra Loy

Canola Oil

[Food Packaging]

Canola oil, also known as "oriental olive oil", is a popular product in China. This design conveys the pure product characteristics through its minimalist packaging, while the pattern on the back adopts the traditional woodblock printing approach. It visually expresses the refinery process of canola oil. At the same time, the environmentally friendly, handmade paper of the external packaging gives the product a tactile quality, while echoing the concept of its natural origin. The overall extraction method is very simple, thus maximising the contemporary character of the brand.

Client
Fengfan Farm Products, Jintan

Design
Rong, Shanghai

→ Designer portrait on page 521

First Night Olive Oil

[Food Packaging]

The task of this packaging design was to emphasise the special features of this olive oil. Its manufacturer believes that only olives harvested during the day and processed during the night within 24 hours can produce extra virgin olive oil of the highest quality. The minimalist design of the double circle against the dark background simultaneously symbolises the moon and the cross-section of an olive. In keeping with the label design, a plain, straight, cylinder-shaped bottle was chosen. The key visual represents the night, the time when the oil is produced, while its colour variants provide differentiation between the olive varieties.

Client
OPG Boris Galic, Zagreb

Design
Designsystem d.o.o., Zagreb

Art Direction
Boris Malesevic

Graphic Design
Boris Malesevic, Linda Golik Horvat

Project Management
Suzana Potrebic

Strong Grip

[Retail Packaging]

Strong Grip is a new type of packaging for two- and three-litre bottles of olive oil, designed for the American market without modifying the existing supply chain. Using the product shape and weight in a smart way to increase resistance, the corrugated cardboard packaging becomes a mono-material solution with no need for an extra handle or additional shrink wrapping. This eye-catching packaging solution leads to high visibility of the primary product and enables communication with the consumer. There is no need for any additional investment in shrink ovens or handle inserters, thus leading to energy cost reduction and savings in transport tray expenses.

Client
Deoleo

Design
Smurfit Kappa Spain

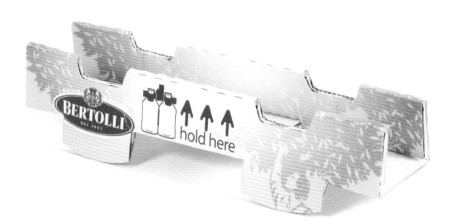

Maggi Bouillon Nature

[Food Packaging]

Maggi Bouillon Nature is the brand's first bouillon with entirely natural ingredients. In order to stand out visually from the classic bouillon range, the agency developed a packaging that is noticeably different. The typography and illustrations, as well as the type of paper, were chosen to emphasise the product's naturalness and simplicity. In order to target a health-conscious audience, the natural recipe and its main ingredients are not only depicted but also named, resulting in a refreshing bouillon packaging.

Client
Nestlé Suisse SA, Vevey

Design
ARD Design Switzerland, Vevey

Art Direction
Alexandre Guignard

Graphic Design
Dylan Abt

Zhangfei Beef

[Food Packaging]

Inspired by the inner temperament of its
own brand culture, the packaging design
of Zhangfei Beef carries the signature of
antique facial make-up from the Chinese
Three Kingdoms culture. The patented
Motai box technology is used to pack irregular pieces of beef, showing the
shape directly in a unique style. In addition, the box is reusable as a mask.
The traditional brand image thus becomes flexible and intimate, deepening
the interaction with the consumer.
The packaging is part of the relaunch of
a traditional Chinese brand against
the background of current fashion and
culture.

Client
Sichuan Guge Dynasty Brand Design
Consultant Co., Ltd., Chengdu

Design
Sichuan Guge Dynasty Brand Design
Consultant Co., Ltd., Chengdu

Graphic Design
Zou Yong, Chen Wen, Pan Xian

→ Designer portrait on page 499

For Kids

[Food Packaging]

For Kids Cheonhajangsa is a sausage snack with a packaging design that depicts children's dreams and hopes using a variety of fanciful motifs. The packaging consists of an octagonal box and a balloon toy, which has been developed and incorporated to attract the attention of the target group. This idea not only successfully upcycles the packaging but also creates an additional incentive to buy. The sausage-shaped balloon toy, as well as the whole packaging, is recyclable in order to help children take care of the environment.

Client
Jinjuham, Seoul

Design
Jinjuham Design Lab, Seoul

Creative Direction
Seunghan Lim

Graphic Design
Eunjung Lim, Junghoon Yang,
Kyoungeun Seo, Suji Kim

Tou Prevezanou

[Food Packaging]

Tou Prevezanou is a new line of ready, pre-cooked fish and crustaceans launched in the Greek market by a small family business in the town of Preveza. The simple design of the packaging conveys the artistry put into the production and cooking of seafood made in a traditional way. Handcrafted linocut prints illustrate the types of fish, and die-cuts highlight the delicacy.

Client
IONIAN FISH, Preveza

Design
2YOLK, Athens

Creative Direction
George Karayiannis

Managing Direction
Emmanouela Bitsaxaki

Graphic Design
Konstantina Benaki, Tobias Möller

Studio Management
Alexandra Papaloudi

Copywriting
Despina Sakellaridi

Marinated
Anchovy

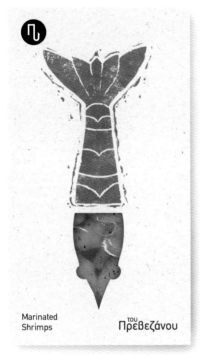

Marinated
Shrimps

Marinated
Octopus

A Bowl of Rice

[Packaging]

This packaging design for organic rice was commissioned by a Chinese brand with a focus on natural farm products. The design concept was inspired by traditional Chinese rice containers used in rural China. With its new structure that reinterprets the traditional look and feel, the container has brought something interesting to daily life. A simple but artfully tied knot encourages consumers to open the box, which alongside the rice contains a traditional porcelain rice bowl. This addition encourages collecting and strengthens brand loyalty.

Client
Lonshare

Design
Shanghai Version Design, Shanghai

Packaging Design
Tengxian Zou

San Mauro

[Food Packaging]

Client
San Mauro, Bloemendaal

Design
Van Heertum Design VHD,
Tilburg

Printing
Drukkerij Tielen B.V.,
Boxtel

Cardboard Supplier
Iggesund Paperboard Europe,
Amsterdam

In the Netherlands, San Mauro is well established as a high-quality brand of Italian olive oil. Currently expanding into the segment of luxury foods, this special packaging was developed for new products. The task was to make the quality and luxurious nature visible, as well as the Italian look and feel of the branding. Inspired by the two main ingredients of the products, artichokes and olive oil, the packaging strategy is based on the collaboration of two separate parts that perfectly fit together. Along with a glass jar, a slide-on box symbolises the symmetry between the ingredients. The packaging design achieves an appealing aesthetic, which gives the product further added value.

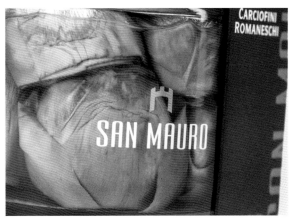

Fein & Fertig

[Food Packaging]

The gourmet manufacturer Fein & Fertig from Hamburg produces à la carte meals and sauces in limited editions. Individually hand-filled into stylish glass jars, each meal is delivered by courier. The packaging not only communicates the premium quality but also clearly identifies the contents. The striped pattern has been inspired by awnings seen at traditional country markets and offers clear colour coding for each product line. Engraved illustrations and text that express pleasure complete the overall appearance and together create a bistro cuisine image.

Client
Fein & Fertig UG, Hamburg

Design
Peter Schmidt Group, Hamburg

Design Direction
Dennis Dominguez

Design Team
Stephanie Rieckmann, Mascha Vögele

Project Management
Celia Brauner, Nicole Bischoff

Production
Tobias Gagelmann

Wagamama Takeout Experience

[Food Packaging]

The objective of this packaging design was to reimagine Wagamama's take-away experience by better connecting the home customer with the excitement, taste and aesthetic value of the restaurant experience. The standard sizes and shapes of the large and small bowls make them stackable for delivery and allow for convenient storage, whilst the choice of materials and form contributes to a holistic, functional system. Each bowl is delivered as a complete package, wrapped in a band that provides a considered place for chopsticks and lists the entire Wagamama menu so that the enclosed order can be accurately marked.

Client
Wagamama, London

Design
Pearlfisher, London

Chief Creative Officer
Jonathan Ford

Managing Director
Darren Foley

Creative Strategy
Jack Hart

Design Direction
Fiona John

3D Design Direction
Mike Beauchamp

Technical Project Management
Jenny Cairns

Client Management
Ally Tyger

→ Designer portrait on page 516

Cardboard Playground

[Food Packaging]

This fruit basket for 3 kg of apples can be used as a toy after the apples have been consumed. There are two different designs in total: the fire department for boys and the princess castle for girls. This improved solution gives a second life to the packaging: it is not thrown away after use but serves as a perfect toy for children. The design inspires children's imagination and encourages them to play with the packaging. In addition, the packaging can be custom-ised by writing down the name of the child, thus giving children an authentic experience. This playful packaging inspires children to ask their parents to purchase healthy apples instead of sweets.

Client
Elbe Obst

Design
Smurfit Kappa Germany

Project Management
Daniel Mansfeld

SoFruPack

[Food Packaging]

The berry punnet set contains four punnet sizes (250 g, 500 g, 1 kg, 2 kg) and special collective trays for facilitating the shipment. They fit precisely into the trays, making palletisation and transportation of the boxes much easier. This solution also provides protection of the berries during the entire supply chain process. Moreover, the special shape of the open bottom of the tray ensures accurate airflow during transport, preventing dampness and mould. The design uses two-colour printing on corrugated cardboard, emphasising its ecological origin and the premium quality of the berries.

Client
SoFruPack

Design
Smurfit Kappa Poland

Concept
Jakub Świętek

The Happy Tomato

[Food Packaging]

The Happy Tomato trademark is used to
sell tomatoes grown on Žitný Ostrov,
which literally translates as Rye Island.
It is a well-known agricultural area in
southern Slovakia surrounded by rivers.
The packaging design is based on a
simple logo concept featuring a large,
softly painted tomato with a smile, set
against a shining turquoise background,
which in combination with the red and
yellow tomatoes catches the attention
of shoppers. The turquoise colour, together with small waves, refers to the
rivers that surround the island, and also
the usage of geothermal water during
the cultivation of the tomatoes.

Client
GreenCoop Družstvo, Zlatná na Ostrove

Design
Pergamen, Trnava

Creative Direction
Juraj Demovič

Graphic Design
Juraj Demovič, Juraj Vontorčík

Photography
Jakub Dvořák

Pre-Press/Final Artwork
Ervin Gejdoš

Beksul Real Brunch Pasta

[Food Packaging]

The Real Brunch Pasta series is an easy-to-cook product, targeting young consumers. The design elements, such as the pasta noodles and the logotype, are portrayed as rough illustrations, while the food is shown in actual images. The free arrangement of the design elements creates a look that is fun and bright. In addition, a brunch recipe on the back of the packaging makes the product easy to use. The packaging type is a standing pouch, which has the advantage of making the product very visible when shelved. The paper material gives it a natural texture and also provides a convenient experience, as it can be torn open easily.

Client
CJ Cheiljedang, Seoul

Design
CJ Cheiljedang, Seoul

Creative Direction
Jisun Kim, Kangkook Lee

Graphic Design
Seungpyo Lee, Hyunjoo Lee

DeliK' –
Delicious Kitchen

[Food Packaging]

DeliK' is a new brand by an established sausage manufactory, offering different meatball snacks. The task was to create a young and creative look with a personal touch that customers can identify with. Accordingly, each logo features a different portrait of a real employee recommending their favourite product. Therefore, the packages show a real face, which makes them personal and approachable for the customer. A slate background highlights the vegetables, photographed from above in a seemingly randomised arrangement. Large hand-drawn chalk lettering for the product names completes the design and gives the line a home-cooked touch.

Client
Rudolf und Robert Houdek GmbH, Starnberg

Design
Markenliaison GmbH, Munich

Art Direction
Diana Friedrich

Graphic Design
Bianca Bunsas

Typography
Martina Süsse

Gustavo Gusto

[Food Packaging]

For the launch of this premium frozen pizza brand, the start-up company only had a small marketing budget available. Therefore, the cartons were turned into advertising space. The packaging design thus shows a range of striking headlines emphasising various product benefits. In line with the brand promise of "freshness", the Gustavo Gusto packaging comes in an eye-catching white. The combination of product images and charming illustrations completes a pool of design elements, giving the company the freedom to create new and original compositions for various media.

Client
Gustavo Gusto, Geretsried

Design
Leagas Delaney Hamburg GmbH, Hamburg

Managing Partner
Stefan Zschaler

Creative Direction
Michael Götz (Text), Jan Wölfel (Art)

Art Direction
Daniel Petterson, Anne von Holten

Illustration
Dennis Lösel

KFC

[Food Packaging]

This KFC packaging design was relaunched in Russia as part of a shift in
global brand platform. The challenge
was "to change everything without
changing anything". The new design
intends to get closer to the consumers.
With strong colours and distinctive
typography, the design achieves an
iconographic effect and has an appealing look. Moreover, the eye-catching
colour coding in itself already enhances
product differentiation and focuses on
the signature dishes and branded products. The incorporation of photos likewise emphasises the brand character.

Client
KFC Russia, Moscow

Design
Depot WPF, Moscow

Creative Direction
Alexandr Zagorsky

Art Direction
Nikita Ivanov

Copywriting
Fara Kuchkarov

Account Management
Elena Kirillova

→ Designer portraits on page 495, 496

Burger King
Halloween Whopper

[Food Packaging]

As a seasonal design for Halloween, Burger King's Whopper packaging high-lights a brand identity which proves that it is in touch with its guests. It's not just the packaging that is inspired by Halloween but also the product it-self, the most iconic being the Halloween Whopper sandwich with its A1 BBQ-flavoured black bun. The packaging to accompany the range needed to cele-brate the festival, as well as be fun and engaging for guests. Accordingly, the Halloween Whopper has been dressed up as a white-bandaged mummy, which contrasts with the black bun Whopper when unwrapped.

Client
Burger King, Miami

Design
Turner Duckworth, London/San Francisco

Head of Design
David Turner, Bruce Duckworth

Creative Direction
Clem Halpin

Graphic Design
David Blakemore, Boyko Taskov

Illustration
Geoffrey Appleton

Production
James Norris

Account Management
Nicola Eager

eicare eggs

[Food Packaging]

The aesthetics of this packaging design
is rooted in the free-range farming
culture of eicare. The main illustrations
feature chickens as protagonists and
communicators of the farming practices.
Playfully looking at each other, two
illustrations interact, while the text
flows in handwritten typography, thus
indicating the humane values of the
brand and completing the composition.
As the chicken is the protagonist,
various complementary illustrations
highlight the quality of the product and
the general feel of the eicare farm.

Client
Barone Food AG, Wohlen

Design
Beetroot Design Group, Thessaloniki

Creative Direction
Alexis Nikou

Art Direction
Marios Georntamilis

→ Designer portrait on page 490

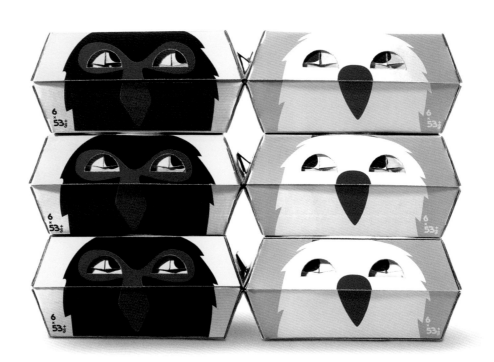

Panorama

[Food Packaging]

The Panorama egg packaging for four eggs combines an open and transparent presentation with a high degree of product protection. Its brown material with the customised sticker gives the product an organic impression, creating a sustainable look and feel. The packaging design concept, unique in the German market, is based on the insight that all customers will open traditional egg boxes to ensure that the product is not damaged. The appealingly shaped element in the centre provides an ideal space for branding the product and is visible from any shelf position in the supermarket.

Client
Holstein Ei

Design
Smurfit Kappa Germany

Graphic Design
Martin Jutzie

SO & JO

[Food Packaging]

So & Jo is a new brand of dips based on traditional Greek recipes, offering a new culinary proposition for the European market. The brand is named after the two business owners and aims to create an association with fun, casual everyday snacking and sharing food with friends. The packaging design follows a pop aesthetic: bright colours that correspond to the main ingredient of each dip and a graffiti font that lends an air of familiarity to the long and quirky Greek food names. Lastly, the Mediterranean ingredients are displayed in the background to convey high quality.

Client
3P SALADS, Karditsa

Design
2YOLK, Athens

Creative Direction
George Karayiannis

Managing Direction
Emmanouela Bitsaxaki

Graphic Design
Filippos Avgeris

Illustration
Panayiotis Vassilatos

Studio Management
Alexandra Papaloudi

Copywriting
Despina Sakellaridi

KARAT

[Food Packaging]

The Moscow cheese factory Karat undertook the first rebranding in its century-long history and redesigned its products, which are familiar to every Russian. The new version of the design retained only the recognisable colour codes, so as to differentiate between the cheese types more easily. A complex design system was turned into simple iconic signs inspired by Soviet Suprematism, an abstract art movement from the early 20th century. The use of bold colours and geometric patterns was intended to be a modern approach to retro heritage and garners a high degree of attention at the point of sale.

Client
KARAT, Moscow

Design
Depot WPF, Moscow

Creative Direction
Alexey Fadeev, Alexandr Zagorsky

Art Direction
Nikita Ivanov

Strategic Planning
Fara Kuchkarov, Anastasia Tretyakova

Account Management
Anna Smirnova

→ Designer portraits on page 495, 496

FINUU

[Food Packaging]

Finuu, the name of a premium butter made in Finland, is a wordplay on "Finland" and the mooing sound of a cow. The packaging design reflects the pure naturalness and Finnish origin of the product. The visual combines geometric aesthetics with the sophisticated engraving of a Holstein-Friesian dairy cow. As a contemporary interpretation of traditional decorative motifs, the colour palette is limited to navy, metallic beige and light blue. Both butter variants are distinguished by colour coding and straightforward verbal communication on the front of the packaging.

Client
ZT Kruszwica SA, Warsaw

Design
Touch Ideas, Warsaw

Creative Direction
Tomasz Kuczma

Graphic Design
Tomasz Kuczma, Marcin Krygier

Strategic Planning
Maciej Biedziński

Account Management
Bartłomiej Serafiński

Artwork
Angus Gray Burbridge

Paris Baguette

[Gift Packaging]

In order to differentiate the gift packages of Paris Baguette from competing products, a series of illustrations of various characters was selected to represent the brand image. The design of each package makes a witty, charming and luxurious impression and features the image of a traditional bakery. Examples of the fun illustrations include a French poodle riding a bicycle with a cake, a patissier bear driving a Citroën car and a Parisian boy in a hot-air balloon. With this imagery and the brand-appropriate colour scheme, the packaging aims to appeal to consumers with its warm and friendly design.

Client
SPC, Paris Baguette, Seoul

Design
SPC, Paris Baguette, Seoul

Creative Direction
Soo Jin Lee

Graphic Design
Yehi Ahn, Min Hyung Seo

Structural Design
Min Ho Dong

Project Management
Hee Soo Her

Official Residence's Pineapple-Longan Cake Gift Box

[Food Packaging]

The focal point of this gift box is the full moon with its golden glow, which harmonises with the gift box's contents: individually packaged longan and pineapple cakes. The pearlescent lamination reflects a warm, soft, lunar glow, with a radiating pattern representing pineapple rinds and fireworks. In contrast to the usual colourful and extravagant packaging, this subtle yet stunning neo-Asian design symbolises the strengthening of Sino-Japanese relations. The spirit of sharing and friendship is reflected in its warm glow and regal sophistication.

Client
Pasadena International Group,
Kaohsiung City

Design
Proad Identity, Taipei City

Creative Direction
Jennifer Tsai

→ Designer portrait on page 520

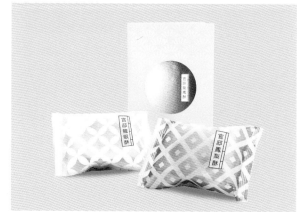

Official Residence's Pineapple-Longan Cake

[Food Packaging]

This individually packaged pineapple cake is used as a stylish welcome present for hotel guests. Pasadena means "crown of the valley" in a Native American language. When the box is opened, a small, exquisite crown glowing with radiant beams of light resembling a pineapple plant appears, dotted with the beautiful lustre of pearls representing a fireworks display. In addition, the packaging design reflects the company values of diligence and passion as defined at its founding; combined with the founder's generous spirit of sharing, it establishes perfect harmony.

Client
Pasadena International Group,
Kaohsiung City

Design
Proad Identity, Taipei City

Creative Direction
Jennifer Tsai

→ Designer portrait on page 520

Xiao-Shi-Mi – Snack Seeker Mushroom Shortbread

[Food Packaging]

Xinshe is a city near the mountainous area in the middle of Taiwan, famous as the place of origin of fresh mushrooms. The Xiao-Shi-Mi shortbread is made of the high-quality dried mushrooms produced in Xinshe. The packaging design adopts hand-drawn illustrations of local characteristics, such as the Sea of Flowers and animals common to the region. Three boxes with different motifs are included in a decorative gift box. Due to their shape and colour scheme, the individual elements combine to form a harmonious whole.

Client
Taichung Xinshe Dist Peasant Association, Taichung City

Design
Hoora Design, Chiayi

Creative Direction
Huang-Yu Xu

Image Editing
Jing-Hui Wang

→ Designer portrait on page 502

Ning Shi Wei

[Food Packaging]

The Tibetan Plateau, which is more than 3,000 meters above sea level, is where the Ning Shiwei highland barley cake is produced. Its pure, untouched ecological environment enables the cultivation of premium highland barley. The pure, natural origin is expressed in the individual barley-shaped cakeboxes and the transparent outer packaging. In the same way, illustrations are used to describe the ecological environment and special ethnic culture of the Tibetan Plateau. In addition, the transparent outer packaging is designed as a storage box for secondary use after the food has been consumed.

Client

Shenzhen Baixinglong Creative Packaging Co., Ltd., Shenzhen

Design

Shenzhen Baixinglong Creative Packaging Co., Ltd., Shenzhen

LINE Café

[Food Packaging, Beverage Packaging]

The Line Café recreated cute mobile messenger characters in the form of desserts to provide customers of all ages with the excitement of reliving their childhood. All packaging has been designed to emphasise both the cuteness of the characters and the unique branding. In addition, the design concept goes a step further by creating packaging that customers want to keep. The popcorn packaging, which humorously parodies the design of Campbell's Soup, can be reused, and the decorative drink bottles are now becoming collectibles among customers instead of being thrown away.

Client
LINE FRIENDS Corporation, Seoul

Design
LINE FRIENDS Corporation, Seoul

The Crumbsies

[Gift Packaging]

The packaging design for The Crumbsies, a corporate Christmas gift by Akis Petretzikis aims to represent the chef's particular style with regard to both content and design. The custom-made box features a set of four characters, representing the biscuit collection inside. These key visuals consist of a common main frame with varying details on each side, thus linking a different character to each of the four biscuit flavours. In addition, by rotating the top, the customer can create new mix-and-match characters, thus offering an option of personalisation in line with the chef's overall image.

Client
Akis Petretzikis Ltd., Agia Paraskevi, Athens

Design
busybuilding, Athens

Creative Direction
Dimitris Gkazis

Graphic Design
Maria Kefala

Text
Sissy Caravia

Account Management
Effie Komninou

Production
Akis Kantartzis

Printing
Paris Orfanos, La Petite Jumelle, Athens

Fortnum & Mason

[Food Packaging]

In order to enhance Fortnum & Mason's confectionery collection, a new trio of chic novelty chocolate boxes conjures up enchanting stories that match the nature of the chocolates inside. The hand-drawn illustrations are full of surprises, such as a black cat with a white mouse hidden between its paws and oyster bubbles that are in fact strings of pearls. Paw prints leading away from a mouse hole and a row of cotton stitches direct the observer around the edge of the package to provide a further layer of engagement. For one final element of discovery, small objects were hidden inside the lid of the box to be found by the customer.

Client
Fortnum & Mason, London

Design
Design Bridge, London

Creative Direction
Holly Kielty, Emma Follett

Graphic Design
Chloe Templeman, Hayley Barrett, Morgan Swain

Account Management
Rebecca Yorke

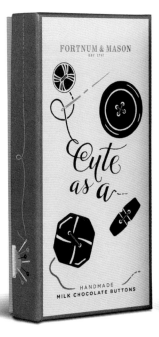

POLA Kireichocolat

[Food Packaging]

The packaging design of the Kireichocolat cosmetics line is based on a concept titled "A Beautiful Gift". Modelled on a gift box, it contains beauty-care products with cocoa butter as an ingredient for skin enhancement. A matching motif on the lid shows cocoa beans in bold colours. This illustration frames the golden print of the product and the brand name. Beautiful hues on the textured paper combine to appeal to both sight and touch, while expressing a new feeling of luxury and distinctiveness.

Client
POLA Inc., Tokyo

Design
POLA Inc., Tokyo

Art Direction
Chiharu Suzuki

Design Team
Takako Kimoto

Smart Buttons

[Food Packaging]

Smart Buttons are small, handmade chocolate buttons in different flavours. In order to make eating little amounts of chocolate with 80 per cent pure cocoa tempting for consumers, a colourful packaging concept was developed. It conveys the health effects of the product in an appealing way, above all through product names such as Power Buttons. The buttons come in a reusable tin that can be kept handy for the occasional treat. The design is printed on the tin container, which is lined with a rose-gold interior and features a metal clasp to complete the simple, elegant packaging.

Client
The Clock, London

Design
Pearlfisher, London

Concept
Louise Nason, Melt, London

Typography
Peter Horridge, Cheshire

→ Designer portrait on page 515

Sparkling

[Food Packaging]

Cacao di Vine is a Portuguese chocolate factory that makes selected wine chocolates. It recently launched Sparkling as a new product line. Using a material that is unique and processed in Portugal, the package of the collection is made out of cork. The reusable package looks like the top of a wine cork and, when opened, the cork can be used as a coaster on dinner tables as well as in the kitchen. It is decoratively branded with the company name in order to remind the customer to buy more wine chocolates.

Client
Cacaodivine, LDA, Coimbra

Design
Episodio Design, Coimbra

Creative Direction
Nuno Baptista

KisKis

[Food Packaging]

Client
Gary & Bros Confectionary Co., Ltd.,
Beijing

Design
Box Brand Design Limited,
Hong Kong

Creative Direction
Joey Lo

Art Direction
Yvonne Chung

Illustration
Michael Kwong

Photography
Ariom Leung

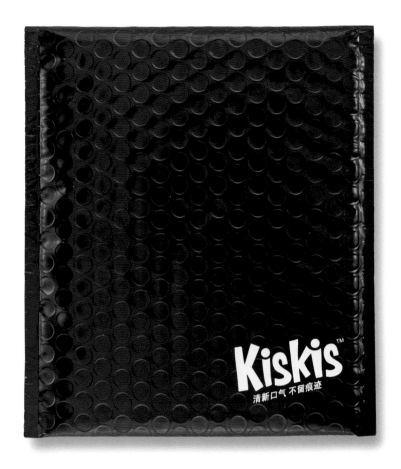

This packaging has been designed for a peppermint candy brand, aiming to become the trendy choice of a young target group. Different from traditional products, KisKis has a unique black container, similar in size to a smartphone. The packaging comes in two patterns, "temperament" and "wilful". The strong brand personality is instantly accentuated by the Chinese street slang printed on the surface. The small rubber lip at the top functions as an opener, corresponding to the brand name KisKis. The packaging comes with two drawing pens, allowing consumers to create their own designs.

Yummy POP!

[Food Packaging]

Chicken floss and shreds are popular foods in Chinese culture; hence there are many similar products on the market. In order to break out of the traditional market, the product has been repositioned not only as an ingredient for home cooking, but also as a snack for all ages. Therefore, the main goal of the new packaging design is to create a unique image. The product characters with their pop hairstyle have been developed to have a trendy, colourful and chicken-like appearance in order to target a younger consumer group.

Client
Non Sheng Co., Ltd., Kaohsiung City

Design
PH7 Creative Lab, Taichung City

KETTLE®
Chef's Signature Range

[Food Packaging]

The task was to create the visual identity
and packaging design for this company's
new premium range, Chef's Signature.
The new design had to communicate the
expertise of KETTLE Chef Chris Barnard,
the source of the ingredients, the lovingly crafted messaging and premium
cues, whilst being differentiated from
other KETTLE ranges. The solution uses
the Chef's chopping board as a holding
device that contains all the product
information and a natural background
for the ingredients. The distinctive colour scheme of the foil bags enables easy
product differentiation, while the key
visual has an appetising look.

Client
Kettle Foods, Norwich

Design
Turner Duckworth, London/San Francisco

Head of Design
David Turner, Bruce Duckworth

Creative Direction
Clem Halpin

Graphic Design
Jessie Froggett, John Randall,
Christian Eager

Photography
Steve Baxter

Artwork
Sebastian Cox

Account Management
Monica Annesanti

MILZU! BIO

[Food Packaging]

MILZU! BIO is an innovative rye cereal
product, created for consumers who
value quality food. The packaging serves
as an effective communication tool for
the brand. The packaging design visually
stands out from competitive products,
mainly because it is coloured black.
However, to make the product easier to
identify, traditionally used cardboard
has been chosen as packaging material.
The characters are robust and the logo
consists of simple, colourful letters and
forms. Thin and constructive lines symbolise the intelligent, meticulous and
innovative approach used in the development of this product.

Client
MILZU! SIA, Riga

Design
DPJN, Diena Pirms Janu Nakts, Riga

Creative Direction
Karlis Kriekis

Graphic Design
Peteris Zihars

Sesamis Bars

[Food Packaging]

F CHOICE was founded with the aim of promoting the traditional pasteli, or sesamis, for the ancient Greeks, a sesame-and-honey bar with a history spanning twenty-five centuries. Honey is the sole sweetener used in the production, while many of the unhulled sesame seeds contained in the bars have been ground, so that their valuable nutrients can be easily absorbed. The attention-grabbing packaging design emphasises the product promise of being a quick source of energy for athletes. The key visuals are animal illustrations, which in combination with colour coding support the product selection.

Client
F CHOICE, Acharnes

Design
k2design, Athens

Creative Direction
Menelaos Kouroudis

HONEY + BERRIES

[Food Packaging]

This packaging design was developed for
creamed honey with berries and dried
fruit. The task was to design jar labels
that are unconventional, while conveying
the contents in a clear and fun manner.
Based on this concept, playful characters – fruit and berries in bee costumes –
are central to the packaging design.
Customers are drawn to the product by
characters that are active, lively and
enjoying themselves. They can be seen
waving and looking up from the jar lids,
so that even if the jars are placed on
the lower shelves in a store, customers
are still attracted to them.

Client
Honey House, Saint Petersburg

Design/Art Direction
Maria Ponomareva, Moscow

3D Visualisation
Pavel Gubin, Moscow

→ Designer portrait on page 518

Nextnest Ice Cream

[Food Packaging]

Cubilose ice cream is based on a dual-purpose packaging design concept. The tinplate material has been used for ice-cream packaging in an innovative way to differentiate it from competing products. Tinplate containers make the ice cream easy to store and use, while also providing enhanced protection against leaks and temperature stability. The second purpose is reutilisation. To achieve the latter, the tinplate ice-cream containers feature black-and-white illustrations with decorative European countryside garden motifs that increase the collector's value, in order to prevent them from being thrown away.

Client
TigerPan Packaging Design Lab.,
Shenzhen

Design
TigerPan Packaging Design Lab.,
Shenzhen

Creative Direction
Hu Pan

→ Designer portrait on page 530

Nextnest
EdibleBird's Nest

[Food Packaging]

EdibleBird's Nest is a high-grade cubilose tonic customised for pregnant women. The imagery shows the twelve animal signs of the Chinese zodiac. Inside the container, a petal-shaped design has been adopted based on the arc of the individual cubilose portion. Thus, the portions can be arranged in a regular pattern, generating more space between the cubilose and the exterior box and lowering the possibility of damage during transport. In terms of materials, an environmentally friendly and renewable wet-pressed pulp moulding method has been used, with white as the main colour of the packaging design.

Client
TigerPan Packaging Design Lab.,
Shenzhen

Design
TigerPan Packaging Design Lab.,
Shenzhen

Art Direction
Hu Pan

→ Designer portrait on page 530

Good Eggwhites

[Food Packaging]

Good Eggwhites is a novel product
for athletes and dieters. The protein-
containing food is made of 100 per cent
organic egg whites. The PET bottle has
been enhanced with white colouring and
varnish, giving it a high-quality look.
Its translucent material shows the fill
level and the texture of the product. The
packaging design, with its attention-
grabbing quality at the point of sale,
has the feel of an egg shell. Instead of a
label, the print on the bottle looks distinctive and convincingly explains the
new product on the back.

Client
Pumperlgsund GmbH, Munich

Design
MING Labs GmbH, Munich

Design Team
Sergey Skip, Christoph Gromer,
Gerhard Seizer

Text
Henning Müller-Dannhausen,
Kristina Würz

Technical Lead
Fabian König, Pumperlgsund GmbH

Project Management
Jan Göktekin, Pumperlgsund GmbH
Stefan Hörmann, MING Labs GmbH

Pure & Mild

[Cosmetics Packaging]

The relaunched botanic cosmetics series Pure & Mild was developed especially for the Chinese market. Its packaging design provides a view of the world in order to inspire modern Chinese women. The outer packaging is characterised by original illustrations in a fairy-tale drawing style, showing cohabiting rare organic plants from around the world that are used as ingredients in this cosmetic series. The product line's high-quality image is reflected in the contour of the bottle, the transparency of which highlights the appealing colour scheme of the skincare products. Inspired by the natural ingredients, the structure of the lid provides an attractive, tactile quality.

Client
Shiseido Co., Ltd., Tokyo

Design
Shiseido Co., Ltd., Tokyo

Creative Direction
Eriko Hirato

Art Direction
Kanako Kawai

Design Team
Kanako Kawai, Akira Muraoka

Illustration
Izumi Matsumoto

innisfree My Body

[Cosmetics Packaging]

The packaging design of this flavour-some cosmetics line focuses on the simple depiction of its main ingredients, such as jasmine or gardenia. Moreover, the simplified illustrations are featured in a hand-drawn style, which communicates a feeling of warmth and comfort. The shape of the flacon was inspired by a reagent bottle, which stands for the distinct identity of the brand. The colourful and transparent bottle glitters like glass as it catches the light. The cap is delicately engraved with the logo, featuring a warm brown hue and a matt finish so as to enhance its natural impression.

Client
innisfree Corporation, Seoul

Design
innisfree Design Team, Seoul
Project Eddy, Seoul

Creative Direction
Mi-Young Park, innisfree

Art Direction/Product Design
Ji-Hye Park, innisfree

Graphic Design
Ji-Hye Park, innisfree
Ye-Da Cho, Da-Yeon Park, Project Eddy

Urban Eco Harakeke

[Cosmetics Packaging]

The SAEM brand has a clear focus on environmental protection in every design. Details of the packaging, such as texture, colour and shape, are designed to convey its nature-centredness to the customer. All packaging uses materials that comply with sustainability and eco-friendliness standards. The container becomes wider at the bottom for increased stability and convenience when testing the product and displaying it in the store. The green colour was chosen to resemble the leaf of the harakeke, the New Zealand flax, while the cap is manufactured using thermal transfer printing to convey the nature-oriented feel.

Client
The SAEM International Co., Ltd., Seoul

Design
The SAEM International Co., Ltd., Seoul

→ Designer portrait on page 529

Chaga

[Cosmetics Packaging]

Chaga is an anti-ageing cosmetics line containing fermented substances. The container has a round design that widens towards the bottom for an easy grip. It features a pump for reliable and convenient use. The pattern of the cap resembles one of the main ingredients, birch, to convey the line's nature-oriented feel. An amber-brown hue is used to emphasise the product's connection with fermentation and nutrition. The box features brown and orange colours only, and it shows a birch tree to convey the characteristics of the product in a simple but powerful manner.

Client
The SAEM International Co., Ltd., Seoul

Design
The SAEM International Co., Ltd., Seoul

→ Designer portrait on page 529

Bi Yun Jin

[Cosmetics Packaging]

This South Korean cosmetics line is a medical product enriched with three oriental extracts to keep the skin hydrated. The design of the container's cap and shoulders was inspired by the shape and colour of a Korean hat called a "got", while its body is delicately expressed with harmonious gradations of green. For the graphic design of the container, a vertical layout was used to create an oriental impression, while the bottom of the case features a comb pattern found on traditional Korean doors. Overall, the product exudes an impression of Korean sensibility.

Client
It's Skin, Seoul

Design
It's Skin, Seoul

Creative Direction
Min-Young Kim, In-Bae Kim

ENTIA LOHB's

[Cosmetics Packaging]

ENTIA LOHB's is a colour-therapy brand that suggests an effective solution to various skin problems through an original approach. The packaging concept differentiates seven skincare lines by combining nature's three essential shades of light and four primary colours, with the stages of chromaticity overlapping. Nature's mysterious colour combinations occurring during sunrise and sunset, as well as horizontal lines, were applied as gradients for the design motifs. The colour palette is eye-catching, and the logo and icons on the front are designed in keeping with the digital signs, attracting a target group in their twenties and thirties. The packaging employs a new material recently spotlighted for its excellent stability, protecting the contents and enhancing its recyclability, while also focusing on a smart brand design with better usability.

Client
Coreana Cosmetics,
Suwon City

Design
Coreana Cosmetics Design Lab,
Suwon City

→ Designer portrait on page 494

Allvit SONG-RA Line

[Cosmetics Packaging]

Allvit SONG-RA is a premium cosmetics line made by fermenting rare, valuable ingredients. With its concise lines, the container motif reinterprets the traditional image of Korean fermenting. The metallic texture of the cap has an artisan look, while the comb pattern symbolises the brand philosophy. The spatula holder at the bottom of the cream container easily and cleanly stores the spatula and was designed to blend in with the shape of the container. The lower component of the outer packaging can be fanned out like a petal once the lid has been removed.

Client
Coway Co., Ltd., Seoul

Design
Coway Co., Ltd., Seoul

Creative Direction
Won Hee Lee

Packaging Design
Soo In Jung, Joo Yeon Lee

ORBIS=U WHITE

[Cosmetics Packaging]

This brightening anti-ageing skincare series aims to prevent excess melanin production and accumulation in the epidermal cells. The blue colour portrays an image of clear skin that compliments the white of the bottle, which is an expression of its brightening effects. The ellipsoidal container symbolises the growth of a circle and also evolution through constant renewal. The off-centre positioning of the logo on the front of the container conveys the desire to look at things from a different angle. Both visually and haptically, the packaging design creates a high-quality look.

Client
ORBIS Inc., Tokyo

Design
ORBIS Inc., Tokyo

Creative Direction
Taku Satoh Design Office Inc, Tokyo

Art Direction
Yusuke Harada, ORBIS Inc.

Design Team
Kanako Maruhashi, Hiromi Kobayashi, ORBIS Inc.

CarrieMe

[Cosmetics Packaging]

Client
Sanqi Biomedical International Co., Ltd.,
Taipei City

Design
Zi Huai Shen, Kun Shan University /
SUMP DESIGN, Tainan City

→ Designer portrait on page 524

The main concept of this packaging design for a cosmetics line is to present product features and stories through a female character called CarrieMe. The imagery is based on the story of a trip to Paris. Thus, six different visual representations have been designed, each in the colour of a macaroon, a French dessert, in order to create a delightful atmosphere. The boxes, which are reminiscent of letter boxes, contain cosmetic products in small packaging units for single use. The empty packaging can be disposed of in the top of the mailbox.

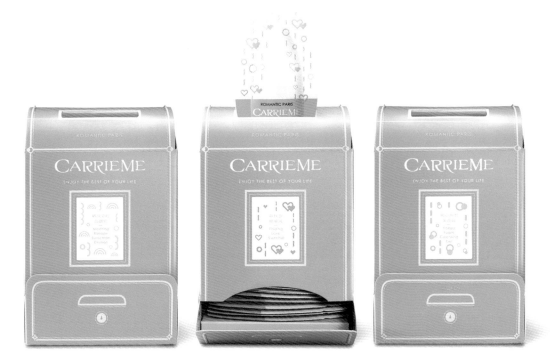

Cha Tzu Tang
Naturally Smooth Series

[Packaging]

In view of the brand Cha Tzu Tang's dedication to farming and environmental protection, this packaging design is characterised by a natural smoothness. A series of artfully drawn motifs adorns the cardboard packaging, while the products are highly regarded thanks to the exclusive images. The packaging materials are made of plain grey cardboard and black-and-white screen printing to highlight the layers of the print production process, which illustrates the brand's focus on nature. Ribbons in harmonious, earthy colours complete the elegant look of the box.

Client
Orientea Enterprise Co., Ltd.,
New Taipei City

Design
Victor Branding Design Corp.,
Taichung City

POLA Kurobihatsu
[Cosmetics Packaging]

These hair products are suited to the needs of Japanese hair, with the packaging design already communicating this concept at the point of sale. An elegant black background and the brand logo in gold lettering imbue the containers with a feeling of premium quality. The seal graphic is based on the Chinese character for hair and fits in neatly with the brand image. The shape of the containers evokes the image of a hair follicle springing up from the root. The minimalist design gives the containers a slightly curved appearance from the front, whereas they look straight from the side.

Client
POLA Inc., Tokyo

Design
POLA Inc., Tokyo

Art Direction
Takashi Matsui

Packaging Design
Rieko Nakamura

Taiwan
Aboriginal Masks

[Cosmetics Packaging]

The Taiwan Aboriginal Masks include
the beauty secrets inherited from six
major aboriginal Taiwanese tribes: Amis,
Puyuma, Saisiyat, Rukai, Thao and Tsou.
The patented formulas include local
plants such as bitter gourd, catjang peas,
and Formosa lilies. The packaging design
is inspired by aboriginal legends, and the
box is printed with non-toxic, soy-based
inks. The shape of the foil bags has been
designed as "orbicular sky and rectangular earth", representing the balance of
yin and yang. The gift box features endangered black-faced spoonbills and is
made of stone paper to express a love
of nature and the earth.

Client
Tenart Biotech Limited, Taipei City

Design
Tenart Biotech Limited, Taipei City

Account Management
Michelle Sung

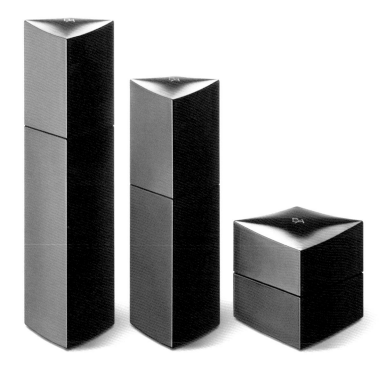

POLA B.A

[Cosmetics Packaging]

The B.A series is a cosmetic anti-ageing product that focuses on the process of how skin forms. Using the prestigious beauty of Japanese lacquer, the packaging design simply places the logo against a glossy black, achieving a tranquil minimalism while also exuding elegance. The front edge of the packaging expresses the determination of the brand to carve out a new era while the contents express innovation. The contrast between the flat sides and the curved top, together with the design of various colourful plants on the inside of the box, represent the many expressions of feminine beauty.

Client
POLA Inc., Tokyo

Design
POLA Inc., Tokyo

Creative Direction
Takashi Matsui

Art Direction
Haruyo Eto

Design Team
Kei Ikehata, Shingo Isobe,
Mai Karin Kamiyama

Cell Renew Bio

[Cosmetics Packaging]

The packaging design of this cosmetics line is aimed at urban men who exhibit both masculine qualities and a caring nature. In line with the recent trend of handmade accessories, the design applies a contemporary leather look to the cosmetics packaging, so that it is perceived as a premium product. The leather structure is embossed on the box along with an image of a forest, which connects with the tree pattern on the cap in order to convey the design concept to the consumer. The contrast between cream and purple hues gives the outer packaging a high-quality look.

Client
The SAEM International Co., Ltd., Seoul

Design
The SAEM International Co., Ltd., Seoul

→ Designer portrait on page 529

FRUDIA

[Cosmetics Packaging]

Named with a compound word consisting of "fruit" and "dia", FRUDIA was created according to the brand ideology of delivering the nutrition of fruit directly to the skin. The packaging design was inspired by a jar of jam, filled with hydrating cosmetics. The side of the lid is curved, mimicking the top of a freshly made fruit jam covered with a wrapper. Moreover, the lower part of the lid resembles the flowing texture of cream. The container is finished with a smooth touch in order to reflect the product's high quality. It aims to appeal to a sophisticated target group in their twenties and thirties.

Client
WELCOS Co., Ltd., Seoul

Project Management
Youngdon Kim

Design
OUTIN FUTURES, Seoul

Deage

[Cosmetics Packaging]

Based on biomimetic molecular structures, the packaging design of this cosmetics line conveys an urban, sculptural
aesthetic, which emphasises the innovative quality of the brand. Haptically
appealing contours are reminiscent of a
worry stone and attract attention at the
point of sale. Due to its colour, the elegant wordmark creates a strong contrast to the dark box and is also tangibly
embossed. The material of the outer
packaging equally reflects the exclusive
concept of this product series.

Client
Legart Forschungsatelier,
Pour Legart GmbH, Raubling

Design
Clormann Design GmbH, Penzing

Creative Direction
Marc Clormann

Art Direction
Michaela Vargas Coronado

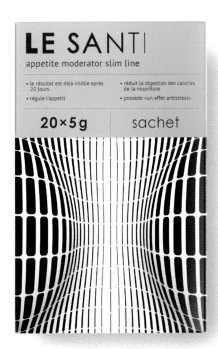

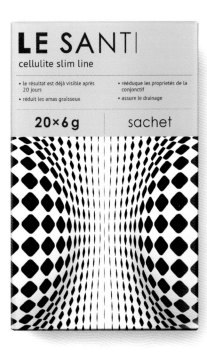

Le Santi

[Packaging]

Le Santi is a trademark for a weight-loss food line. The distinctive packaging design aims to appeal to both women and men who want to lose weight in a pleasant way. In order to convey that one can lose weight anytime, a pictorial language has been created which vividly illustrates the weight-loss process. The packaging presents graphic shapes subjected to a visual metamorphosis of becoming thinner in the "waist". By means of this visual metaphor, the brand message is communicated in a unique and convincing manner.

Client
Vertex, Saint Petersburg

Design
:Otvetdesign, Saint Petersburg

Creative Direction
Vladimir Fedoseev

Art Direction
Arina Yushkevich, Ksenia Alekina

Concept
Veronica Toropsova

Account Management
Aleksandr Bakin

237

t: by tetesept

[Cosmetics & Care Packaging]

The sub-brand "t: by tetesept" focuses on pleasure instead of medical benefits. As its most important communication tool, the packaging design stands out at the point of sale and increases consumers' willingness to buy it. For four bubble-bath products, different packaging variants were created to communicate not only the new sub-brand, but also their respective attributes. The bubble baths were designed as eye-catchers for the bathroom. Each design uses key visuals related to the fragrances and ingredients of the respective type, connecting the brand with a modern lifestyle. All packaging consistently follows the same two-part design: a colourful banderole above and a section in solid colour below.

Client
Merz Consumer Care GmbH, Frankfurt/Main

Design
WIN CREATING IMAGES, Aachen/Cologne/Munich/Berlin

→ Designer portrait on page 533

Bath & Nature

[Cosmetics Packaging]

Bath & Nature is a body-care line by the brand Nature Republic. In order to express a mysterious atmosphere, five types of natural fragrances are embodied in concise yet fairy-tale-like imagery. Colourful illustrations are portrayed to take customers on an imaginary journey to an exotic island, to enrich their experience when showering. Colour gradation has been used on the packaging in order to convey a sweet and fresh aroma. The colour applied to each lotion and wash packaging is different, so that customers can easily distinguish the products.

Client
Nature Republic, Seoul

Design
Nature Republic, Seoul

Creative Direction
Suk Jae Jung

Product Design
Tae Min Kim, Hyemi Kim

Graphic Design
Young Jun Jeon, Wan Tae Kim
Momentum, Seoul

Ponio

[Cosmetics Packaging]

Ponio is a young brand of handmade natural cosmetics. The task was to re-design its logo and product packaging. The design of the latter is minimalist, with the use of pleasant-to-touch craft paper and an undertone colour palette that reflects the ingredients of the product. Small details define the product groups: horizontal lines for massage cubes, small waves for deodorants and bubbles for soaps. All these details distinguish the trademark from similar products on the market. The new logo with a sans-serif font uses an irregular letter "O", which refers to the handmade character of the products.

Client
Ponio s.r.o., Zvolen

Design
Pergamen, Trnava

Creative Direction
Juraj Demovič

Graphic Design
Lívia Lörinczová

Photography
Jakub Dvořák

Pre-Press/Final Artwork
Samuel Ryba

Enzyme Cleansing Powder Wash

[Cosmetics Packaging]

The packaging design concept for the Enzyme Cleansing Powder Wash appeals to the target group and essentially achieves two effects. First, the single-dose packaging simplifies one-time use for effective facial cleansing. Second, the form and colour of the individual packages express the refreshing feeling as a key point of this enzyme cleansing. The cover design of the packaging features a charming hand-drawn illustration in blue and white. The cloud as a key visual conveys the lightness of the product. Moreover, the triangular outer packaging can be stacked in a space-saving and attention-grabbing way at the point of sale.

Client
Blisspack Co., Ltd., Siheung City, Gyeonggi Province

Design
Blisspack Co., Ltd., Siheung City, Gyeonggi Province

innisfree Jeju
Perfume Note

[Cosmetics Packaging]

Client
innisfree Corporation, Seoul

Design
innisfree Design Team, Seoul

Creative Direction/Graphic Design
Mi-Young Park

Product Design
Mi-Young Park

The Jeju Perfume Note is a perfume line consisting of five scents inspired by the flair of the Korean holiday island Jeju. Based on a travel diary, the packaging follows a clear design concept. When opened, the packaging is reminiscent of a book cover. The written record of scents on the inside of the packaging accentuates the high-quality impression. The transparent perfume bottle allows the decorative image behind it to shine through. After the product is taken out of its book-like cover, the cover can be reused for storing small items.

Intelligent –
Natural Enzymes
Toothpaste

[Cosmetics Packaging]

Intelligent is a Taiwanese toothpaste brand which uses natural enzymes for healthy dental care. The packaging design combines the spirit of the brand with innovative product characteristics. The concept of rare active enzymes is incorporated into the graphic symbols of elements, thus visually highlighting the effectiveness of active enzymes. The packaging material is foil cardboard. The bright and metallic look of the outer packaging emphasises the strength and health of teeth as the key message while enhancing the tactile product impression.

Client
Free Bio Technology Corp., Taipei City

Design
Proad Identity, Taipei City

Creative Direction
Jennifer Tsai

→ Designer portrait on page 520

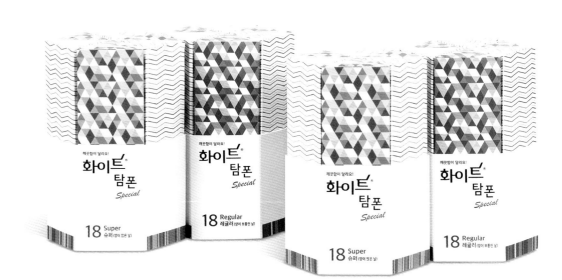

Chic and Light
the New White!

[Cosmetics Packaging]

The packaging design for White Tampons was created so that women can carry these tampons around openly. The patterns and colours of the triangular boxes look trendy and chic, thus lacking any association with sanitary products. The combination of the two different designs in the product set achieves a visually appealing effect. The tampon packaging is available as a pack of two or six, which easily fit into a handbag. Each triangular package contains three tampons with applicators.

Client
Yuhan-Kimberly, Seoul

Design
Yuhan-Kimberly, Seoul

Creative Direction
Jungwoo Choi

Art Direction
Haein Kim

Concept
Yoonseon Kang, Sara Lee

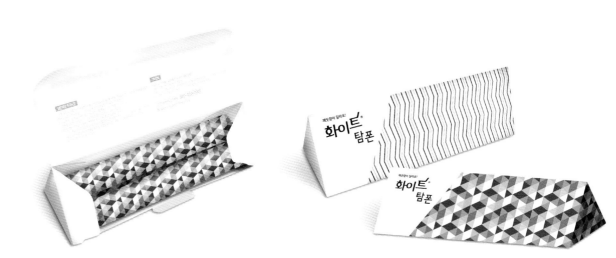

LongFeng Dafa

[Packaging]

In China, the traditional table game mah-jong is a popular nationwide pastime, with players often smoking cigarettes during the game. Hence, the packaging design of this cigarette brand uses the pictorial language of known gaming tiles to visualise the brand name LongFeng. The shape of the well-known character "Fa" is formed using the dragon and phoenix totems from Chinese mythology, employing the technique of mah-jong pattern carving. Furthermore, the white-and-green classical combination immediately conveys the connection with the game.

Client
TigerPan Packaging Design Lab.,
Shenzhen

Design
TigerPan Packaging Design Lab.,
Shenzhen

Art Direction
Tiger Pan

→ Designer portrait on page 530

Tianzi No. 1

[Packaging]

Tianzi No. 1 is a cigarette brand with a packaging design that reinterprets expressive motifs from Taoist culture. In China, Tianzi is a dragon. The key visual creates the shape of a flying dragon by using the two Chinese characters "tian" and "zi" written in calligraphy. A delicate embossing is applied to the pure white and textured paper in order to highlight the white colour and space. With regard to structure, the outer cigarette packaging is designed to slide open to one side, while the inside is lined with aluminium foil featuring the design of a wave and cliff pattern from traditional emperor costumes.

Client
TigerPan Packaging Design Lab., Shenzhen

Design
TigerPan Packaging Design Lab., Shenzhen

Art Direction
Tiger Pan

→ Designer portrait on page 530

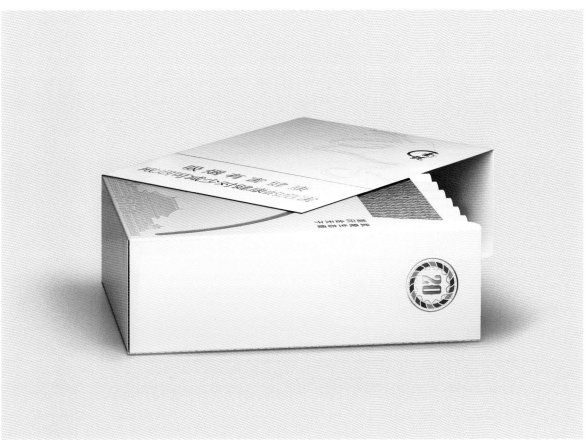

Marking Memory

[Packaging]

LKP's Marking Memory series adopted the concept of a wooden flash drive and extended it to the packaging. The design concept uses tree rings as markings of memories. This is equated with the flash drive as a device for memory storage. Hence, its surface is designed to look like wood grain. In order to open the premium cardboard packaging, a sleeve made of semi-transparent paper has to be removed first. The interior of the packaging is an extension of the markings on the flash drive and the related motto – "Don't measure yourself by what you have accomplished but by what you should have accomplished with your ability" – is echoed in the concept of the markings.

Client
LKP, Taipei City

Design
Proad Identity, Taipei City

Creative Direction
Jennifer Tsai

→ Designer portrait on page 520

Uprising Sounds

[Music Packaging]

The 2nd BenQ Foundation Music Camp album is named "Uprising Sounds", not only to imply that these musicians are young, but also to indicate their connection with the ocean. The music camp was held on the eastern coast of Taiwan and invited songwriters to compose new songs. The cover design is based on an aboriginal tradition of using the shell-flower leaf for packaging. The lyrics pages show a decorative wave pattern painted in watercolour to enable people to dive deeper into the songwriters' minds and experience their love for the eastern coast and music.

Client
BenQ Foundation, Taoyuan City

Publisher
Jennifer Chen

Design
Chia-Wei Lai, Taipei City
Wei-Chia Lu, Taipei City

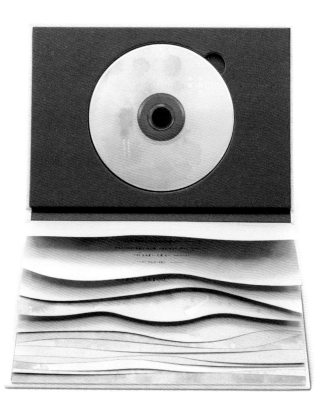

The Dash –
Truly Wireless
Smart Earphones

[Packaging]

Client
Bragi GmbH, Munich

Design
Bragi GmbH, Munich

Creative Direction
Matthias Lackus, Arne Loermann

Graphic Design
Elisabeth Wagner, Katja Riley

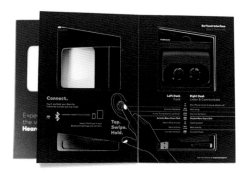

The Dash are wireless smart earphones controlled either by gestures via the EarTouch interface or by using the free Bragi app. As this innovation sets a new standard for interacting with technology, the packaging is critical for guiding customers through their first use of the product. It opens like a book, each page displaying product use illustrations. With each turn of the page, a new step or feature is revealed. Printed on an entirely black background, the text and the illustrations have a distinctive effect. A trendy blue, as a contrasting colour, completes the concept.

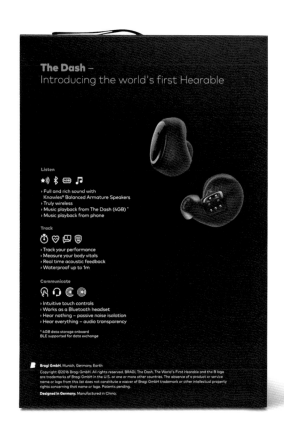

OTT Box

[Retail Packaging]

The overall concept of this retail
packaging design is based on the slogan
"Go Green" and has been applied to
three product groups. The packaging is
entirely made from recycled paper,
watercolour ink and other eco-friendly
materials, such as cornflour, which is
used as glue. The H1 box can be reused
as a product stand, by cutting along
the dotted lines. The H2 packaging is
designed so that the product is displayed when users slide the sleeve aside,
with accessories hidden underneath.
In the case of the H3 packaging, the
product pops up when the user opens
the cover. Product differentiation is
made easy through eye-catching colour
accents.

Client
HUMAX, Seongnam City

Design
HUMAX, Seongnam City

Concept
DK Kim

Solar Crackle
Glass Ball Light

[Packaging]

This semi-enclosed packaging box has been designed to highlight the solar light bulb. Available in five different colours, it symbolises the specific colour of the light. Geometric motifs in various sizes and different shades of the same colour are used to indicate the special visual effects created by the crackled look of the bulb. Squares in various colours on two sides of the bulb create connections with boxes in different hues like a fun jigsaw puzzle, which also encourages customers to purchase more products. The round hole at the bottom of the box adds another function to the product by allowing it to be hung on the wall in addition to hanging from a string or being placed on a desk.

Client
TEST RITE GROUP, Taipei City

Design
TEST RITE GROUP, Taipei City

Creative Direction
Wen-Hsiang Wei

Art Direction
Shuai Zhang, Ming-Chien Chen

Concept
Yun Huang

Graphic Design
Meng Lu, Yu-Wen Chiu, Liming Shu

Artwork
Yongjian Tu, Fangyi Zhen

I-1 Analog
Instant Camera

[Packaging]

The launch of the I-1 camera aims to take the tactile magic of analogue instant photography into the digital age. The packaging is inspired by both the industrial design of the camera and the tactile experience of using instant film. The zip pull tab, the cardboard stock, the screw connecting the camera to the packaging and the debossing all have been designed to provide as tactile of an experience as possible. The yellow shipping box provides protection during transport, but stores have the option of removing it and using the grey box as a point-of-sale display. The inner box is also intended for displaying the photographer's instant creations.

Client
Impossible Camera GmbH, Berlin

Design
Impossible Camera GmbH, Berlin

Art Direction/Graphic Design
Danny Pemberton

Concept
Danny Pemberton, Oskar Smolokowski,
Jesper Kouthoofd, Debbie Vesey,
Felix Yarwood

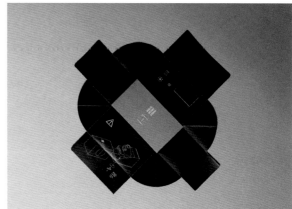

Impossible Instant Film

[Packaging]

Impossible Project, the company that purchased the last Polaroid factory in 2008, now produces nearly 20 editions of instant film. The packaging has to allow the customer to quickly identify the technical aspects of each film (such as format, chemistry), and also inject a sense of fun back into the brand. A primary colour system was developed to help solve both challenges, anchored by the main brand shade of black. The inside of the packaging was reworked with a newly designed tip sheet and a series of creative briefs, created to guide new users and inspire experienced photographers.

Client
Impossible Camera GmbH, Berlin

Design
Impossible Camera GmbH, Berlin

Creative Direction/Graphic Design
Danny Pemberton

Concept
Danny Pemberton, Oskar Smolokowski

Memorieslab

[Packaging]

Client
Memorieslab, Hong Kong

Design
LOOVVOOL, Hong Kong

Creative Direction
Hannes Unt

Graphic Design
Neil Watson, Hannes Unt

Account Management
Jaime Chua

→ Designer portrait on page 510

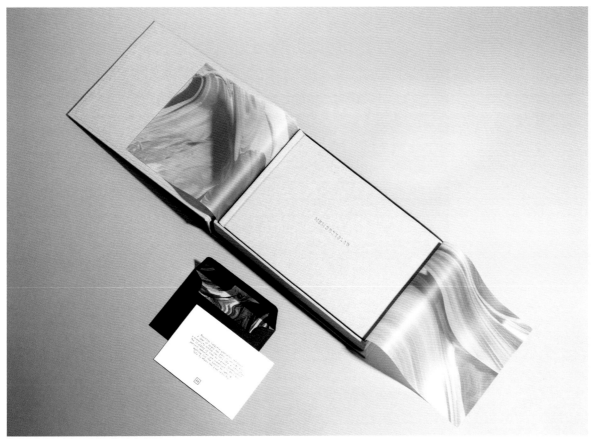

Memorieslab is a high-end online photo lab and gallery, dedicated to the exploration of photographic preservation. The packaging for their product range had to be unique with premium touches in order to represent the brand's positioning and concept. The overall look and feel of the packaging was kept intentionally minimal and contemporary. The brand patterns were created as accents referring back to chemical processes that take place during traditional photo development in the darkroom.

Dr. Reckhaus Fly Trap

[Packaging]

The Dr. Reckhaus fly trap represents insect repellent for indoor use with high ecological standards, thus reducing or avoiding the use of biocides. The packaging design also raises awareness for the value of insects. The product packaging has two components in order to clarify both the ecological aspects and the control aspect for the consumer. The outer packaging component in orange has a signal effect at the point of sale, while the interior white packaging component underlines the insect-friendly properties. The product promise is successfully conveyed by the quote, the text and also a reference to further information on the Internet.

Client
Reckhaus AG, Gais,
Appenzell Ausserrhoden

Design
Alltag, St. Gallen

Camera
Jelena Gernert,
Jelena Gernert Productions,
St. Gallen

Harvest Bag

[Sustainable Packaging]

Woven bags are the most traditional packaging used for cereals in China, due to their low price and ease of production. However, used woven bags create a huge amount of non-recyclable waste, posing a severe burden on the environment. Harvest Bag can be easily recycled into a fashion bag for shopping due to its high durability. Combined with stylish visual effects and reinforced material properties, the empty bag is given a new life. The simple bag, without excessive patterns and colours, is in keeping with the core design, indicating the concept of environmental protection as advocated by the brand.

Client
Fengfan Farm Products, Jintan

Design
Rong, Shanghai

→ Designer portrait on page 521

Green Catch

[Packaging]

The packaging for Green Catch has been designed for potted plants and consists of two simple layers. Considering that these goods are mainly sold online, the packaging has to protect the plants and their glass vessels during transport. In order to display simplicity and ecological awareness, there is no outer packaging. The two parts of the package display beautiful plant patterns in a watercolour design. The interior cardboard tray has a small curve matching the shape of the container. When the outer box is lifted up, the interior cardboard tray imitates the process of a plant growing.

Client
Guangzhou Flower Qing Feng
Landscaping Co., Ltd., Guangzhou

Design
Box Brand Design Limited,
Hong Kong

Creative Direction
Joey Lo

Art Direction
Yvonne Chung

Graphic Design
Joey Lo, Taylor Shum

Photography
Ariom Leung

Green Dream

[Packaging]

The concept of "The Green Dream" is to grow a combination of plants in a glass container. Customers can enjoy and experience the fun of putting individual plants together to create their own combinations. The product packaging appears like a colourful puzzle box. It incorporates different requirements related to the safe shipping of fragile goods ordered online. Unlike regular cardboard or rough packaging, the plants come in a cushioning bag that also highlights the plants and enables customers to clearly see what they have purchased before opening it. In addition, the air-filled bag will prevent damage during shipping thanks to its unique cushioning effect.

Client
Guangzhou Flower Qing Feng
Landscaping Co., Ltd., Guangzhou

Design
Box Brand Design Limited, Hong Kong

Creative Direction
Joey Lo

Art Direction
Yvonne Chung

Graphic Design
Kyran Chan

Photography
Ariom Leung

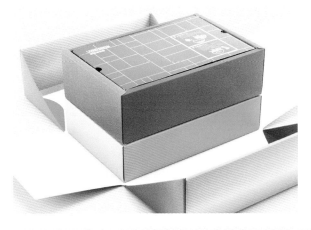

Holcim Agrocal

[Sustainable Packaging]

Agrocal powder is a natural, eco-friendly source of calcium and magnesium that increases soil fertility. In order to reach urban gardeners, it is now launched in small packages of 4 kg made from ecological, easily degradable paper, with a decorative single-colour print. Each package comes in a wooden box that is intended to be reused by gardeners. Different motivational sayings are carved into the box. Thanks to its stackability, this product becomes an independent entity which need not fight for a place on the shelves in the usually crowded agricultural supply stores.

Client
Holcim Croatia

Project Management
Julija Škoro

Design
STUDIO SONDA, Vižinada

Creative Direction
Jelena Fiškuš, Sean Poropat

Art Direction
Martina Sirotić Pavletić

Graphic Design
Andrej Glavičić

Illustration
Eugen Slavik

Filemon

[Transport Box]

Filemon is a transport box that doubles as a cosy and natural cathouse. The design concept is based on cats' love for hiding in cardboard boxes. Accordingly, the "travel box" was created out of a simple sheet of corrugated cardboard, so that every trip becomes stress-free for both the animal and its owner. The three-element construction is fast and easy to assemble. The cat is placed in the transport box from above and locked in with a single movement. Additionally, the changeable front and back allow users to easily turn the transport box into a cathouse.

Client
Cosy & Dosy

Design
Smurfit Kappa Poland

Project Management
Artur Wisniewski

ADVERTISING

Red Dot: Grand Prix

The 2 Euro T-Shirt –
A Social Experiment

[Out-of-Home & Ambient]

With the aim of drawing consumer attention to the inhumane work conditions in the textile production industry, a social activation campaign was launched as part of the Fashion Revolution Day. As such, an attention-grabbing turquoise-coloured T-shirt vending machine was built and placed on Berlin Alexanderplatz in Germany. The teaser was a T-shirt for only 2 euros. On inserting the coin into the machine, the display showed a 20 seconds long video with nightmarish images showing the conditions under which textiles are often produced. Potential customers were then given a "Buy" or "Donate" choice on the display, meaning they could choose between buying the T-shirt or donating the inserted money. About 90 per cent of all people who had wanted to buy a T-shirt cheaply at the vending machine ended up deciding against the purchase. The results of the experiment were documented in a video, which sparked a big discussion amidst consumers and between consumers and producers.

Statement by the jury

This campaign manages to emotionally touch people, who at first only thought about grabbing a bargain, and then to make them reconsider. Particularly noteworthy is that the campaign did not stop there, but the video documentation was shared and thus contributed to the multiplication of the momentum via social media. Thus, this one-off campaign generated high awareness of a grave social concern.

reddot award 2016
grand prix

Client
Fashion Revolution, Berlin

Design
BBDO Berlin

Chief Creative Officer
Wolfgang Schneider

Creative Managing Direction
Jan Harbeck, David Mously

Executive Creative Direction
Jan Harbeck, Michael Schachtner

Art Direction/Script
Jessica Witt, Michail Paderin

Account Management
Mike Kannowski

Chief Production Officer
Steffen Gentis

Agency Producer
Silke Rochow

Film Production
UNIT9, Berlin

Post-Production
CraftWork – a brand of
ad agencyservices

Film Direction
Robert Bader

Camera
Alessandro Rovere, Kevin Krefta

Film Editing
Kevin Krefta

Animation
Nicolas Molès

→ Designer portrait on page 487

Red Dot: Best of the Best

Design Your Time

[Social Media Campaign]

With the Gear S2, Samsung has presented its first round smartwatch. Prior to the launch and under the motto "Design your time", the Samsung community was invited via Facebook, Instagram, tech bloggers and opinion leaders to design a new individual watch face for each minute of the day. There were no particular rules, allowing everything from drawings and paintings to collages. Within just a few days, thousands of unique watch faces were created and submitted. The most original 1,440 designs among all submissions were integrated into the dynamic "Samsung Watchface" and published as an app. Thus, the watch features a different image for each minute of the day. This campaign generated a high awareness of the new product in the social web and led to the development of an innovative content tool.

Statement by the jury
With this social media campaign, Samsung has managed to both reach a creative target group and position itself as a design-oriented manufacturer. The campaign is based on a strong and clever idea. The community was invited to take part in creating the dynamic watch face through individual submissions – a kind of "crowd illustrating" – with a result that simultaneously demonstrates the potential of the new product to impressive effect.

Client
Samsung Electronics, Schwalbach

Design
Leo Burnett Germany, Frankfurt/Main

Chief Creative Officer
Andreas Pauli

Executive Creative Direction
Christoph Riebling

Creative Direction
Helge Kniess (Art), Benjamin Merkel (Text)

Art Direction
Thomas Koch

Copywriting
Christian Urbanski

Red Dot: Best of the Best

The Guy Who Cut Everything in Half
[Digital Campaign]

In Germany, a divorce can cost you up to 50 per cent of your belongings. Consulting a lawyer and getting a prenuptial agreement before the wedding can help to prevent that. In order to sensitise unmarried couples to the topic, the Deutscher Anwaltverein (German Bar Association) commissioned this campaign. A purposefully amateur-style video was created for streaming on YouTube, showing fictitious character Martin G., who after splitting up with his wife takes the notion of "splitting up" literally and cuts the entire shared household in halves, sarcastically thanking his ex-wife for "12 beautiful years". He then continues to sell all cut up items on eBay. This story made it around the world, generating high attention in social media and on the web. After revealing who stood behind the story, the traffic on the German Bar Association's online platform increased by 173 per cent.

Statement by the jury
This viral campaign is a truly powerful way of getting a heavy message across in a very light-hearted and entertaining way – a highly humorous and clever canvass. By resorting to social media as a channel, the campaign also has exemplarily managed to place the topic in traditional media in order to generate the highest possible degree of attention.

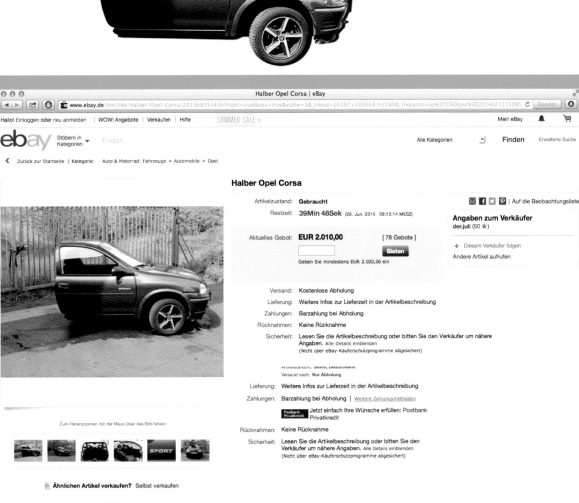

Client
Deutscher Anwaltverein, Berlin

Design
Serviceplan/Plan.Net

Executive Creative Direction
Benedikt Göttert

Creative Direction
Franz Röppischer, Lorenz Langgartner

Art Direction
Julius Steffens

Copywriting
Philipp Stute

Creative Innovation Direction
Franz Röppischer, Lorenz Langgartner

Graphic Design
Azim Abasbek

Motion Design
Dennis Fritz

→ Designer portrait on page 523

Red Dot: Best of the Best

smart – Shock

[TV Commercial]

This TV commercial promotes the new smart forfour by focusing on and staging the peculiarity of the car in an entertaining manner. A small turning circle, agility in city traffic, seating space for four and outstanding parkability – all these are characteristics that mark the car as truly "smart". The concept of the spot delivers both entertainment and surprise: three men are driving through the city in this four-seater, when the driver suddenly spots a parking space at the other side of the street. The driver turns the car around and sets out to park the car backwards. On turning his head, a shrill yell escapes him for the shock of seeing the third man sitting in the back he had forgotten about – reassured, he then finishes the parking manoeuvre sovereignly. In a charming manner, the video thus conveys its message that "driving the smart forfour feels so much like driving the iconic smart fortwo that you forget you have a back seat". The video gets this message across in just a few seconds and is therefore far from over-straining the attention span of viewers.

Statement by the jury
This advertising video stays entertaining even after watching it repeatedly. The story, the direction, the actors, the acting and the sound – all aspects are implemented perfectly. At the same time, the video also pointedly communicates the unique selling proposition of the smart forfour in an extremely funny yet brief manner. "Shock" brings everything together to reach the target group and create a memorable impression.

>> So smart you forget it's a fourseater.

Client
Daimler AG, smart, Böblingen

Design
BBDO Berlin

Chief Creative Officer
Wolfgang Schneider

Creative Managing Direction
Jan Harbeck, Ton Hollander

Executive Creative Direction
Michael Schachtner, Jan Harbeck

Creative Direction/Copywriting
David Missing, Ricardo Wolff

Art Direction
Angelo Maia

Account Management
Jan Hendrik Oelckers, Joris Jonker,
Lindsay Jönsson

Chief Production Officer
Steffen Gentis

Agency Producer
Silke Rochow

Film Production
Anorak, Berlin

Film Direction
Calle Astrand

Camera
Thomas Kürzel

Post-Production
Slaughterhouse, Berlin

→ Clip on DVD
→ Designer portrait on page 489

Red Dot: Best of the Best

smart Parking Ramps

[Print Campaign]

The message of this print campaign reads "The city is one huge parking space" – at least when driving the new smart fortwo with its short length of only 2.69 metres. Each motif of the campaign conveys this message through a dense illustration, showing the cities of Berlin, Rome and London compressed into parking ramps with a smart just about to drive into them. The top floor features distinctive landmarks and parts of the skyline to indicate which city it is. The lovingly crafted illustrations in the form of hidden object images fascinate with their richness of detail. In addition, they motivate viewers to take their time to explore and spot minutiae, thus taking full advantage of the possibilities offered by print. The visually striking campaign does without text, while the smart logo at the top edge looks like a bookmark.

Statement by the jury
The print campaign for the new smart outstandingly illustrates the essence of the smart idea. The drawings convey an immediate impression of how smart drivers feel when driving into a big city and being able to find a parking space almost everywhere, unlike drivers of other cars. The illustrations are magnificent and full of witty details, keeping you engaged once you get the idea.

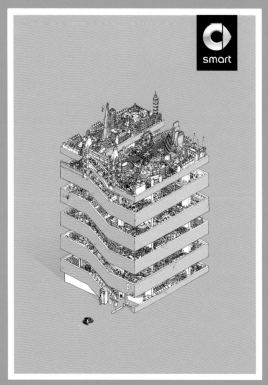

Client
Daimler AG, smart, MBD, Berlin

Design
BBDO Berlin

Chief Creative Officer
Wolfgang Schneider

Creative Managing Direction
David Mously, Jan Harbeck

Executive Creative Direction
Ton Hollander, Jan Harbeck

Creative Direction
Daniel Haschtmann, Tobias Feige

Art Direction
Felix Boeck

Text
Samuel Weiß

Illustration
Chrisse Kunst, Berlin
Upper Orange, Berlin

Managing Director
Dirk Spakowski

Account Management
Sebastian Schlosser, Casper Pongs

→ Designer portrait on page 488

Saturn Shop Clock

[App]

The Saturn Shop Clock is a smartphone clock widget. It was created to demonstrate that the tech retailer offers highly competitive deals around the clock. The mobile app displays all deals that match the current time. Thus, at 09:35, it shows a TV for 935 euros, and a camera for 1,617 euros at 16:17. The tool is intuitive to understand and offers high consumer benefit according to the idea that every time the user checks the time, an opportunity to save money is provided. In addition, the brand is thus presented up to 150 times a day on customer smartphones.

Client
Saturn, Munich

Design
Serviceplan/Plan.Net, Munich

Chief Creative Officer
Alexander Schill

Executive Creative Direction
Alexander Nagel, Christoph Everke, Michael Wilk

Creative Direction
Franz Röppischer, Lorenz Langgartner

LG 55UH600V, 139 cm (55 Zoll), UHD 4K, LED TV

1099.-

inkl. Mwst. zzgl. Versand € 35,00

» BUNDLE AKTION

+ **JUKE!**

A+

Online auf Lager

In den Warenkorb

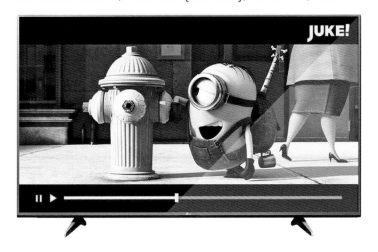

LG 55UH600V, 139 cm (55 Zoll), UHD 4K, LED TV

1099.-

inkl. Mwst. zzgl. Versand € 35,00

» BUNDLE AKTION

+ **JUKE!**

A+

Online auf Lager

In den Warenkorb

Sneak Preview

[Digital Campaign]

Juke! offers access to more than 15,000 movies and series. The goal of this campaign was to promote the streaming service's quantity and quality of entertainment content, alongside generating new subscriptions. For that purpose, visitors of the Saturn online shop were to be surprised with an eye-catching experience: the placeholders of the TV preview screens were turned into ad spaces by showing the latest content of the streaming service. The result of the promotion was that 80 per cent of the customers took the offer of buying a TV plus streaming subscription.

Client
Saturn, Munich

Design
Serviceplan/Plan.Net, Munich

Chief Creative Officer
Alexander Schill

Executive Creative Direction
Matthias Harbeck, Sandra Loibl

Creative Direction
Franz Röppischer, Lorenz Langgartner

Art Direction
Damian Sturm, Thomas Heckenberger, Thomas Wiegand

Text
Sebastian Meyer

Vector Coded Ads

[Integrated Campaign]

Vector is a huge employer in the IT
sector and a technology partner to the
global automotive industry. However,
it is virtually unknown among career
starters. With the aim of lending
the company a striking appeal as an
employer brand, this campaign speaks
directly to potential applicants in their
programming language of choice –
from Java to C++. The self-made feel
of the campaign does not come across
as advertising but rather as a dialogue
between experts – with confident statements that repeatedly highlight the
unique mindset of the people at Vector.

Client
Vector Informatik GmbH, Stuttgart

Design
Publicis Pixelpark, Munich

Executive Creative Direction
Stephan Ganser

Creative Direction
Manfred Feiger

Art Direction
Maja Lindemann

Text/Concept
Reinhard Putscher

Production
Stefan Pulster

Account Management
Beate Ernst

```
#include<iostream>
void main()
{
    int myJob;
    std::cout<< "Ist es noch Arbeit, "
            << "wenn es Spaß macht?";
    myJob = jobCode(1,0);
}

/* Vector -
   Automotive. Software. Engineering.
   jobs.vector.com */
```

VECTOR >

```
static class JobSearch
{
    static void Main(string[] args)
    {
        Job nextJob = CreateChallenge("Sie passen nicht zu uns. Du schon.");
        nextJob.StartCareer();
    }

    private static Job CreateChallenge(string details)
    {
        Console.WriteLine("Ein 'Sie' schafft Distanz." +
                        "Ein 'Du' macht ein Team. Das sind wir." +
                        "Vom Praktikanten bis zur Geschäftsführung.");
        Console.WriteLine("Software-Engineer gesucht. jobs.vector.com ");

        return Jobs.GetJobOffers().BestMatch(job => job.Details.Contains(details));
    }
}
/* Vector - Automotive. Software. Engineering. */
```

VECTOR >

Eyes on Gigi

[Digital Campaign]

Created under the direction of Hollywood director Marc Forster, the digital campaign for the new BMW M2 Coupé takes the form of a fast nutshell game. Shot on an airfield located in the Mojave Desert in California, the video shows five vehicles constantly changing positions, and challenges viewers to track and not lose sight of the car into which supermodel Gigi Hadid stepped. The right answer is indicated on the campaign-related microsite that also offers viewing of the video shot with 360-degree movie technology.

Client
BMW Group, Munich

Design
Serviceplan/Plan.Net, Munich
KBS, New York

Chief Creative Officer
Alexander Schill, Serviceplan
Jonathan Mackler, Dan Kelleher, KBS

Executive Creative Direction
Michael Wilk, Serviceplan
Paul Renner, KBS

Creative Direction
Kolja Danquah, Serviceplan

I Hate My Job

[TV Commercial]

Audi was looking for an entertaining and light-hearted way to bring up the issue of piloted driving. This commercial therefore plays with the idea that robots also like to have fun. In the past, all the tasks they did for humans were rather unpleasant ones. Now, however, robots are finally allowed to do a job that is enjoyable, namely driving the RS 7, the first autonomous racecar. The message of the video is supported by distinctive background music, a specially recorded gospel song, in which the robots lament the hardship of their work.

Client
AUDI AG, Ingolstadt

Design
thjnk ag, Hamburg

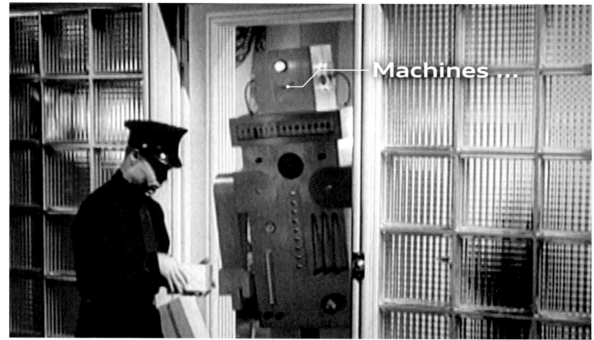

Pulse
[TV Commercial]

The RS models by Audi stand for acceleration rates that make the heart beat faster. The TV advertisement is aimed at demonstrating this emotion vividly. The video tells the dramatic story of a heart transplantation, a situation in which every second counts. An Audi R6 is used to transport the freshly donated organ from one hospital to another. When the surgeons open the cooling box on its arrival after a fast-paced ride through the night scenery of a big city, they are surprised: it contains a heart that beats all by itself – exalted by the ride in the sportscar.

Client
AUDI AG, Ingolstadt

Design
thjnk ag, Hamburg

Do Something against Climate Change

[Cinema Commercial]

This commercial by the waste disposal service company Berliner Stadtreinigung (BSR) promotes the look and feel of a Greenpeace appeal. The images of melting glaciers and arctic animals – musically accompanied by Mozart's Requiem – demonstrate the dramatic changes suffered by our planet. Normally, such type of ad calls for donations. The turning point here, however, comes with a surprising twist: the donation boxes are waste containers. The message is that everybody can do a little every day to help reach global climate targets by separating waste.

Client
Berliner Stadtreinigung (BSR), Berlin

Design
Peperoni Werbe- und PR-Agentur GmbH, Potsdam

Film Production
trigger happy productions GmbH, Berlin

Abfalltrennung in Berlin spart jährlich 403.000 Tonnen CO_2. Danke.

IKEA – The Great Sleep

[Integrated Campaign]

This campaign for IKEA under the motto "Und wie schläfst du?" (And how do you sleep?) focused on the importance of individual sleeping comfort and positioning the furniture house as a partner for good sleep. A TV commercial introduced this topic. Over various online channels, users were then asked how they sleep best. Four of the respondents were selected and invited to sleep in beds located at unusual places, in locations that were customised to meet best their individual answer – be it deep underground, in a forest, high on a cold mountain peak or at the beach.

Client
IKEA Deutschland GmbH & Co. KG, Hofheim-Wallau

Design
thjnk hamburg gmbh, Hamburg

The Daily Catch

[Promotion]

To demonstrate the freshness of Metro's fish, this promotion uses the most established way to show being up-to-date: the daily newspaper, which also happens to be the traditional way to wrap fish. In cooperation with the partner fishermen, selected quantities of freshly caught fish are shipped together with the latest issue of their local newspaper. Every time a customer in the store buys a fish from that special batch, the purchase is wrapped in a page from this very newspaper. Additionally, a specially designed sticker highlights the date of the catch.

Client
METRO AG, Düsseldorf

Design
Serviceplan/Plan.Net, Munich

Chief Creative Officer
Alexander Schill

Executive Creative Direction
Christoph Nann

Creative Direction
Hendrik Schweder

Art Direction
Annlka Gude

Text
Bernhard Labitzke, Benjamin Krause

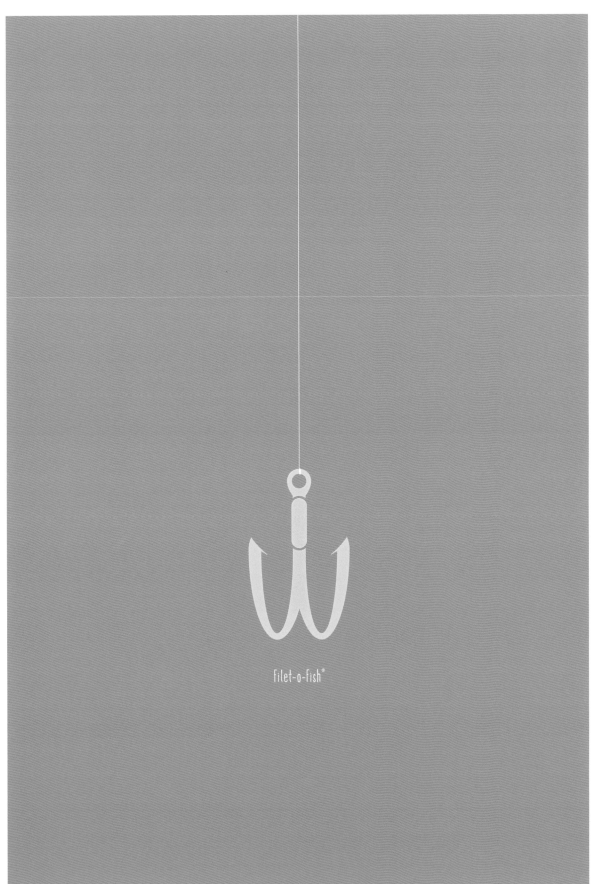

Fishing Hook

[Print Campaign]

As part of a quality campaign, the fast food chain McDonald's wanted to emphasise the freshness of its Filet-o-Fish burger made of 100 per cent fish filet. By simply turning the iconic brand logo upside down, the message was conveyed in a striking manner. The "golden M" was adjusted only so much as to keep the high recognition value of the logo intact. Apart from the unobtrusive label "Filet-o-Fish", the advertisement does without text. The backdrop of the advertisement features entirely in blue to harmonise perfectly with the logo colour.

Client
McDonald's Deutschland Inc., Munich

Design
Leo Burnett Germany, Frankfurt/Main
thjnk ag, Hamburg

Chief Creative Officer
Andreas Pauli, Armin Jochum

Creative Direction
Helge Kniess (Art), Benjamin Merkel (Text)

Art Direction
Thomas Koch

Graphic Design
Michael Fluhr

Nobody Has to
Drive a Mercedes

[Print Campaign]

Client
Daimler AG, Stuttgart

Design
Sarah Illenberger, Emeis Deubel GbR,
Berlin

Creative Direction
Martin Pross, Matthias Schmidt,
Tilman Gossner

Art Direction
Damon Aval,
Mark Taylor (Junior Art Director)

Copywriting
Judith Preker

Account Management
Sophie Hansen

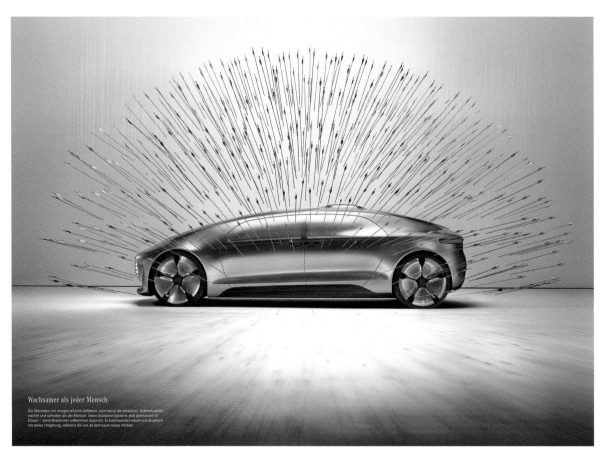

Weil ein Mercedes schon bald allein fahren kann.

For the ad campaign of the Mercedes-Benz F 015, artist Sarah Illenberger was commissioned to produce five installations. Her creative task was to translate the features of the self-driving research car into an expressive pictorial world. To do this, she had to work between the poles of technological future and artistic handiwork. The subjects take a leap into the new era of autonomous driving, rendering the associated changes touchable and comprehensible. Every installation is real, completely without using CGI – just like the car itself.

Aber nur, wenn Sie wollen.

Fiat Panda 4x4 –
Surprised Animals

[Print Campaign, Poster Campaign]

The aim of this campaign is to promote the off-road qualities of the new Fiat Panda 4x4. Thanks to the new selectable four-wheel drive, the car is suited for reaching even the most remote places on earth. The photographs show snapshots of exotic animals like koalas and monkeys literally dropping their jaws on seeing this vehicle driving through the off-road "wilderness". By only showing the facial expressions of the animals – which look almost human – the campaign piques the interest of viewers to find out what exactly made them react in such amazement.

Client
Fiat Group Automobiles Germany AG, Frankfurt/Main

Design
Leo Burnett Germany, Frankfurt/Main

Chief Creative Officer
Andreas Pauli

Creative Direction
Benjamin Merkel,
Hans-Jürgen Kämmerer, Andreas Stalder

Art Direction
Hugo Moura

Account Management
Rafael Koldewey

 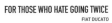

For Those Who Hate Going Twice

[Print Campaign]

This print campaign for the Fiat Ducato is inspired by the phenomenon that people, when they have to bring many items from one place to another, rather carry everything at once instead of going twice. That is particularly true for the clients of this brand, including craftsmen, construction workers and small business owners. The image motifs depict people who stack their tools and wares in an almost artistic way to transport them. This series of ads thus demonstrates the load capacity of the commercial vehicle in a surprising and memorable manner.

Client
Fiat Group Automobiles Germany AG, Frankfurt/Main

Design
Leo Burnett Germany, Frankfurt/Main

Chief Creative Officer
Andreas Pauli

Creative Direction
Jörg Hoffmann, Daniela Ewald

Art Direction
Hugo Moura, Till Rothweiler

Text
Andreas Daum

Frankfurt Zoological Society – Statues

[Print Campaign]

This print campaign by the Frankfurt Zoological Society, which dedicates itself to the protection of endangered animals and their environments, features majestic lions, huge elephants and imposingly strong rhinoceros. These motifs reveal the intended concern about the issue of poaching only at a second glance. The shown animals are in fact only statues, not real animals, and the number of statues already exceeding their living relatives. The advertisements irritate without being shocking and thus underline the objective work of the organisation.

Client
Frankfurt Zoological Society,
Frankfurt/Main

Design
Leo Burnett Germany, Frankfurt/Main

Chief Creative Officer
Andreas Pauli

Creative Direction
Hans-Jürgen Kämmerer

Art Direction
Christopher Buers, David Apel

Text
Florian Fehre

Art Buying
Cornelia Richter

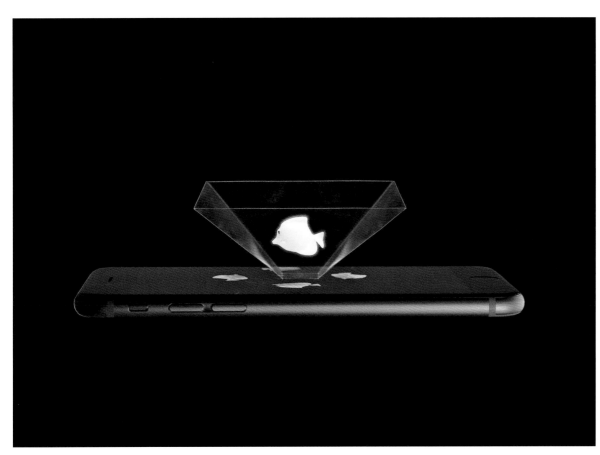

Frankfurt Zoo – Holoquarium

[Print Ad, 3D Video]

Frankfurt Zoo has one of the most beautiful aquariums in Germany. However, most visitors do not know about it. To change this, a traditional print ad was brought to life with a 3D video. All that is needed is a smartphone with QR code reader and the piece of plastic film that comes with the print ad. By bending the film into a pyramid and placing it on their smartphone, viewers create a mini-aquarium with its underwater inhabitants as a 3D projection. Anyone who wants to see more of the underwater world is thus invited to visit Frankfurt Zoo aquarium.

Client
Frankfurt Zoo, Frankfurt/Main

Design
Leo Burnett Germany, Frankfurt/Main

Chief Creative Officer
Andreas Pauli

Creative Direction
Hans-Jürgen Kämmerer

Art Direction
Hugo Moura, Michael Fluhr

Creative Technology
Viktor Kislovskij

Film Editing
Kai Rossbach

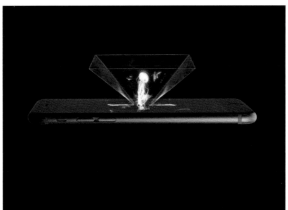

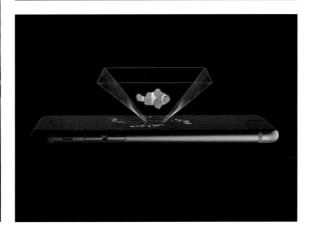

First Movers

[Print Campaign]

Tools and devices have always fuelled both innovation and evolution. This print campaign by Samsung gives an eye-twinkling nod to the first movers in the history of early humankind. The images show a Neanderthal man dressed like a fashion model posing with the company's products, communicating that the brand is an accelerator in technical advancement. The advertisement ran in fashion and men's magazines during the world's largest consumer electronics fair IFA in Berlin, complementing a special brand promotion in the KaDeWe luxury department store.

Client
Samsung Electronics, Schwalbach

Design
Cheil Germany GmbH, Schwalbach

Chief Creative Officer
Roland Rudolf

Executive Creative Direction
Thomas Schröder, Jörn Welle

Art Direction
Miriam Preissinger, Daniel Gumbert

Marketing Service Director
Hong Seuk Lim

Copywriting
Christopher Daniel Drücks

Akk*ul (Creator of the Erect Walk) wearing the new **Samsung Gear VR**

SAMSUNG MADE FOR FIRST MOVERS

*Kk atok (Designer of the Wheel) wearing the new **Samsung Gear S**

SAMSUNG MADE FOR FIRST MOVERS

G'awh (The Discoverer of Fire) wearing the new **Samsung Level On**

SAMSUNG MADE FOR FIRST MOVERS

Tha'g (Speaker of the First Word) using the new **Samsung Galaxy Tab S2**

SAMSUNG MADE FOR FIRST MOVERS

Innovating Evolution

[Out-of-Home & Ambient]

During the IFA trade show in Berlin, Samsung staged a promotional campaign at the KaDeWe luxury department store. The promotion followed the conceptional idea of "re-imagining human evolution by fusing past and present". The key figure was a stylish Neanderthal man embodying the fusion of times. This was reflected in the ten shop windows aiming at "reinventing evolution" by fusing prehistoric times with interactive design in impressive art installations. Inside the store, visitors were invited to dive into a prehistoric underwater world.

Client
Samsung Electronics, Schwalbach

Design
Cheil Germany GmbH, Schwalbach

Chief Creative Officer
Roland Rudolf

Creative Direction
Hannes Deutsch

Art Direction
Miriam Preissinger

Retail Design
Ron Stasch

Marketing Service Director
Hong Seuk Lim

Marketing Service Management
Sabrina Müller

293

Rethinking the Modular

[Promotion]

The USM Haller is a design classic. However, today, this modular furniture system has become part of mainstream. For
its 50th anniversary, the campaign
"Rethinking the Modular" was launched
to make the item desirable again among
a young target group. Student groups
of seven renowned universities of design
were invited to reinvent the concept
of modularity. Each participating team
developed a project which then was
integrated in an exhibition. More than
60 young designers and architects became part of the initiative and as such
ambassadors for the brand.

Client
USM U. Schärer Söhne AG, Münsingen

Curator
Tido von Oppeln, Berlin
Burkhard Meltzer, Zurich

Design
Scholz & Friends Schweiz, Zurich
Atlas Studio, Zurich

Creative Direction
Lukas Frei

Strategic Planning
Tobias Baumann

Project Management
Michèle Gutmann

Digital Concept
Dan Nessler

Web Design
Manuela Miksa

Team 2090

[Direct Mailing]

In times of digital photography and e-mail communication, Berlin photographer Darius Ramazani came up with the idea of sending out a printed poster to his clients. The image on the poster is a group photo of four old people, representing "Team 2090", as a reference to the photographer and his team in the future. Following the amusing instructions, recipients are asked to hang the poster in their offices and send Ramazani a photo of how it looks by mail. This final step is aimed at making clients remember him whenever they need a photographer.

Client
Darius Ramazani Photography, Berlin

Design
Jule Roschlau, Berlin

Creative Direction
Darius Ramazani
Jule Roschlau

Illustration
Jule Roschlau

Photography
Darius Ramazani

Text
Paula Hedley, Trend Translations, Cologne

Women Who Made History

[Integrated Campaign]

Client
ZDF Zweites Deutsches Fernsehen, Mainz

Head of Marketing
Thomas Grimm

Head of Programme Marketing 1
Astrid Kämmerer

Project Management
Sandra Hebel

On-Air Editor
Alexandra Schulte

Design
KNSK Werbeagentur GmbH, Hamburg

Creative Direction
Tim Krink (Art), Ingo Müller (Text)

The TV series "Women Who Made History" by German public-service television broadcaster ZDF portrays six highly influential women in world history. The campaign stages these women as self-assured characters on the cover of a modern glossy magazine. These magazine covers in tabloid style are the focus, backed up by photos taken in an editorial style and journalistically pointed headlines that provide ironic teasers on the life stories of these historical women with the aim of promoting the documentary to potential viewers.

BVG #weilwirdichlieben
[Integrated Campaign]

Client
Berliner Verkehrsbetriebe (BVG), Berlin

Head of Marketing
Martell Beck

Design
GUD. GRÜNER UND DEUTSCHER, Berlin

Creative Direction
Katja Scholze

Strategic Planning
Jens Grüner

Digital Concept
Christian Artopé

Gesehen in der U8, 20.06.2013.
Teile deine besonderen BVG-Momente auf: 🇫 🐦 📷 YouTube

#weilwirdichlieben

Gesehen im M41, 05.07.2013.
Teile deine besonderen BVG-Momente auf: 🇫 🐦 📷 YouTube

#weilwirdichlieben

Zur Fashion Week mal wieder den Style hochfahren.

BVG

WEIL WIR DICH LIEBEN.

Berliner Verkehrsbetriebe (BVG) is one of Germany's major municipal public transport companies. More than one billion passengers used the bus, underground, tram and ferry services in 2015. Boasting the divisive hashtag #weilwirdichlieben (because we love you), this campaign was developed to strengthen the brand's image and make it more likeable. With disarming humour and charming self-irony, these advertisements pick up daily scenes and strange stories by and with passengers. Besides traditional media relations such as collaborations with leading media outlets, ambient and large surfaces, image films, vehicle branding and floor graphics on platforms, the focus is particularly on social media channels.

Gesehen an der U1, 12.05.2013.
Teile deine besonderen BVG-Momente auf: [f] [t] [i] [YouTube]

#weilwirdichlieben

Hol dir lieber das Original.

Das BVG-Abo.

ABO sichern und **247 €** sparen

BVG

WEIL WIR DICH LIEBEN.

Jetzt mit dem Abo sparen
und sich und was Echtes gönnen.

www.BVG.de/Abo

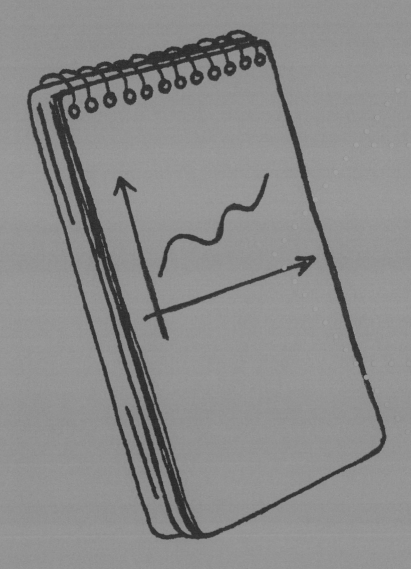

ANNUAL REPORTS

Red Dot: Best of the Best

HOERBIGER Yearbook 2015/2016

The 2015 yearbook by HOERBIGER Holding AG focuses on communicating the performance claim that binds all people working at the company. Furthermore, it also aims at promoting the company that sets standards with technologically challenging key components and services. At various points, the yearbook introduces employees from the different corporate divisions as well as representatives of the corporate management team. On four-page inserts, they present their developments, describe the essence of their work and talk about their drive and motivation. The introductory pages of the inserts, which are kept in a warm red tone, form the bridge with their clear statements from the text level of the yearbook to the people shaping the company. The typographic look has been fundamentally revised and renewed. Considerably stronger emphasis has been placed on the use of the corporate colour red, which stands for the people.

Statement by the jury
The HOERBIGER yearbook fascinates with an unobtrusive, yet distinctive cover design, as well as with a clear and consistently implemented page layout on the inside. The concept of shorter insert pages is particularly convincing, as they liven up the layout to appealing effect. The overall impression is rounded off by the use of beautiful and subtly refined paper.

Client
HOERBIGER Holding AG, Zug

Project Management
Ludwig Schönefeld

Design
Jäger & Jäger, Überlingen

Creative Direction
Regina Jäger

Graphic Design
Michelle Miesel, Tanja Weich

Text
Ludwig Schönefeld, Sophie Blasberg
(inserts)

Photography
Manfred Klimek (inserts),
Nicolaus Schäffler (products),
TRIAD Berlin (intro pages)

Printing
Druck-Ring, Kirchheim

→ Designer portrait on page 504

Red Dot: Best of the Best

How We Create the New –
adidas Group Annual Report 2015

Under the title "How We Create the New", this annual report sets out to introduce the "Strategy 2020" by the adidas Group. The reporting comprises a magazine and the actual report, interpreting the strategy by focusing on the issues of "how we create the new" and "how we create value". The Group's sustainability report follows the same pattern with „how we create responsibly". The aim is to give concrete answers to what is to be achieved within the 2020 targets and how the adidas Group wants to create the "new". The magazine thus presents initiatives and approaches that the adidas Group has launched and tracked. In addition, the first successes in 2015 regarding adidas' three strategic choices of "Speed", "Cities" and "Open Source" are presented. The content is visualised through a deliberately striking design complemented by powerful images. The dynamic appearance of these publications is achieved through the use of different materials and the principle of a slanted cut.

Statement by the jury

The design of the adidas Group annual report successfully manages to lend each page an exciting rhythm, turning the pages into perfect compositions that each tells their own story. Typographic elements are used as illustrations to impressive effect, while a sans serif font is used on the image level. Opting for reduction, the colour design comprises beautiful grey tones and embodies a convincing implementation.

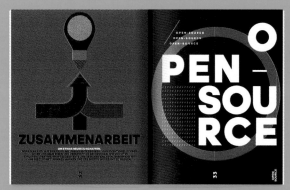

Client
ADIDAS AG, Herzogenaurach

Design
Strichpunkt Design, Stuttgart/Berlin

→ Designer portrait on page 527

Red Dot: Best of the Best

BESTSELLER
Sustainability Report 2015

The design of the 2015 sustainability report for the Danish fashion company BESTSELLER focuses on visualising corporate social responsibility as a deeply integrated part of the company's business operations. Creating a meaningful link between the communication of this engagement and the reporting from the core business fields, the design is inspired by the simple look of icons on care instruction labels hidden in the clothes. These icons were turned into infographics that, at the same time, form a visual bridge to the garments and fashion objects of the company. Throughout the report, they are used to translate abstract figures and data into easy-to-understand, visual messages. Furthermore, they are used to highlight important facts including key figures, percentage distributions and advancements. Last but not least, they also feature in a motion graphics film, which was produced in parallel with the sustainability report, and where they convey highlights from the report.

Statement by the jury
The design of the BESTSELLER sustainability report 2015 suits the fashion brand perfectly. The figures are presented to appealing effect, fascinatingly complemented by careful image selection and refined use of pictograms. The concept is overall convincing and the choice of paper is also ideally suited to a sustainability report. Its well-balanced colours are pleasing to the eye.

Client
BESTSELLER A/S, Brande

Design
Pravda A/S, Aarhus

Art Direction
Vibeke Krag Rasmussen

Concept
Karim Frølund Jarrar

Project Management
Malene Korsholm

→ Designer portrait on page 519

Bauhaus and HUGO BOSS – HUGO BOSS Annual Report 2015

The design of this business report is inspired by the maxim of precision, clarity and aesthetic perfection as the central elements of the Bauhaus movement. Alongside implementing campaign motifs and window decorations of a collection by artistic director Jason Wu, the key visual elements and colours of grey, orange and white from the "The Bauhaus #itsalldesign" exhibition also inspired the design of the annual report. A playful approach to typography, as well as to the form and colour of basic elements, is in harmony with the visual world of the company.

Client
HUGO BOSS, Metzingen

Design
hw.design gmbh, Munich

Creative Direction
Sandra Gieseler

Art Direction
Felicetta Manicone

Project Management
Saskia Themans

Production
Katja Knahn

Artwork
Raimund Verspohl, Inske Rottmann

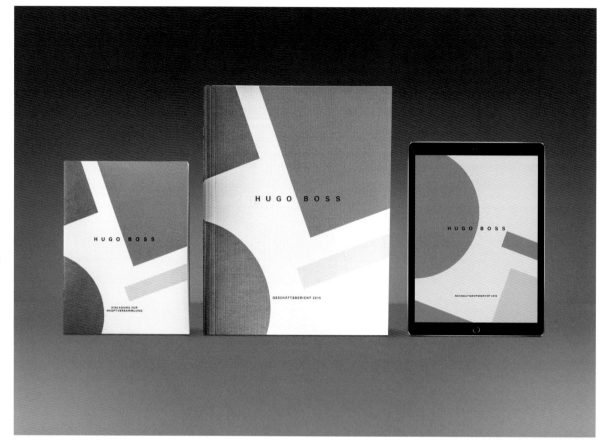

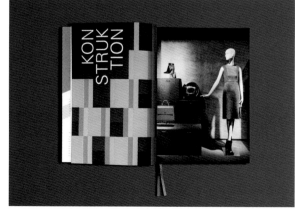

Open-Minded –
METRO Group
Annual Report
2014/2015

"Open-minded" is the motto of this annual report, meaning that being open to new ideas is a prerequisite for driving in novation, as well as developing products and solutions that create value for customers. The report combines strong and authentic images with short and concise texts. Internal and external projects are presented, along with the innovators, creators, market experts and customer-care specialists, who are the driving force behind the future development of the company. The full annual report has been published in digital form exclusively. A shorter version is also available in printed form.

Client
METRO AG, Düsseldorf

Design
Strichpunkt Design, Stuttgart/Berlin

Rethinking Efficiency – Schuler Annual Report 2015

The motto of Schuler AG's annual report 2015 is "Effizienz neu denken" (Rethinking efficiency). Based on reports, interviews and graphics, the magazine section provides clear, authentic imagery proving how the company increases its efficiency and promotes the internationalisation of the value chain. The article "Go East" gives a more in-depth account of this topic, focusing on the Chinese company Yadon, which Schuler acquired to boost production in Asia. The overall aim is to communicate that exact knowledge of the entire process chain, as well as expertise of materials and markets are all essential prerequisites for increasing efficiency.

Client
Schuler AG, Göppingen

Design
Strichpunkt Design, Stuttgart/Berlin

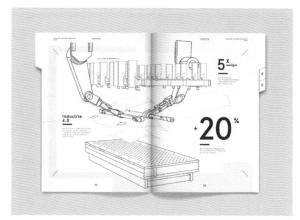

Attentive –
TRUMPF Annual Report
2014/2015

The topic of attentiveness forms the framework for this annual report by the globally active laser and machine tool manufacturer TRUMPF. In the form of a brand story, it communicates the message of a clear, value-oriented attitude as well as a corporate and innovative culture. TRUMPF is to be perceived as a company with a palpable entrepreneurial spirit and an uncompromising forward-looking approach. Six lively photo features, along with two essays, reflect various facets of the word "attentiveness".

Client
TRUMPF GmbH + Co. KG, Ditzingen

Design
Strichpunkt Design, Stuttgart/Berlin

52/2015 –
Gebrüder Weiss
Annual Report 2015

Client
Gebrüder Weiss GmbH, Lauterach

Design
GROOTHUIS. Gesellschaft der Ideen
und Passionen mbH, Hamburg

Printing
BULU – Buchdruckerei Lustenau GmbH,
Lustenau

By speaking of people, places and projects in an authentic and entertaining manner, this yearbook aims to inform readers about the international activities of the logistics company Gebrüder Weiss GmbH. In 52 chapters, one for each week of the year, the design of the report illuminates the day-to-day company culture and presents the company staff in profiles. Easy-to-follow footnotes and fact boxes contextualise the company goings-on and geography within the perspective of global events. The company mission statement of "We are where you are" thus comes alive.

Enabled – ALSO
Annual Report 2015

In the annual report for ALSO Holding AG, a Swiss company specialised in IT, telecommunications and consumer electronics, a variety of ALSO's customers discuss the services and solutions the company offers from their perspective and share what they value about their collaboration with the company. For the portraits of the customers and the board of executives, a generative design was chosen and animated for the web version. Therefore, the portraits were reduced to an RGB grid of points and then dynamically visualised through attractors, with a bright neon green as the signal colour.

Client
ALSO Holding AG, Emmen

Design
Strichpunkt Design, Stuttgart/Berlin

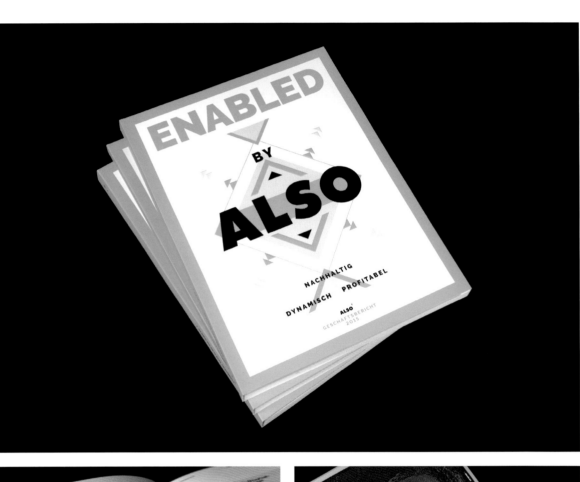

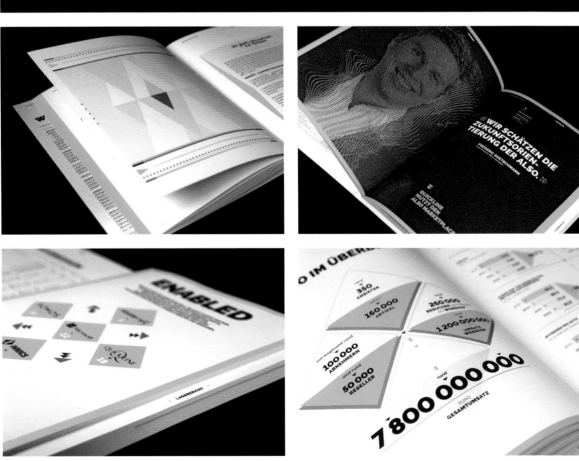

Liechtensteinische Landesbank Annual Report 2015

The LLB Group's successful completion of its corporate strategy in the 2015 business year inspired this annual report aimed at promoting the dynamic impact of its StepUp2020 strategy. The new strategy is visualised through the figure of a traceur who sees opportunities, not obstacles, as he makes his way through an urban parkour landscape. When balancing skilfully on a wall or using momentum to glide along a railing, the traceur hints at the qualities of inventiveness, skill and discipline so important to the LLB Group in stepping towards the future.

Client
Liechtensteinische Landesbank AG, Vaduz

Design
Eclat AG, Zurich

Project Management
Werner Rudolf

Creative Direction
Anna-Caroline Pflug

Art Direction
Lorenzo Geiger

Graphic Design
Tina Braun

Photography
Scanderbeg Sauer Photography, Zurich

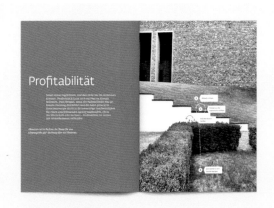

akf bank
Annual Report 2015

The design of this annual report for 2015 visualises the theme of growth, which also lends the report its title. This was achieved by developing an attention-grabbing concept that centres on dynamic graphics for conveying the subject through shifting coloured surfaces. These abstract illustrations seem to extend beyond this format, with the aim of creating an invigorating contrast to the "simplicity" of the typographic grid and the clear, comprehensible architecture of information.

Client
akf bank GmbH & Co KG, Wuppertal

Design
herzogenrathsaxler design, Düsseldorf
Büro für Design, Petra Hattab, Wuppertal

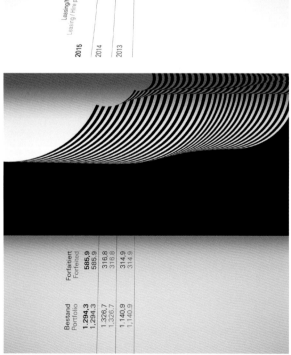

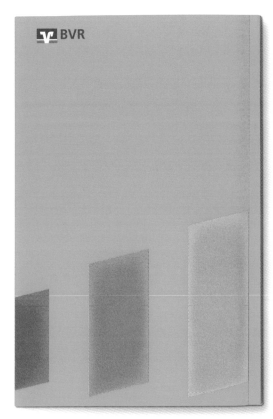

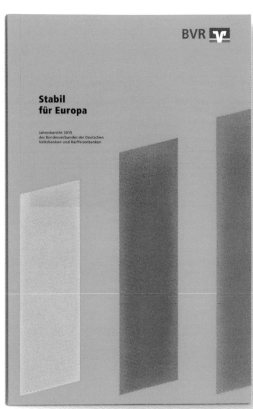

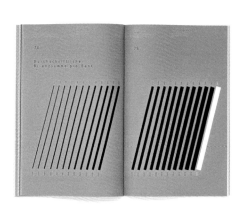

BVR
Annual Report 2015

The annual report of the National Association of German Cooperative Banks (BVR) provides information about the business performance of the 1,021 (as of 2015) financially independent local cooperative banks in Germany. The design approach had to reflect not only the demands of the modern association, but also its profile and position as an umbrella organisation. The content of the report was visualised in both the print and online versions to eliminate the need for "external" design means. Particular attention was paid to a condensed arrangement of the key figures and content.

Client
BVR, Berlin

Concept
Tim Zuchiatti

Publisher
Melanie Schmergal

Design
VERY, Frankfurt/Main
wemove digital solutions gmbh, Berlin

Creative Direction
VERY, Frankfurt/Main

Synthon
Annual Report 2015

The pharmaceutical company Synthon puts its cutting-edge science, ability to innovate and talented people into action to provide affordable medicines, both by producing generics and by developing innovative products like bio-pharmaceuticals. This year, the company got organised and equipped to be "in position" to achieve results in the years to come. Within the annual report "in position" is being reflected in photographs of people from around the world: all in the same position, with bare shoulders, without make-up and looking straight into the camera. To underscore the claim "for everyone", four different covers have been created, featuring a total of eight portraits on the front and back.

Client
Synthon Holding, Nijmegen

Design
Zuiderlicht, Maastricht

Project Management
Eline Dekker

Art Direction/Graphic Design
Ruud Temmink

Photography
Hugo Thomassen, Maastricht

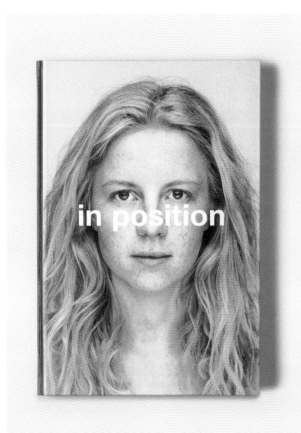
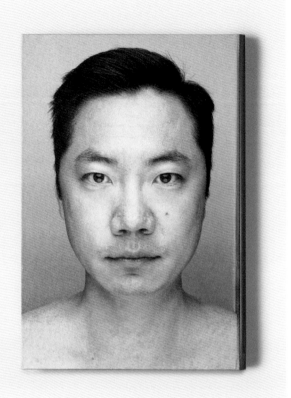

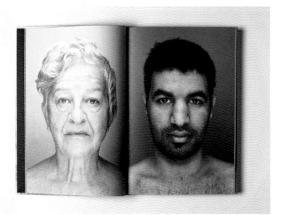
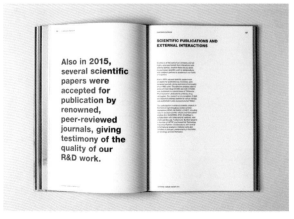

Understand What Counts – Fresenius Medical Care Annual Report 2015

With the claim "Verstehen was zählt" (Understand What Counts), this annual report focuses on the four strategic objectives of the company. It communicates that the Fresenius Medical Care group possesses an understanding that will guarantee success regarding its markets, its fields of business, its patients and the direction in which the company will develop in the future. Therefore, the magazine focuses on core issues, divided between the group's four strategic orientations, encompassing storytelling that delivers an appealing juxtaposition to the growth and communication levels. Large, striking images and photoessays round off the graphic representation.

Client
Fresenius Medical Care AG & Co. KGaA, Bad Homburg

Design
hw.design gmbh, Munich

Creative Direction
Sandra Gieseler

Graphic Design
Felicetta Manicone, Julia Molina Romero

Project Management
Silke Blattner

Production
Katja Knahn

Clubstiftung
Annual Report 2014

The "Stiftung zur Stärkung privater Musikbühnen Hamburg" (Foundation for the Promotion of Private Music Venues) was founded by the City of Hamburg and the Clubkombinat Hamburg to support the city's live music venues with investment costs. The 2014 annual report comprises a folder in white and neon orange with an aim to bring the foundation's motto "Promoting loud noise" to life. Folded up, it is a handy-sized A3 report, while folded out it has the format of an A0 poster. The heading of each section in the annual report is a line from song lyrics.

Client
Stiftung zur Stärkung privater Musikbühnen Hamburg

Design
loved gmbh, Hamburg

Art Direction
Julia Kerschbaum

Editorial Work
Catrin Florenz, Alessandra Sardo

RUFA
Annual Report 2015

This annual report collects the most meaningful activities, moments and creations of the Rome University of Fine Arts (RUFA), an advanced professional training institute and a major centre for culture and the arts in Rome. The report's cover puts together the technological and manual sides of the academy's modus operandi. QR codes recall external digital content, becoming silkscreened graphic patterns. Inside the report, data and figures are reported, along with a selection of the academy's best projects, a review of the main events and partnerships, and a complete list of the leading personalities.

Client
RUFA, Rome University of Fine Arts, Rome

Design
Intorno Design, Rome

Creative Direction
Guido Lombardo, Tommaso Salvatori

Editorial Work
Elena Pagnotta, Alessandro Caruso, Insideart, Rome

Graphic Design
Gianluca Vicini, Linda Marchetti, Diletta Damiano, Roberta De Cristofaro, Irene Guarino, Matteo Sampaolo

Photography
Stefano Compagnucci, Christian Rizzo, Rome

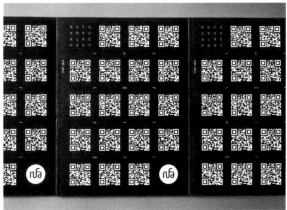

The Safety of Things – DEKRA Annual Report 2015/2016

Following the concept of "The Safety of Things: a magazine from the future!", the publications surrounding the 2015 annual report by the German expert organisation DEKRA promote its future-oriented competence in safety matters. With the additional function of brand and image formation, the publications also point to three focus areas – on the road, at home and at work – for exploring fascinating opportunities and the potential risks of digital transformation. The result is a multifaceted picture of the world of tomorrow, in which the organisation acts as a responsible thinker and initiator in a massive global growth market.

Client
DEKRA e.V., Stuttgart

Design
Strichpunkt Design, Stuttgart/Berlin

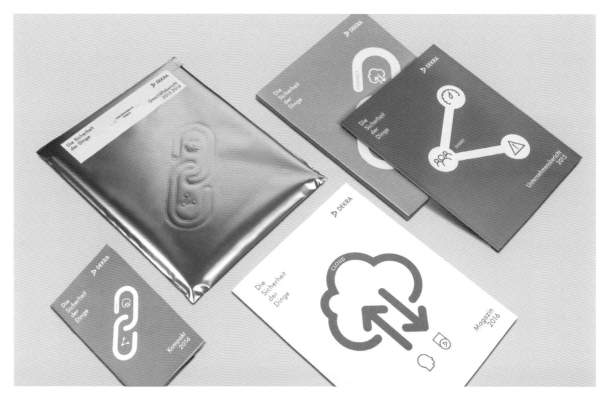

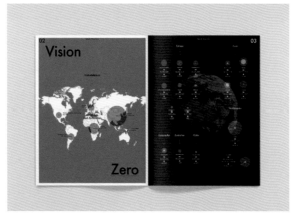

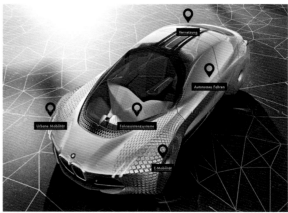

Growing to the Next Level – ProSiebenSat.1 Media SE Annual Report 2015

Employing the corporate design first introduced in 2014, this annual report by ProSiebenSat.1 Media SE highlights the company's dynamically growing success over the past few years. Simultaneously, it is meant as an incentive to continue pursuing a diversified growth strategy in the future. Interviews and reports from various business segments show how this dynamism in profitability and growth can be further increased in the future by integrating the TV and digital businesses. Essays on the topics of courage, entrepreneurship, responsibility and luck draw not only on personal experiences but also on the media group's strategy.

Client
ProSiebenSat.1 Media SE, Unterföhring

Design
hw.design gmbh, Munich

Art Direction
Thomas Tscherter

Graphic Design
Lukas Millinger, Carola Plappert

Project Management
Bettina Kroth

Production
Benedikt Bäumler

Artwork
Rudolf Hartwig

Simply.Connected.
Bosch Annual Report
2015

Client
Robert Bosch GmbH, Stuttgart

Design
heureka GmbH, Essen

Art Direction
Gorden Koschel

Editorial Work
Bettina Langer, C3 Stuttgart Creative
Code and Content GmbH, Stuttgart

Camera
Maik Scharfscheer, Frankfurt/Main

Digital Concept
Gorden Koschel, heureka GmbH, Essen
Peter Smyczek, SapientNitro, Cologne

Coding
heureka GmbH, Essen

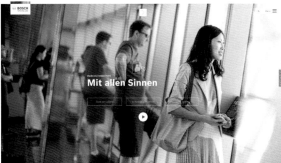

Bosch 2015: Umsatzsprung von 44%

Following the storytelling approach of "digital first", this annual report intends to show, by means of an interactive online magazine, that the company Bosch has already made significant contributions to the "Internet of Things". Four main stories on the subjects of connectivity, mobility, industry and home, as well as seven further stories from different business areas, take users on a journey through a "connected world" visualised with videos, interactive 360-degree perspectives, animations and playful features. Large images, small text segments, animated icons and illustrations make this publication a more engaging experience.

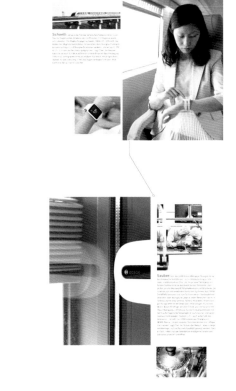

Stadtwerk am See
Annual Report 2015

This digital annual report wants to
sensitise people to the fact that pro-
curing electricity, water and gas is
resource-intensive. The aim was to create an annual report that is entertaining
and well-structured so that anybody
can easily read and enjoy it. This idea was
implemented in the form of animated
3D infographics and a design tailored to
a smooth user experience. Users simply
have to scroll through the different business divisions of Stadtwerk am See to
automatically obtain all relevant information. Since the report is browser-
based and therefore can be accessed by
every online device, it also manages to
reach a diverse target group.

Client
Stadtwerk am See GmbH & Co. KG,
Friedrichshafen

Design
Gessulat/Gessulat GmbH & Co. KG,
Munich

Digital Concept
Stefan Gessulat

Account Management
Christina Wieder

Art Direction
Rustam Sayfutdinov

Graphic Design
Andreas Müller

Programming
Steffen Thiede

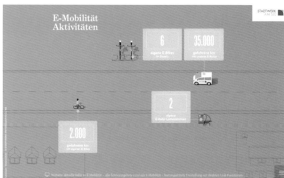

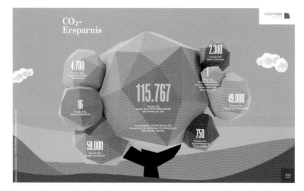

Deutsche Post DHL Group Annual Report 2015

Using the example of the life sciences and healthcare sectors, this digital annual report sets out to illustrate the meaning of "smart logistics". The company's innovative logistics operations are demonstrated to striking effect along the lines of the supply chain, complemented by an intuitive information architecture that allows focused reading and highly purposeful searches. As a start, core topics in logistics such as security, transparency and competence are individually staged and presented in a manner suited to online media. The site's responsive web design facilitates easy navigation reminiscent of the principles of an app.

Client
Deutsche Post DHL Group, Bonn

Design
21TORR GmbH, Reutlingen
hw.design gmbh, Munich

Project Management
Sylvia Rost

Account Management
Carsten Lörzing

Concept
Andreas Bauer

Programming
Boris Bojic, Timo Günthner

Web Design
Daniel Heidecke

Interaction Design
Jennifer Glaser

Hager Group
Annual Report 2015

The 2015 annual report by the Hager Group is dedicated to the "art of listening". It is aimed at increasing the ability to listen and, at the same time, inviting employees, customers, business partners and interested parties to join in an intensive dialogue. Both the exciting, responsive online version and the apps for iOS/Android were created using the new corporate design and offer numerous elements for exploration, including animation, information bubbles, location maps, videos, picture galleries and audio files. Each element is made to present a different example of the concept of listening.

Client
Hager Group, Blieskastel

Design/Concept
hauser lacour kommunikationsgestaltung gmbh, Frankfurt/Main

Text/Concept
Textbüro Harald Willenbrock, Hamburg

**Digital Implementation/
Film Production**
Mhoch4 – Die Fernsehagentur, Hamburg

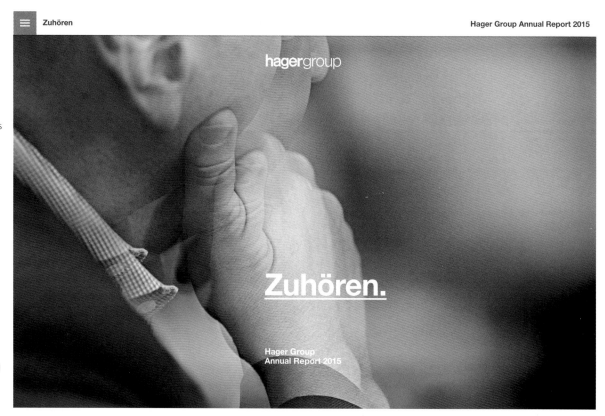

DIE MÖGLICHMACHER.

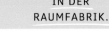

IN DER
RAUMFABRIK.

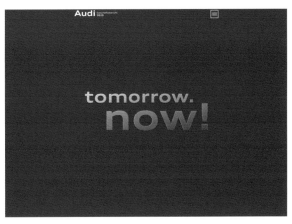

Audi
Annual Report 2015

The Audi annual report 2015 focuses on the central theme of "Tomorrow. Now!" to place experiencing the brand centre stage. Consisting of a magazine and a financial section, it is used not only as a pure reporting tool but also employed internationally as a means of brand communication. The aim is to communicate that Audi offers its customers progressive solutions that are always "one step ahead". This progress through technology was also to feature on a responsive website for customers to experience across various media. The topics and design of the digital version are modelled on the print version of the annual report and enhanced by additional content.

Client
AUDI AG, Ingolstadt

Design
kdgroup GmbH, Stuttgart
21TORR GmbH, Stuttgart

Creative Direction
Isabel Hamann, Kerrin Nausch,
kdgroup GmbH

Art Direction
Thomas Schrempp, kdgroup GmbH
Isabell Höffner, 21TORR GmbH

Project Management
Marc Neubauer, kdgroup GmbH
Daniel Horvath, 21TORR GmbH

MLP
Annual Report 2015

Client
MLP AG, Wiesloch

**Head of Investor Relations/
Financial Communication**
Andreas Herzog

Design
heureka GmbH, Essen

Art Direction
Gorden Koschel

Account Management
Sebastian Schulz

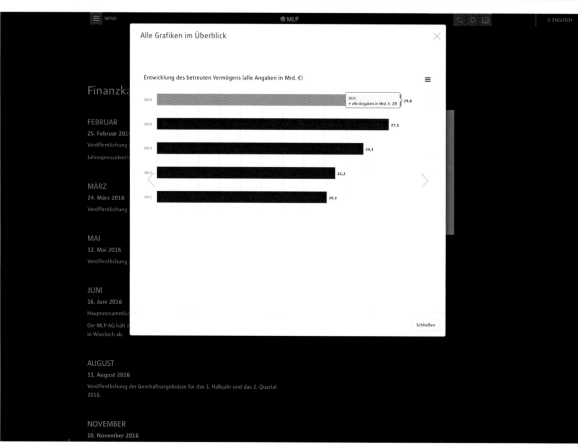

The annual report by MLP AG was published as a digital-only version for the first time in 2016. It includes, among other things, a 90-second video on the events of 2015 and an interactive comparison of the key figures. The graphic implementation with large images and colour blocks follows the new appearance of the corporate website. Topic-specific tiles, informative graphic and text slides, as well as a fold-out letter to shareholders, are all clearly arranged on the home page. The responsive web design facilitates a user-friendly presentation of the contents through animated graphics and clearly structured tables, and text that can also be viewed on any mobile device.

REWE Group
Annual Report 2014

The annual report titled "Our World in Motion" presents the economic development of the company REWE Group. It is published exclusively online, focuses on the topic of "trends" and, in addition to the corporate figures, also offers a magazine. Readers can learn about the trends and drivers of the group's business, ranging from omni-channel sales and store brands to regional products and "conscious consumption". Reflecting the title of the report, each section of the magazine features large-format images. Articles are written in a journalistic style, featuring photography and multimedia content, and are aimed at informing and entertaining readers.

Client
REWE Group, Cologne

Design
KD1 Designagentur, Cologne

REWE Group Sustainability Report 2013/2014

With the claim "Wir sind mittendrin" (We are in the midst of it), this online sustainability report points out the market presence of the REWE Group. It welcomes users to a responsive microsite aimed at showing the group's responsibility via the central topic of sustainability. Alongside important performance indicators, the site offers information on the company and five interactive supply chains, as well as on the "four pillars of sustainability": Green Products; Energy, Climate and the Environment; Employees; and Social Involvement. The site is barrier-free with a clear design. Colourful and varied, it features authentic visuals, graphs, videos and animated figures.

Client
REWE Group, Cologne

Design
3st kommunikation GmbH, Mainz

Creative Direction
Marcel Teine

Art Direction
Tobias Gebert

Concept
akzente kommunikation und beratung gmbh, Munich

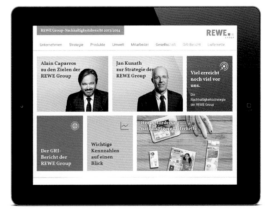

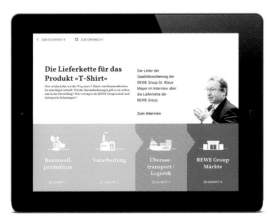

PUBLISHING & PRINT MEDIA

Red Dot: Grand Prix

PHILIP

[Customer Magazine]

The anniversary magazine "PHILIP" celebrates the 100th birthday of the visionary entrepreneur Philip Rosenthal. Designed as a high-quality hardcover oversized book, the magazine comprises nearly 200 pages. Featuring expressive photography, it visualises the life and work of the entrepreneur, complemented by numerous anecdotes and incidents that render a vivid image of his eventful life. The special friendship to architect and designer Martin Gropius has inspired the distinctive cover design element. Since the motif of the "pig" played a role in a bet between the two about the emergence of the gold rim on porcelain, it was made to feature on a porcelain plate fully decorated in gold, attached to the front cover as a special eye-catcher. Aside the three solid colours, a colourfully designed "happy birthday folder" and truncated pages, a photo story by photographer Joachim Baldauf enriches the liveliness of the magazine that comes in a protective box made of the same material.

Statement by the jury

This magazine traces and illustrates the eventful life of entrepreneur Philip Rosenthal. Each of the excitingly told stories in the book represents an epoch of innovative porcelain design, which is also visualised by the porcelain plate consistently integrated into the cover. The surprising combination of pictorial material and graphic elements with a congenial typography is infused with high-level design skills.

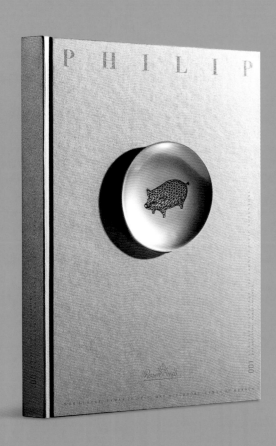

reddot award 2016
grand prix

Client
Rosenthal GmbH, Selb

Design/Artwork
MILCH+HONIG designkultur, Munich

Printing
Gotteswinter und Aumaier GmbH,
Munich

Packaging
Hertel Kartonagen, Bayreuth

→ Designer portrait on page 511

Red Dot: Best of the Best

Korrekturspuren – Traces de correction

[Exhibition Catalogue]

Since every creative work, be it in architecture, design, painting or literature, is usually marked
by many revisions, changes and corrections in the process up to the final stage, the Centre national de littérature in Luxembourg set out on a search for these corrections. An exhibition was
created to document such "traces" in different literary works, translating them into systematic
categorisation. It shows the works of the authors in their struggle of finding the right words and
forming them into the right sentences. The exhibition displays feature one original work each
for visitors to look at and explore through a tiny window serving as a magnifying glass. The exhibition catalogue in 24 x 30 cm format comprises 400 pages and is bilingual, covering German
and French. The design conveys the exhibition concept of presenting original works through
coloured notes of paper inserted into the pages. Readers thus have the feeling of holding an
original work in their hands.

Statement by the jury

This exhibition catalogue adopts an air of the provisional to invite readers into the intimate
thoughts and minds of the authors. It makes clear that the individual literary works are strongly
influenced by the authors' environments. As exciting as the topic itself, the outstanding design
of the catalogue convinces with a beautiful materiality and an open stitch binding that leaves
the spine of the book visible.

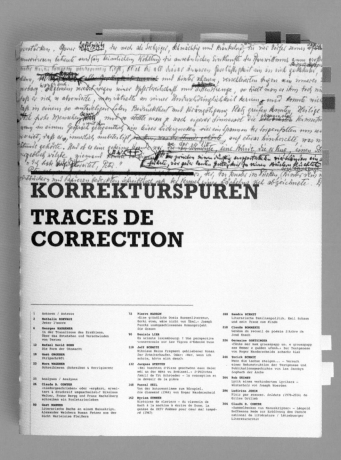

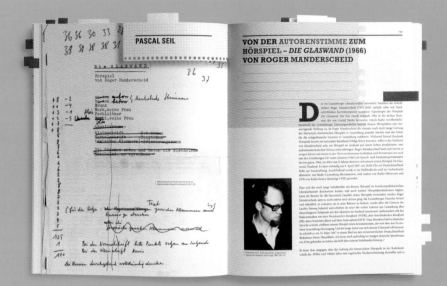

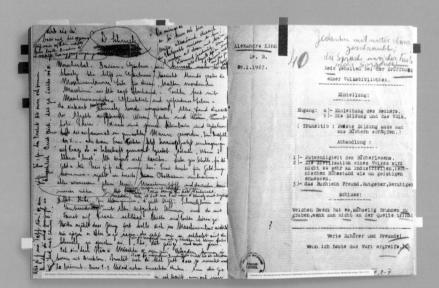

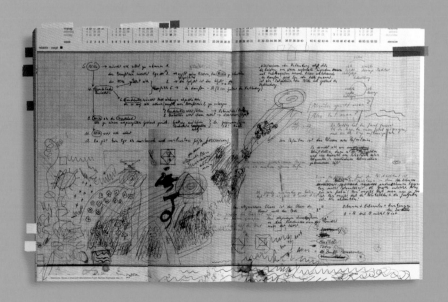

Client
Centre national de littérature,
Luxembourg

Design
Rose de Claire, design., Luxembourg

Graphic Design
Albert Seyser, Delphine Forcher,
Rita Godinho

Planning/Production Management
Babeth Neiers

Image Editing
Daniel Rassel

Photography
Christof Weber

→ Designer portrait on page 522

Red Dot: Best of the Best

Carved Names Vol. 2

[Book]

The book "Carved Names Vol. 2" accompanies the inauguration of a monument called "Names in Mortar Joints". Consisting of a 200-metre bronze strip in a brick wall, the monument at Eötvös Loránd University in Budapest is dedicated to university staff and students who fell victim to the anti-Jewish laws, the Holocaust and World War II. The book features a black cover and contains lectures given at a conference related to the work. Its purist appearance is aimed at visualising the humility of science and the calmness of thinking, and thus draws attention exclusively to the content. A homogenised typography with only one single font and size was chosen as a metaphor referring to the destruction of diversity. "Carved Names Vol. 2" is defined as a space experiment that was designed to correspond to the monument's architectural space experiment. The "typographical silence" of the design aims to represent the loss caused by the Holocaust.

Statement by the jury

No more than a black box at first glance, "Carved Names Vol. 2" presents on the inside typography at its purest. The book fascinates with design details such as refined indentations and lines that run across pages. In addition, the book is beautifully bound and convinces as an overall concept for conveying a difficult and delicate topic. It manages to establish an emotional relation with readers.

Client
Eötvös Loránd University,
Faculty of Humanities, Budapest

Project Supervision
Péter György

Design
Lead82, Budapest

Art Direction
Zalán Péter Salát

Graphic Design
Dániel Németh L.

→ Designer portrait on page 508

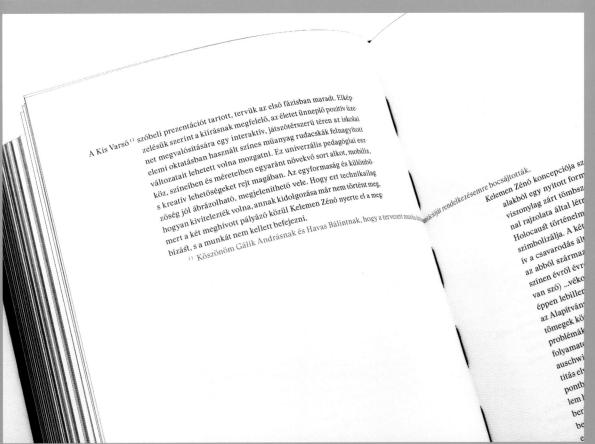

Red Dot: Best of the Best

FEUER & RING

[Cookbook Set]

This book set documents the possibilities of the "Feuerring" (Fire Ring), a versatile barbecue and grill tool with an innovatively designed outer ring (patented). The two books in the slip-case compile over 70 recipes ranging from smaller dishes to entire courses. With the idea of presenting an authentic as well as culinarily inviting appearance, the photographs of the dishes in this publication were shot in daylight without enhancement by artificial aids. They visualise the communal experience of grilling and feature step-by-step explanations of the dish prepar-ation processes. The books of the set exude a high-quality appearance thanks to the all-round matte black edge colouring and the spine being screen-printed in black. Made of thick black cardboard and featuring the title embossed in gold, the cover underlines the book's elegant appearance. The lay-flat binding offers an optimal presentation of both photos and artwork.

Statement by the jury
This book set fascinates readers with a selection of photographs that instantly appeal to the senses. Matched by the typography, the set stages a vivid product and living environment that creates an emotional approach. Both the design and the printing convey high quality stand-ards with double pages making good use of the space. These books are an overall piece of art.

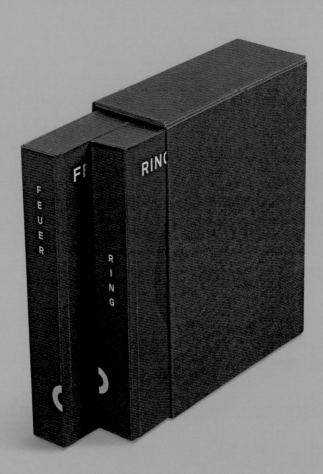

Client
Feuerring GmbH, Immensee

Design
Andreas Reichlin, Beate Hoyer, Immensee

→ Designer portrait on page 497

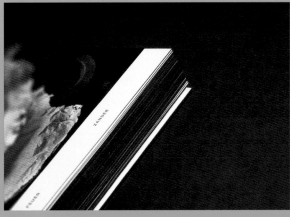

Red Dot: Best of the Best

BOOK – best architects 16
[Book]

An annual publication accompanies the "best architects" award, compiling the award winners together with their architectural projects. The latest edition, "BOOK – best architects 16", was created against the backdrop that the award itself allowed submissions from all over Europe for the first time. On 424 pages, it presents the 89 winners subdivided according to the six different award categories. The design realises the concept of removing the title from the book and transferring it onto the accompanying slipcase. This allowed the book itself to be covered with a geometric pattern on all sides. The result is an exciting optical irritation that challenges the spatial perception of the viewer. Each award-winning project is presented on two double-page spreads featuring photos, carefully sketched plans and descriptions. Thus, the book gives a good overview of the current best works in the architecture scene in Europe.

Statement by the jury
This book has an invigorating effect and allows delving deeply into the world of contemporary architecture. It fascinates with an appealing page layout, a well-balanced selection of photographs and a typography that guides readers through the pages with ease. A consistently realised concept that convinces as a whole, completed with a cover design idea that is particularly outstanding.

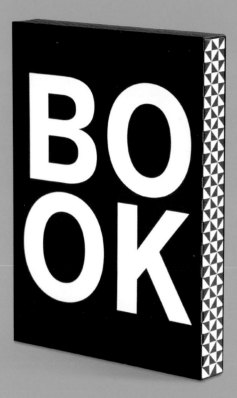

Client
best architects Award,
zinnobergruen gmbh, Düsseldorf

Design
zinnobergruen gmbh, Düsseldorf

Creative Direction
Bärbel Muhlack, Tobias Schwarzer

→ Designer portrait on page 537

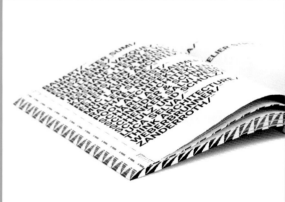

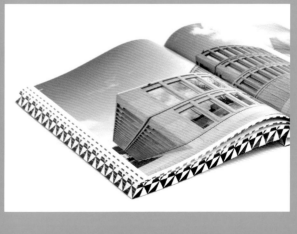

FPS VIEWS

[Client Magazine]

Under the motto "A strong connection", this client magazine wants to strengthen connections between a business law firm, which has approximately 140 lawyers across Germany, and its partners. The magazine therefore takes readers on a short journey to the founding year of 1846 and provides an outlook on the future. Current developments and contemporary topics are presented in an informative and entertaining manner. The existing corporate design has been refined and an uncluttered, sophisticated editorial layout created. Forming a stylistically defining part of the concept, the illustrations are used in a creative way.

Client
FPS Fritze Wicke Seelig
Partnerschaftsgesellschaft,
Frankfurt/Main

Design
APPEL NOWITZKI GmbH, Frankfurt/Main

Creative Direction
Anne Julia Nowitzki

Art Direction
Lisa Stein

Project Management
Eva Maria Nowitzki

Concept
Ulf Appel

→ Designer portrait on page 485

Gotteswerk 5.2015

[Magazine]

The "Gotteswerk 5.2015" customer magazine deals with various stages of people meeting, exemplified by "You look great!" (first flirt), "Nice to meet you" (become acquainted) and "Clap your hands, say yeah" (be thrilled), with the aim of illustrating the steps of approach between customers and the printing house. The publication itself promotes various typographic refinements, such as embossing and scented paper. A personal interview with Florian Kohler, the director of the Büttenpapierfabrik Gmund, completes the content of the magazine. The red colour cut, with inlaid metallic-yellow fine paper, lends the publication a strong visual appeal.

Client
Gotteswinter und Aumaier GmbH, Munich

Printing
Helmut Gahse, Bernd Weber

Design
MILCH+HONIG designkultur, Munich

Graphic Design
Christina John, Rafael Dietzel

→ Designer portrait on page 511

Audi Magazine
No. 03/2016

The aim of "Audi Magazine", as a platform
published quarterly for customer
communication, is to showcase the Audi
brand in line with its values. Defined as
technology, sports driving and high
quality, the brand values are presented
in sections named "drive", "move" and
"inspire". As a mix of information and
entertainment, the concept of this magazine uses powerful images, interviews,
reports and sophisticated writing. It thus
aims at finding new ways to bring customers closer to the world of the Audi
brand. Overall, the magazine is focused
on the brand's future.

Client
AUDI AG, Ingolstadt

Design
loved gmbh, Hamburg

Creative Direction
Rouven Steinke, Julia-Christin Holtz,
Mieke Haase

Art Direction
Julia Kerschbaum, Frauke Engler

Editorial Work
Patrick Morda

Account Management
Daniel Albrecht, Peter Matz

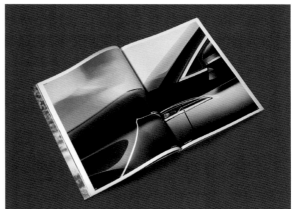

43einhalb MAG

[Customer Magazine]

The customer magazine "43einhalb MAG" was conceived for a specialist sneaker store that emphasises a close relationship to its customers. Aimed at complementing the company's communication portfolio, the magazine is based on the corporate philosophy that each sneaker shoe also has a story to tell. The design for telling these stories has been implemented with company-typical attention to detail in order to open up a realm in which customers can learn about a variety of things in the daily business of the company, get to know the people the company works with and read about the "weird stuff" the company does.

Client
43einhalb GmbH, Fulda

Design
43einhalb GmbH, Fulda

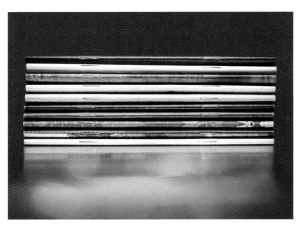

TUI AG
Corporate Magazine

Client
TUI AG, Hannover

Design
3st kommunikation GmbH, Mainz

Creative Direction
Florian Heine

Art Direction
Ruth Kalicki

Editorial Work
Cornelia Theisen

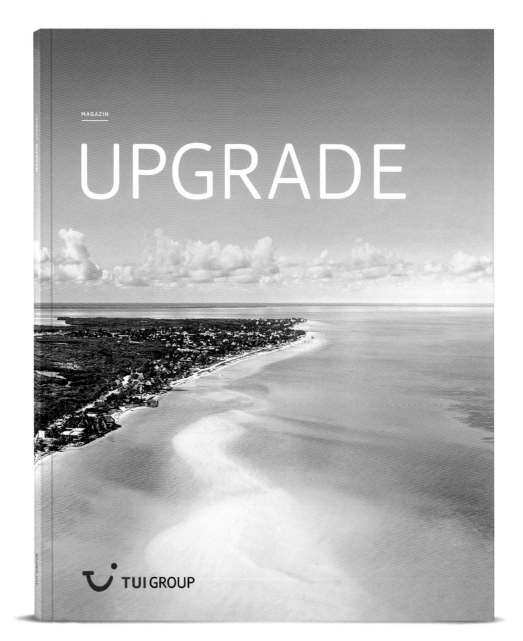

In excitingly narrated stories, the "Upgrade" corporate magazine by TUI Group sketches a scene in which company employees are working on ensuring the best possible tourist experience for customers. The cover features a visual of a South Sea island as well as an easily recognisable layout with colourful images to awaken people's wanderlust. The title statement is visually enhanced by blind embossing, emblazoning the cover. In addition, the magazine also includes the group's sustainability report. Originally, the corporate magazine came out as part of the 2014–15 annual report, but it is also available separately.

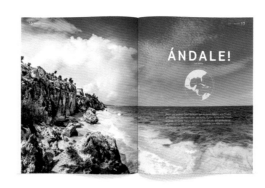

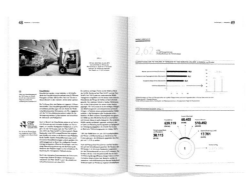

Pure Cycling

[Magazine, Product Catalogue]

With the aim of inviting readers to explore the experiences of Canyon cyclists and conveying a vivid impression of the passion for this sport, the magazine "Pure Cycling" documents a ride with mountain bikers Fabio Schäfer and Jannik Hammes through the US state of Utah. The minimalistic design philosophy of the company was translated into a compact format, a streamlined layout and progressive typography. Since the product catalogue contains the technical data for the 2016 bikes in the form of an insert, it can also serve as a practical resource for use at trade shows and events.

Client
Canyon Bicycles GmbH, Koblenz

Design
KMS TEAM, Munich

Managing Partner
Knut Maierhofer

Managing Director
Patrick Märki

Design Direction
Jessica Krier

Graphic Design
Aurelian Hallhuber

Project Management
Kathrin Bach

Production
Matthias Karpf

Pre-Press
Angela Keesman

→ Designer portrait on page 505

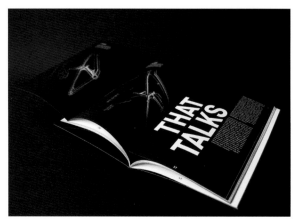

skantherm elements

[Magazine]

The skantherm "elements" magazine aims at visualising the variety of possible architectural arrangements that can be realised with the manufacturer's fireplaces. It promotes the latest product developments by presenting different scenarios of individual arrangement in the home environment. The large-format magazine with integrated flap thus illustrates how the fireplaces can be given a unique personal stamp. A play-fully designed insert stimulates the creativity of readers and enables them to customise their own dream fireplace.

Client
skantherm Wagner GmbH & Co. KG, Oelde

Design
cyclos design GmbH, Münster

L'Hommage

[Special Publication]

Designed to take the form of a classic newspaper, the photo magazine "L'Hommage" by bicycle manufacturer Canyon debuted at the Eurobike trade show 2015. The design portrays the raw emotions and stories of the world's most important bicycle race, the Tour de France, in meticulously curated images. Each picture captures and tells the tale of exciting, legendary bicycle racing. The "L'Hommage" magazine thus visualises passion and excitement for cycling, which extend far beyond the racing to also reflect the core of the brand.

Client
Canyon Bicycles GmbH, Koblenz

Design
Canyon Bicycles GmbH, Koblenz

Creative Direction
Frank Aldorf, Canyon Bicycles GmbH

Art Direction
Thomas Laschet, Canyon Bicycles GmbH
Axel Kippenberg, Hamburg

Photography
Tino Pohlmann, Berlin

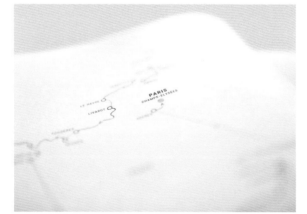

Fortuna Cycles –
Made by Skilled Hands

[Catalogue]

This publication for the brand Fortuna Cycles expands on the original character of the bicycles by this still young company. The style and appearance of these handmade bicycles are reminiscent of the "good old times". This folder/magazine/product catalogue for customers was conceived during the redesign of the entire corporate image. The design aims to ensure consistency by harmonising the look, textual content and images. The goal is to convey the message that each Fortuna cycle is customised to meet individual customer demands.

Client
Kraftstoff Handmadebikes, Dornbirn

Design
Haselwanter Grafik_und Design, Dornbirn

Context Issue No. 4

[Magazine]

This redesign transformed VCUQatar's annual report into a more interactive piece that engages readers and looks back at the major happenings over the past academic year. The goal was to create a new identity that is in line with the recent rebranding of the school. The design re-envisioned the annual report as a yearly magazine to make it a more visually compelling piece. The title "Context" was chosen for the magazine to reinforce the university's commitment to providing a design education that is multidisciplinary in nature and structured to take into consideration the "local context".

Client
Virginia Commonwealth University in Qatar (VCUQatar), Doha

Design
Sara Shaaban

Editor-in-Chief
Meike Kaan

Writer
Lauren Maas

Photography
Markus Elblaus, Raviv Cohen

TWELVE – A Magazine by the Serviceplan Group

"Twelve" looks back at the people and topics that motivated and accompanied the firm Serviceplan Group last year. Since every issue is created in collaboration with a different young artist, the second edition highlights small and larger drawings by German illustrator Frank Höhne throughout the magazine. Together with the neon-orange colour, they give this annual review magazine its own personality. The specially compiled soundtrack comes as a surprising innovation. Also referenced in the cover illustration, it runs through the individual chapters as a common thread.

Client
Serviceplan, Munich

Design
Serviceplan, Munich

Chief Creative Officer
Alexander Schill

Executive Creative Direction
Beate Gronemann

Head of Marketing
Julia Becker

Chief Communication Officer
Christiane Wolff

Text
Alexandra Berger, Munich

Illustration
Frank Höhne, Berlin

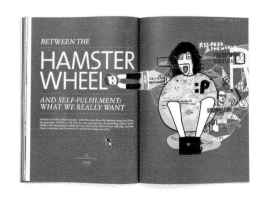

Nord & Süd

[Business Magazine]

The business magazine Nord & Süd was born out of the needs of South Tyrol's location development agency BLS. In order to call attention to the multifarious local economy, it compiles features by authors, journalists, photographers and artists from the region. The economic situation is thus portrayed in relation to a larger whole through high-quality journalism. The magazine is published annually and builds on a basic graphic grid allowing the visual appearance of each edition to evolve in terms of typography, imagery and colours.

Client/Publisher
Business Location Südtirol · Alto Adige AG,
Bozen

Director
Ulrich Stofner

Head of Marketing
Birgit Mayr

Design/Art Direction
CH Studio, Vienna
Lupo & Burtscher, Bozen

Content Design/Editorial Work
Ex Libris, Bozen

Content Design
Angelika Burtscher, Thomas Hanifle,
Christian Hoffelner, Thomas Kager

Editor-in-Chief
Michaela Namuth (2014)

Marimbondo Magazine

The aim in designing "Marimbondo" magazine was to visualise complex art and culture themes in an easy-to-understand graphical manner. Landscape and portrait formats of vivid appeal project an iconographic significance that monitors the relationship of readers to the subject. The individual covers distinguish themselves through a visually powerful design and colouring. The hornet, which lends the magazine its name, is represented in the reductive symbolic form with high recognition value. Derived from the logo, the choice for the typographic texts opts for visual comfort and tranquillity.

Client
Canal C – Comunicação e Cultura, Belo Horizonte

Design
OESTE, Belo Horizonte

Art Direction
Mariana Misk

Graphic Design
Aline Ribeiro, Anne Patrice

Production
Joana Alves

nomad

[Magazine]

The "nomad" magazine with the subtitle "The Magazine for New Design Culture, Business Affairs and Contemporary Lifestyle" is published in print and digital versions. It offers a multifocal perspective on the topic of design by viewing it within the context of society, the economy, lifestyle and culture, and by asking how it relates to future trends and developments. The title "nomad – where to go?" is an expression of a contemporary way of life, while also standing for the search for new topical, personal and societal stances. Renowned authors and journalists feature in interviews and essays dealing with questions related to the future.

Client
hw.design gmbh, Munich

Design
hw.design gmbh, Munich

Creative Direction/Concept
Frank Wagner

Art Direction
Veronika Kinczli

Project Management
Elke Hey

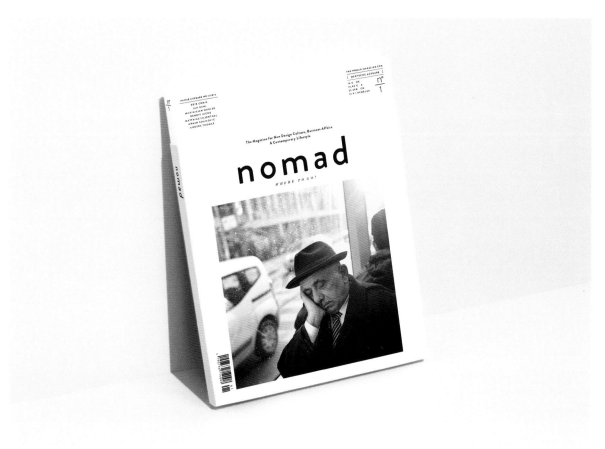

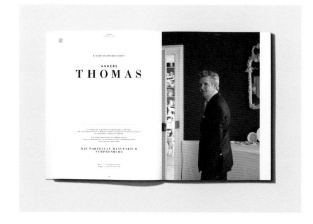

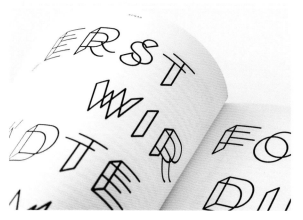

agenda design

[Magazine]

"agenda design" is a magazine published by the Alliance of German Designers (AGD). It discusses the changing role of design and its influences on the technical, ecological, economic and social aspects of today's world. Issue 1 is dedicated to the topic of "visibility" and divided into three sections. The section titled "Diskurs" (discourse) is focused on dialogue with experts of different disciplines; "Projektor" (projector) features the best projects by selected AGD members; and "Augenblick" (moment) talks about contemporary issues and introduces phenomena of the World Wide Web. The target audience includes 3,000 members of the AGD.

Client
Alliance of German Designers (AGD),
Braunschweig

Design
BUNTESAMT, Berlin

Editor-in-Chief
Florian Alexander Schmidt, Berlin

Pre-Press
Heiko Preller, Hannover

Printing
Jochen Wanderer,
Wanderer Werbedruck GmbH,
Ronnenberg

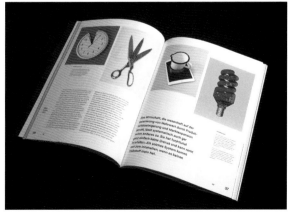

DEUTSCH MAGAZINE

The redesign of DEUTSCH MAGAZINE, an international lifestyle magazine published by Art Verlag Berlin since 2003, is marked by typographic borrowings from the world of encyclopedias. The objective here was to give the magazine an independent visual character, as it is a constantly evolving reference book that redefines itself with each published issue. This edition addresses the question of what it means to be German and concludes that "German" has a different meaning for every individual and that the notion itself undergoes permanent change indefinitely. This idea served as the basis for the design concept.

Client
DEUTSCH MAGAZINE, Berlin

Design
Strichpunkt Design, Stuttgart/Berlin

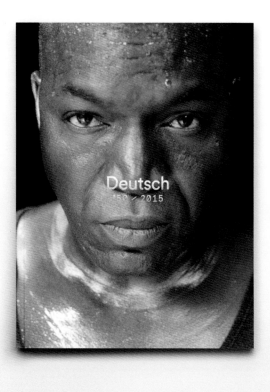

LOVED&FOUND –
The Sex Issue

[Magazine]

The "LOVED&FOUND" sex issue was released on 1 December to coincide with World Aids Day. The Jugend gegen AIDS (Young People against AIDS) association used this special issue as a platform to educate both young people and adults in an accessible way, talking openly and directly about sex on 80 pages. It promoted the slogan "Do it with love, respect and condoms" and featured the Jugend gegen AIDS corporate identity, with visual elements of that corporate design running throughout the magazine. In line with the slogan "Sex is fun", the issue's design featured stylised penises, vaginas and fun, as well as colourful shapes.

Client
Jugend gegen AIDS e.V., Hamburg

Design
loved gmbh, Hamburg

Creative Direction
Mieke Haase

Editorial Work
Eva Bolhoefer, Ava Carstens

Graphic Design
Kim Arendt, Tom Schuster,
Ruben Scupin, Dominique Brodel

Chandra Kurt's Weinseller Journal

[Magazine]

Chandra Kurt's "Weinseller Journal" magazine is derived from the "Weinseller" guide, which has existed for 19 years now and is targeted directly at wine aficionados. Each edition starts with a personal and educative report accompanying the wine expert Chandra and her team while visiting a winery in a famous wine region. The story is personal and illustrated with pictures. The visual appearance is characterised by chapters with bold typographic elements to lend the magazine a clear language and aesthetic layout, providing readers with know-how and information about wine-related topics.

Client/Editor
Chandra Kurt AG, Zurich

Publisher
Werd & Weber Verlag AG, Thun

Design
clear of clouds gmbh, Zurich

Transhelvetica

[Travel Magazine]

Transhelvetica is an independent travel magazine for Switzerland, which aims at lending the subject a high degree of authenticity through high-quality presentation. Published since 2010, the magazine also features a design concept distinguishing it from other publications in the tourism industry. The goal is to promote sophisticated, responsible tourism for the "Lohas generation", combining fun, adventure and a good sense for the hidden treasures at the doorsteps of its readers. It thus joins valuable information with well-designed packaging.

Client
Passaport AG, Zurich

Design
Fabian Leuenberger, Zurich

Creative Direction
Jon Bollmann, Michèle Fröhlich,
Fabian Leuenberger, Pia Marti

Editorial Work
Michèle Fröhlich

Account Management
Karl Grauhans

Customer Advisory Service
Sabeth Bollmann

Supervision
Neil Oliver Harte, Gina Marti

b – Nº 6
Ballett am Rhein

[Magazine]

The sixth edition of the Ballett am Rhein magazine "b – Nº 6" centres on the history of dance. A report on the German Dance Archives Cologne revives the art of dance in the 19th and 20th centuries, while the current trends in artistic discourse are illustrated against the background of a filmic portrait on choreographer Martin Schläpfer. The future of dance is addressed in sketches and notations by six Ballett am Rhein dancers who are debuting as choreographers in the choreography platform. The generous use of images in the layout is aimed at breaking up the essays and facilitating an easy reading flow.

Client
Ballett am Rhein Düsseldorf Duisburg

Ballet Director/
Chief Choreographer
Martin Schläpfer

Design
Markwald Neusitzer Identity,
Frankfurt/Düsseldorf

Art Direction
Nina Neusitzer, Nicolas Markwald

Photography
Gert Weigelt, Susanne Diesner,
Nadja Bournonville et al.

Editorial Work
Anne do Paço

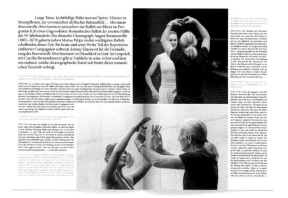

Objektiv

[Magazine]

The design of over 60 covers for Dnevnik's Saturday supplement in Slovenia was created following the maxim that covers are not simply a comment on the writing, or a synopsis of it. Instead, they often go a step beyond the power of the word, or the lack thereof. These covers are aimed at provoking and making the readers smile or angry, with titles such as "Promotion of junk food", "The Vatican broom", "Functional (i) literacy in Slovenia", "Srebrenica, 20 years of holocaust", "New hope: Slovenia after another early election", "Cybercrime" or "Climate changes & us". As such, the covers also intend to pay respect to the readers of this newspaper, since, instead of being passive recipients, they usually deal with media content consciously.

Client
Dnevnik d.d., Ljubljana

Design
Tomato Košir s.p., Kranj

Creative Direction/Concept
Tomato Košir

Graphic Design/Photography
Tomato Košir

Art Direction
Samo Ačko, Dnevnik

Editorial Work
Miran Lesjak, Dnevnik

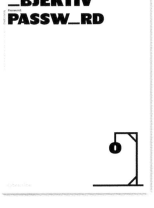

National Museum of Korea

[Magazine]

This quarterly magazine introduces the National Museum of Korea's exhibitions, academic activities and cultural projects. The aim is to deliver artistic value and meaning related to the NMK's collection in intriguing ways, as well as to introduce the museum's various programmes. The publication follows the design of a magazine that is visually beautiful and also informative through well-written text. It wants to shed light on the origins of today's Korean culture and people's emotions in an in-depth way from multiple perspectives, complemented by content that depicts major exhibitions held at the museum.

Client
National Museum of Korea, Seoul

Design
National Museum of Korea, Seoul
Ahn Graphics, Seoul

vorarlberg museum – Artist Talks

[Book Series]

This book series documents events, installations and exhibitions in and around the vorarlberg museum in Bregenz, Austria. Although rigorously structured, the series leaves plenty of room for presenting the individual artistic works. Each publication of the series always starts with an artist inter-view, followed by a section with pic-tures. The design picks up elements of the museum's architecture. This is paired with interesting details, such as vari-ation of paper inside as well as a binding technique that is characterised by open thread stitching with fitted covers.

Client
vorarlberg museum, Bregenz

Design
Kurt Dornig Grafikdesign & Illustration, Dornbirn

Photography
Markus Tretter, Lindau

Pre-Press
Günter König, Dornbirn

Printing
Thurnher Druckerei, Rankweil

Touch

[Exhibition Catalogue]

The publication "Touch" documents the Saastamoinen Foundation Art Collection by presenting topical Finnish and international contemporary art. The exhibition was divided into three thematic entities, all of which related to humanity. This publication approaches the artworks in the exhibition from a variety of perspectives. The writers include members of the staff at EMMA (Espoo Museum of Modern Art, Espoo, Finland), experts and artists, as well as museum visitors. The aim was to design a publication that is as interesting and tangible as the exhibition.

Client
EMMA – Espoo Museum of Modern Art, Saastamoinen Foundation

Design
Kuudes Kerros, Helsinki

Art Direction/Editorial Design
Tony Eräpuro

Account Management
Sonja Söderholm

Production
Vesa Viljakainen, József Kiss

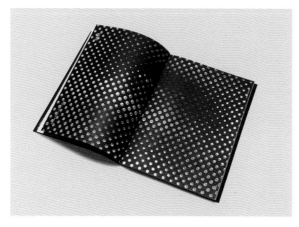

Mind The Gap

[Exhibition Catalogue]

"Mind The Gap" is an exhibition focused on mapping, featuring three artists commissioned to create artworks based on the data of their chosen findings and research. The catalogue documenting the exhibition is segmented into three irregular, individual sections for each artist. The design plays with space as a visual pun to reflect the title carefully coming together to form the cover. Bars and monospaced fonts evoke the sensation of cold hard data.

Client
National Library Board, Singapore

Design
studioKALEIDO, Singapore

Graphic Design
Winnie Wu

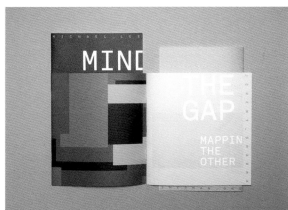

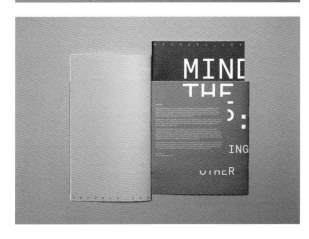

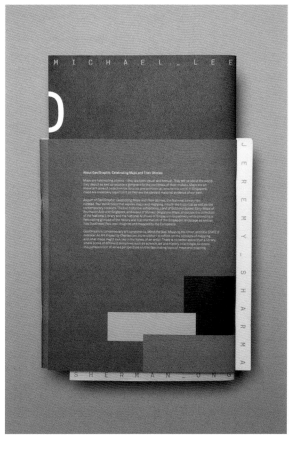

Writing Pictures – Picture Writing. Chinese Poster and Book Design Today

[Book]

The book is a catalogue designed for an exhibition at the Museum Folkwang in the city of Essen, Germany, in which more than 70 designers presented their works in contemporary Chinese poster and book design. The design of this book is inspired by the form of folded pages found in traditional Chinese books. Therefore, it features a rectangular shape with inserted posters that unfold forward in a unique manner. This approach breaks with the tradition of folding all book pages inward: it folds only a small number of pages, making the book itself take on a trapezoidal form, as it ends up being thicker toward the binding side.

Client
Museum Folkwang, Essen

Design
Jianping He, hesign International GmbH, Berlin

→ Designer portrait on page 501

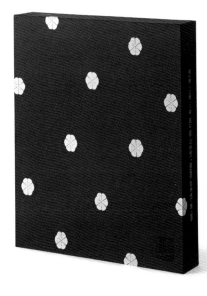
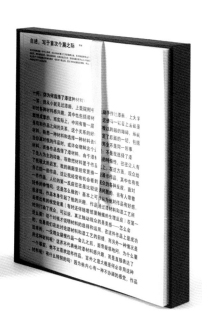

Qiao Jia –
Lacquer Painting &
Lacquer Ping-Feng

[Book]

Designed for a solo exhibition by
Qiao Jia, a Beijing artist of lacquer art,
this picture book dedicates itself to the
future of her artistic work. Following
a similar approach as in her lacquer art,
the exhibition and book merge heredi-
tary lacquer art skills with a personal
style, aimed at showing the special characteristics of the artist's work. The
publication has been designed to comprise three volumes that structure the
content according to her oeuvre. One of
the volumes features only text. The
other two volumes compile the artist's
output, subdividing it into four categories and highlighting the special
feature of being readable from both
front to back and back to front.

Client
Qiao Jia, Beijing

Design
Jianping He, hesign International GmbH,
Berlin

→ Designer portrait on page 501

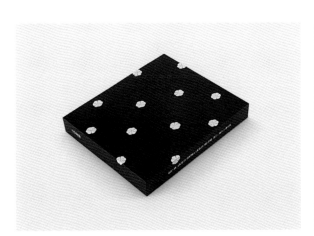

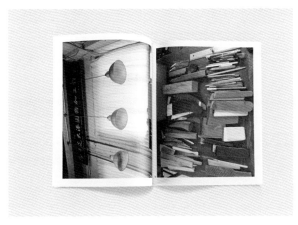
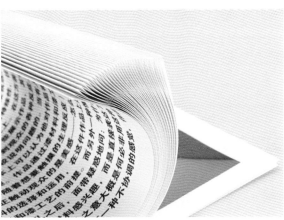

Tasmeem 2015 – 3ajeeb!

[Special Publication]

Client
Virginia Commonwealth University
in Qatar (VCUQatar), Doha

Design/Art Direction
Sara Shaaban
Nathan Davis, Arcadian Studio
("Tasmeem in the Classroom" Publication)

Design Team
Haya Daher, Moza Khalifa Al-Suwaidi

Editor-in-Chief
Meike Kaan

Writer
Lauren Maas

Photography
Markus Elblaus, Raviv Cohen,
Rachele Storai

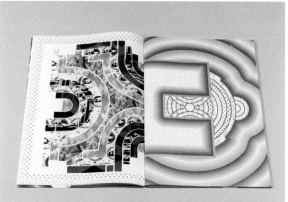

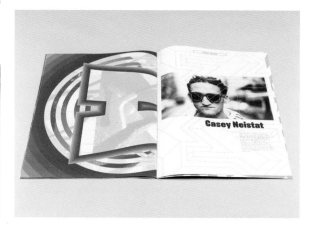

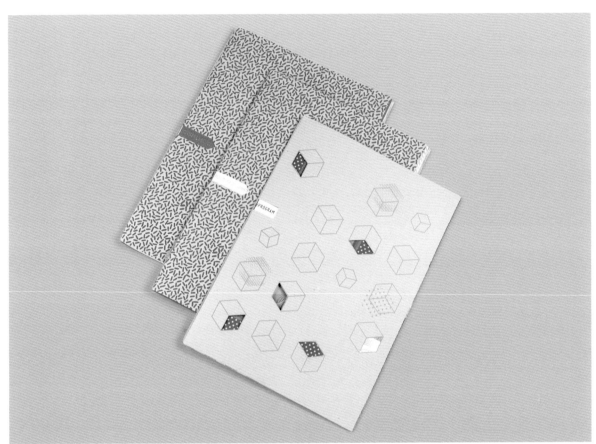

The 2015 edition of the "Tasmeem Doha Conference: 3ajeeb!" focuses on "playfulness" as a methodology to create interesting and unexpected outcomes in art and design. This notion of playfulness is reflected in all aspects of the conference and most notably in the publications. "Tasmeem in the Classroom (TIC)", a series of semester-long pre-conference projects, is the first part in a series of three publications. The second, "Tasmeem 3ajeeb! Program", covers the speakers, workshops and activities. The third, "Take Me With You", is the post-conference publication and conveys the conference spirit, reusing parts of the two previous publications.

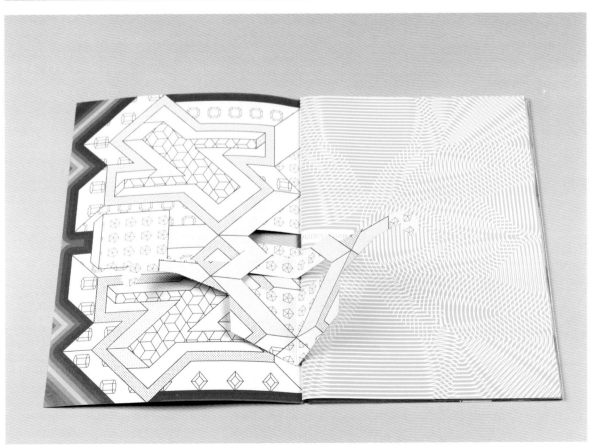

Staatstheater Mainz
Season Guide
2016/2017

[Booklet]

Visualising the world of theatre both on and off the stage, the season programme 2016–17 of the State Theater in Mainz, Germany, opens with a collection of photographs of its members. The compact format allows every single face to fill an entire page, thus allowing them to naturally feature centre stage. Constituting half of the season programme booklet, the portrait gallery deliberately precedes the information section. The second half of the booklet is characterised by large lettering, clear graphics and the theatre's distinctive star logo. It features a clearly structured overview of the upcoming opera, drama, dance and concert premieres and repertoire pieces.

Client
Staatstheater Mainz GmbH

Design
Neue Gestaltung GmbH, Berlin

Graphic Design
Pit Stenkhoff, Anna Bühler, Nina Odzinieks

Photography
Andreas J. Etter, Hüben und Drüben Mainz

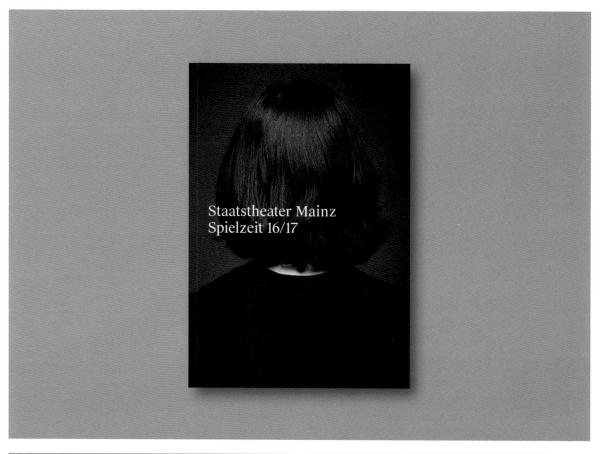
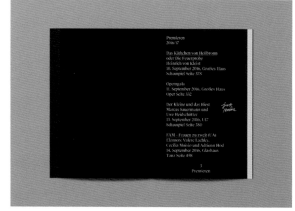

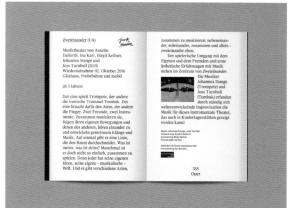
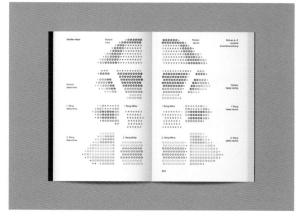

Onassis Cultural Centre 2015–2016

[Booklets]

This book documents the agency's design work for the Onassis Cultural Centre in Athens, Greece, ranging from promotional publications to videos and catalogues, as well as various digital and analogue applications for a large and diverse series of events for the 2015–16 season. The visual identity is based on illustrations composed of solid-coloured cut-out shapes. The illustrations evoke the impression of "handmade" collages due to the rendering of the shadow cast by a piece of cardboard superimposed upon another.

Client
Onassis Cultural Centre, Athens

Design
Beetroot Design Group, Thessaloniki

Creative Direction
Alexis Nikou, Vangelis Liakos

Art Direction
Giannis Gougoulias, Ilias Pantikakis

→ Designer portrait on page 490

Image Ethnography –
Zhuang Xueben
Photographs
[Book]

Client
Ethnic Costume Museum, Beijing
Institute of Fashion Technology, Beijing

Editor-in-Chief
Yuanfeng Liu

Chief Director
Yang He

Design
Hang Hai, Meng Jie, Beijing

Publisher
SDX Joint Publishing Company, Beijing

Editor
Guoqiang Xv

→ Designer portrait on page 500

This book presents a collection of photographs by Zhuang Xueben, an important Chinese anthropology photographer of the early 20th century. The photos were taken between 1934 and 1942, documenting the daily life-styles, religions, costumes, products and geography of the time. The book design was based on noninterference in order to be able to accurately record the precious minority culture. The aim is to reflect the plain, natural and elegant style and the toned colour of that period in the Republic of China. In addition, the book cover is made from handmade blue-dyed calico, featuring a typical vertical typography.

Warm Modernity

[Book]

The book "Warm Modernity" focuses on the urban architecture of India by placing it in a spatial context so as to take readers on an architectural adventure. It conflates scientific research on contemporary issues with the origins and history of participatory architecture. The design retraces the process of architectural development in India, leading to the creation of a book that illustrates a kind of graphical identity of the country. Thus, the colour code is a warm duotone of auburn and brown, typical of Indian textiles, while the logotype is derived from an original typeface inspired by Gandhi's glasses.

Client
Triennale di Milano, Milan

Concept
Maddalena d'Alfonso, Milan

Design
Stefano Mandato, Milan

Photography
Marco Introini, Milan

Publisher
Michele Pizzi, Silvana Editoriale, Cinisello Balsamo (Milan)

Exhibition Production
Isa Consonni, UNIFOR S.p.A., Turate (Como)

Exhibition Architecture
Samuel Colle, Giacomo Gatto, Pierpaolo Tonin, Milan

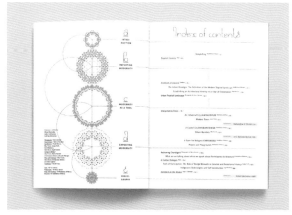

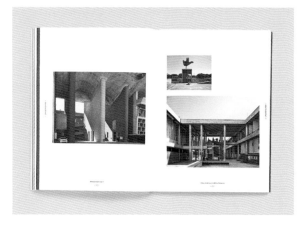

A Living Space –
The Homes of Pak Sha O
[Book]

This book is created as part of an art project called "A Living Space", which aims to explore the intrinsic quality and possibility of life through a range of observation, exploration and research. The Chinese title, literally meaning "a liveable house", is named after a house that artist Suk Ki Wong discovered in Hong Kong and which inspired her to ponder what life is. By depicting life in a traditional Hakka village in Pak Sha O, Sai Kung, Hong Kong, this book raises thought-provoking questions about what is essential for a place to be considered "home" and how a "living space" of one's own can be created.

Client/Publisher
kaitak, Centre for Research and Development, Academy of Visual Arts, Hong Kong Baptist University, Hong Kong

Design
kaitak, Centre for Research and Development, Academy of Visual Arts, Hong Kong Baptist University, Hong Kong

Art Direction
Suk Ki Wong

Graphic Design
Lai Ping So

Creative Team
Wai Lun Hsu, Long Hei Matthew Kwan

Printing
Sunny Ng, Suncolor Printing Co., Ltd., Hong Kong

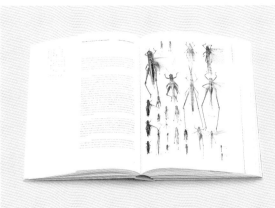

HOERBIGER
Illustrated Books

[Corporate Publishing]

After moving to a new location, Christiana Hörbiger, family shareholder of the HOERBIGER Holding AG, issued two illustrated books. The challenge was to transfer the personality and spirit of the 85 year old former site into the future. The first book captures the unique charm of the Group's previous head office and the bording production facilities in architectural photographs – supplemented by memories of selected employees whose contributions can be either read in the book or listened to via QR codes. The second book deals with the new site, documenting its construction and settling. It also features interviews with employees who now share their thoughts for the future.

Client
HOERBIGER Holding AG, Zug

Project Management
Ludwig Schönefeld

Design
Jäger & Jäger, Überlingen

Creative Direction
Olaf Jäger

Art Direction
Regina Jäger

Graphic Design
Michelle Miesel

Text
Ludwig Schönefeld, Zug
Sophie Blasberg, Wuppertal
Patricia Grzonka, Vienna

Photography
Brigida González, Stuttgart
Manfred Klimek, Vienna

Printing
Druck-Ring, Kirchheim

→ Designer portrait on page 504

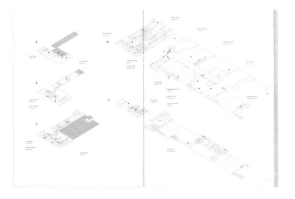

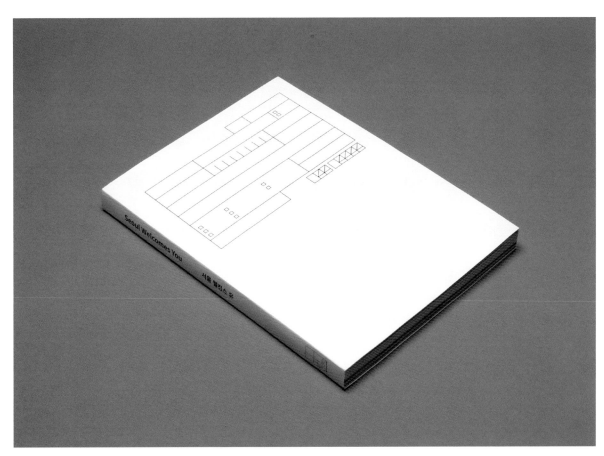

Seoul Welcomes You

[Book]

The book titled "Seoul Welcomes You" was designed as part of an invitation to the Typojanchi International Typography Biennale, held under the theme "City & Typography". The book was published by various designers coming from six different teams, after cooperatively planning and participating in the event as either author or artist under the common "Seoul Welcomes You" theme. The book features nine chapters and is structured from the cover page to the last page in the order of a schedule for a visit to Seoul by a foreigner, including the time when that person returns to his or her country.

Client
KCDF, Typojanchi 2015 & Doosung Paper, Seoul

Design
Project Team "Seoul Welcomes You", Seoul

Graphic Design
Daeki Shim, Choong Ho Lee, Hyun Cho, Sangpil Lee, Jungmo Nam, Yongjun Park, Hyojun Shim

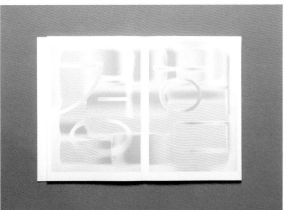

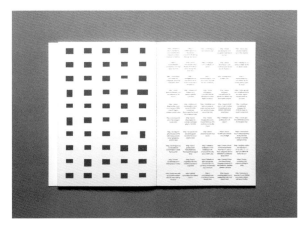

A Hopeful Story about Our Future

[Brochure]

This brochure for the Swedish Forest Industries Federation is designed to communicate the possibilities that the forest has to offer in the pursuit of a sustainable future. The assignment was to create a visionary story with the forest as the hero and character, a story that is intriguing and uncomplicated. Tactile and innovative materials play an important role in illustrating the opportunities for innovation provided by the forest. The cover is printed on Fibre-Form®, a material that can even be used for recyclable paper bottles. To increase the tactile feel, the cover is also embossed, debossed and foiled.

Client
The Swedish Forest Industries Federation, Stockholm

Design
BVD, Stockholm

Text
Mattias Jersild

Photography
Lennart Durehed

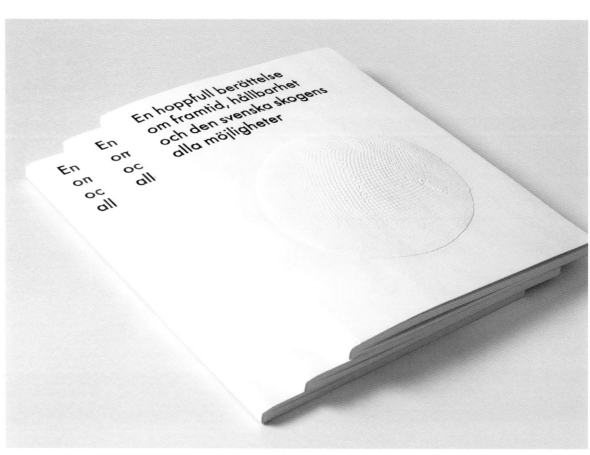

Act of Love

[Book]

"Act of Love" is a visual dictionary based on over seven years of research into animal courtship behaviour. The featured images were shot by various international photographers and re-photographed for the purpose of integrating the tone within the design context of a photography book. The goal was to create a visual dictionary that is easy to read, using catchy copy and simple explanations rather than difficult terms targeted towards experts. Paying careful attention to bookbinding, the publication uses lightweight paper for its large-format design to deliver a physically comfortable reading experience.

Client
Sagami Rubber Industries Co., Ltd.

Design
Chieko Zaitsu, Tokyo
Kei Ishimaru, London

Art Direction/Planning/Editing
Chieko Zaitsu, Tokyo

Creative Direction
Koichiro Tanaka, Projector Inc., Tokyo

Production
Atsuki Yukawa, Rock'n Roll Japan Inc., Tokyo

Project Direction
Hideaki Oki, Hakuhodo Kettle Inc., Tokyo

Supervision
Keisuke Ueda, Rikkyo University, Tokyo

ILR 14 20

[Book]

Client
Goya Choi, London

Design
Goya Choi, London

Creative Direction
Adrian Shaughnessy,
Royal College of Art, London

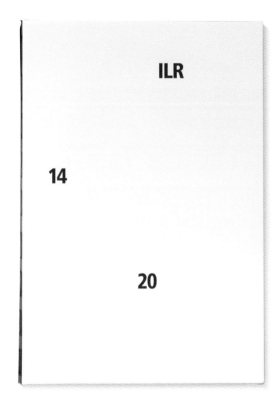

ILR

14

20

INDEFINITE LEAVE
TO REMAIN (ILR) IS
A FORM OF AMNESTY
WHICH ALLOWS
OVERSTAYERS
TO LEGALISE THEIR
STAY IN THE UK AFTER
14 YEARS.

HOWEVER, IT HAS
BEEN ABOLISHED.

AND NOW
REQUIRES 20 YEARS.

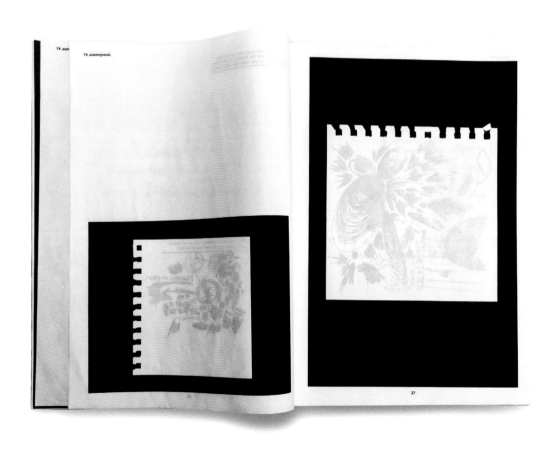

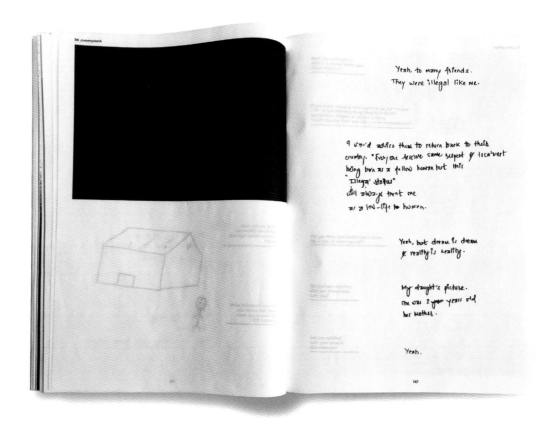

This book tells the "hidden" stories of seven formerly illegal immigrants in the UK who were the last people able to legalise their overstay as Indefinite Leave to Remain (ILR) according to the Amnesty Act 14-year rule before it was changed to 20 years. The aim of implementing elements like reverse printing and cut-outs was to visualise the associated socially problematic time of uncertainty between illegal overstay and officially recognised right to stay. In order to visualise both this shadow world and the keywords of "anonymous", "obscure" and "double-edged" characterising this publication, the book features a transparent design.

YOUCAT Bible

[Book]

The development of this Catholic Bible integrates and expands on the communicative and aesthetic means as well as the strategic principles of a previous project (an international Youth Catechism). Tools such as branding, illustration and infotainment elements were integrated by following a process of target group participation. Therefore, most of the photographs were taken by young people to have them participate actively and directly in the making of this Bible. The "Youth Bible of the Catholic Church" is being translated into 35 languages and inculturated into local participation projects.

Client
YOUCAT Foundation gGmbH,
Aschau im Chiemgau

Design
Alexander von Lengerke, Cologne

Publisher
Christoph Schönborn,
Archdiocese of Vienna
Michael Schönberger,
YOUCAT Foundation

**Strategic Planning/
Editorial Management**
Bernhard Meuser, YOUCAT Foundation

Editorial Work
Clara Steber, YOUCAT Foundation

Writer
Thomas Söding, University of Münster

→ Designer portrait on page 532

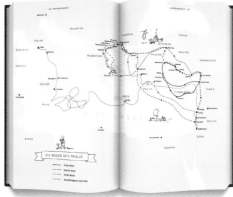

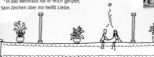

Auf der Erde leben
Living on Earth

[Book]

Celebrating the 250th anniversary of the Freiberg University of Mining and Technology, this book pays tribute to the institute's history and scientific renown. The idea was to enable readers to immerse themselves in the world of geology and to pique interest for this field of study. The design creates a coherent overall concept from a multitude of different individual papers and supports this with high-quality images. Abstract geological maps are used as a graphical element throughout to depict the stratification of the earth in an alienated manner. A ruler at the edge of the page represents the connection to scientific work.

Client
TU Bergakademie Freiberg,
Fakultät Geowissenschaften,
Geotechnik und Bergbau,
Freiberg

Concept
Ute Baumgarten, Textwerkstatt

Design
element 79, Bergisch Gladbach

Art Direction
Anke Klasen

Graphic Design
Luisa Möbus

Mori's Bookstore Short Story Series

[Book]

The Mori's Bookstore Short Story Series follows an unusual design approach to narrating a Korean short story. The story is formed by compiling a number of papers featuring written words. The intrinsic meanings of letters, sentences, situations and paragraphs are interpreted as a sequence, thus leaving creative leeway for readers to individually edit the story. This book is light in weight and carefully bound. The pages are easy to turn, as the book uses high-quality paper with a natural surface texture.

Client
dotcompany, Seoul

Design
dotcompany, Seoul

Creative Direction/Editorial Work
Donggil Kim

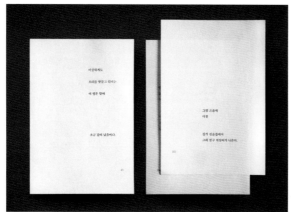

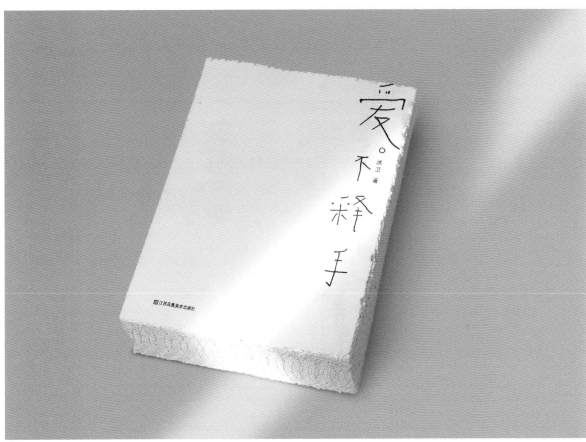

Enchantment of Handwriting

[Book]

The book "Enchantment of Handwriting" takes the form of a diary reflecting the daily notes of a designer. This editorial concept not only carefully records the designer's daily routine, learning notes, creative inspiration and philosophical thinking; it also conveys a sense of the designer's understanding of and attitude towards life. In order to make the multifaceted content appear vivid in content and natural in style, monochromatic print and unadorned blinding were adopted throughout the book.

Client
Phoenix Fine Arts Publishing Ltd., Nanjing

Design
Day Day Up Design Consultancy, Zhongshan City, Guangdong Province

Art Direction
Hong Wei

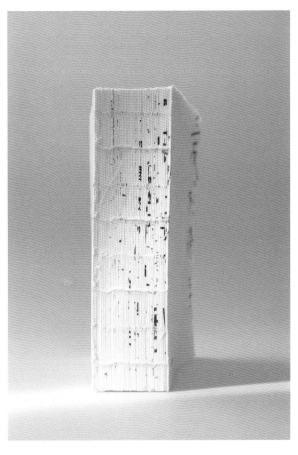

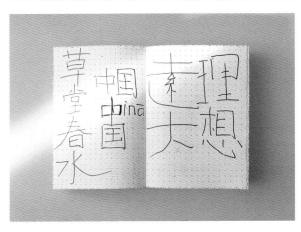

Vanishing Materials

[Book]

This second book of the "Vanishing Series" is designed to promote the awareness of traditional crafts. It was conceived to serve as a memory project of Singapore, sharing stories of the last remaining artisans. Readers are invited to partake as co-creators. The pages are designed with lots of blank space for their curatorial input, their memory records and photographs of any traditional artisan and vanishing trade from around the world. In order for this valuable history to pass down for generations to come, a children's storybook is included to introduce this heritage to the younger generations.

Client
National Library Board, Singapore

Design
Nanyang Technological University, Designing Cultures Studio, Singapore

Creative Direction
Jesvin Yeo

Graphic Design/Editorial Design
Alvin Ng

Illustration
Jesvin Yeo, Tengwan Quek

Project Management
Yuhui Cheng

Research
Tengwan Quek

Publisher
Abdul Nasser, Basheer Graphic Books, Singapore

Printing
Sky Liu, Neo-Brands Co., Ltd., Shenzhen

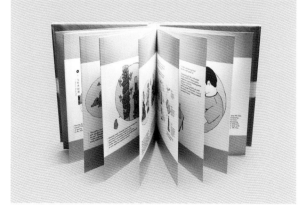

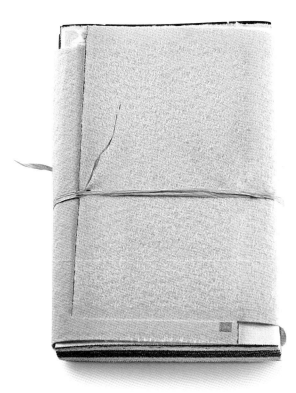

Pleasure of Learning

[Book]

The book "Pleasure of Learning" is de-signed like a bundle of secret documents with folded, ultra-delicate pieces of rice paper on the inside. A soft swathe of felt is wrapped around its body and tied with a thread of raffia. Calligraphic daubs of ink darken the creamy natural white of the paper page by page, aimed at immersing the reader in a new world. The strong, tough paper of this book contains texts in filigree Chinese type, with some smears of watery ink here and there. Implemented as a book that challenges the perception, readers wonder whether these smears are traces of the artists' work or printing ink that has seeped through.

Client
Phoenix Fine Arts Publishing Ltd., Nanjing

Design
Minmin Qu, Nanjing
Qian Jiang, Nanjing

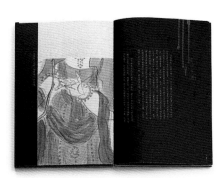

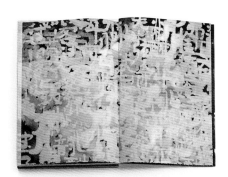

Lululux

[Book]

Client
Lote 42, São Paulo

Design
Casa Rex, São Paulo

Art Direction
Gustavo Piqueira

Graphic Design
Gustavo Piqueira, Samia Jacintho

Design Assistance
Marianne Meni

Lululux was conceived as a humorous game of re-signification that questions players' perceptions. It features 20 napkins, six place mats and eight coasters, each silk-screened with one of the 34 fragments, creating a multiplicity of reading possibilities. As such, it is designed to serve as a transformative element of the reading experience. Lululux is unbound by fixed structures, but rather spread across a narrative dining set. Readers are invited to read it sequentially, one format at a time. However, if readers decide that this book is not their thing, they can use it for setting the dinner table.

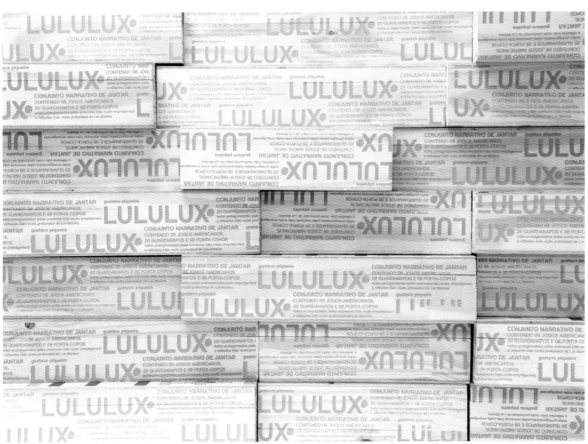

Discovery Foundation Awards 2015

[Book]

In the form of a coffee-table book, this publication documents the winners of the Discovery Foundation Award 2015. The awards are made annually to specialists who serve rural communities. To celebrate the 10th bestowal of the awards, the design was meant to focus on the aspects of look and feel and to emphasise the humanitarian angle. Large-scale photographs contribute to presenting the nominees as heroes. The aim was to portray a series of epic stories dedicated to special individuals reaching out to communities. The book thus also conveys an optimistic outlook for the future.

Client
Discovery Pty. Ltd., Johannesburg

Design
Roering Creative Kin, Johannesburg

Creative Direction
Ivan Kirstein

Concept
Simone Meyburgh

Graphic Design
Martin Winter, Marcel Buerkle, Kim Clift

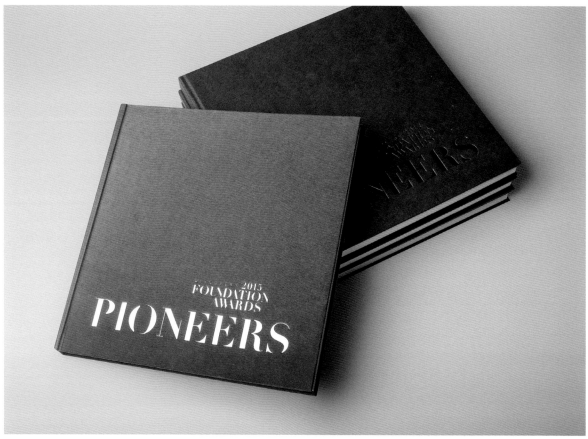

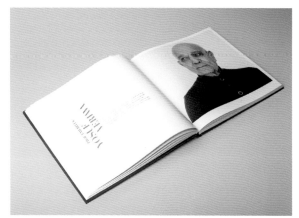

Man muss ein Spiel auch lesen können
Reading the Game

[Corporate Publishing]

For the 2014–15 season, the principal
sponsors of Borussia Dortmund, Evonik,
decided to invite a group of writers –
the German Football Association
National Writer's Side – to accompany
the Bundesliga team. The outcome was
a paean to the club known as BVB,
illustrated in its trademark black-yellow
colour scheme and featuring pieces by
well-known authors such as Thomas
Brussig. In the course of the year, the
writers take a literary look at the various
dimensions of the game, leading the
reader on a journey through this exciting
season, cheering, celebrating, and suf-
fering with the club. "Reading the Game"
was released as a bookstore edition
and in an Evonik corporate version.

Client
Evonik Industries AG, Essen

Design
Aufbau Verlag GmbH, Berlin

Graphic Design
studio grau, Berlin

Illustration
Tim Dinter, Berlin

Project Management
BISSINGER[+] GmbH, Hamburg/Essen

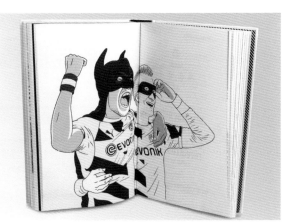

Absoliuti Tekstilė
Absolute Textile

[Book]

This book is dedicated to the contemporary textiles of Lithuania, which, as a synthesis of meticulous craft and innovation, represent one of the country's most creative industries. The division into four chapters corresponds to the four papers written by Lithuanian researchers on the four periods that the local textile industry has experienced. One illustration from each chapter features on the book cover. The book has double covers, with the third one highlighting simple typography marked by a gradient from red colour to green, while the second cover features typographical holes forming the words "Absoliuti Tekstilė".

Client
Publishing House of Vilnius
Academy of Arts, Vilnius

Design
Ausra Lisauskienė, Vilnius

Editorial Work
Eglė Ganda Bogdanienė, Vilnius

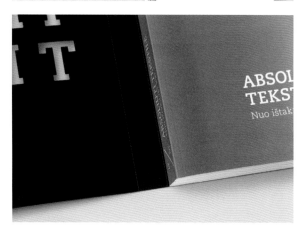

minimum Monographs

[Catalogue]

The five monographs of this series provide an overview of the past 100 years of evolution in furniture design. They chronologically document the work of designers like Marcel Breuer, Charles & Ray Eames and Arne Jacobsen. A blend of historic and contemporary interior design examples visualises the sovereign timelessness of the furniture they created. The series' sixth instalment "Design from Berlin" introduces 30 contemporary designers who continue the tradition of the masters with their own exciting projects. The monographs come in a sophisticated slipcase featuring metallic hot-foil stamping.

Client
minimum einrichten gmbh, Berlin

Design
Rosendahl Berlin

Creative Direction
Lars Borngräber

Art Direction
Florian Hauer

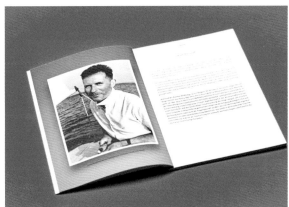

Tresides Asset Management

[Image Book]

This imagebook for the company Tresides Asset Management adopts a storytelling approach focusing on the number three, which builds part of the name. It delivers facts, which aim at giving readers information on numbers that can be encountered in daily life. The second part of the book offers and illustrates in-depth know-how on asset management. Addressing a sophisticated target group, the book features a discreet yet precious design. The combination of consistent storytelling with the presentations of in-depth market information delivers high credibility to the brand.

Client
SÜDWESTBANK AG, Stuttgart

Head of Marketing
Jochen Sautter

Project Management
Thomas Hovemann

Design
Keim Identity GmbH, Zurich

Strategic Planning
Christine Keim

Creative Direction
Matthias Keim

Art Direction
Benjamin Stetter

Editorial Work
Jochen Wolf,
Tresides Asset Management,
Stuttgart

Text
Nadja Mayer, Frankfurt/Main

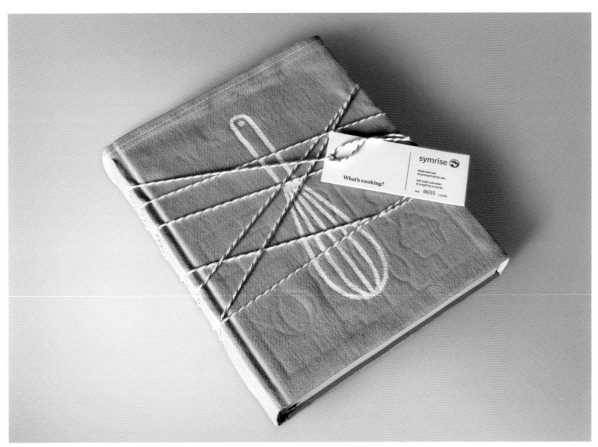

What's Cooking?

[Image Book]

The imagebook for Symrise visualises the company's diverse portfolio in the area of scent and aroma production. The book "What's Cooking?" illustrates in images and on 256 pages of in-depth texts the process of how culinary trends around the world are turned into final products. Originating from about a dozen locations, the stories are written in a journalistic style and illustrated in a documentary way. Materials such as linen and uncoated paper, as well as refinements like hot-foil and blind embossing, support the typographically detailed design.

Client
Symrise AG, Holzminden

Design
Heine Warnecke Design GmbH, Hannover and Münsterland

Creative Direction/Concept
Dirk Heine

Project Management/Production
Wiebke Alm

Text/Concept
Marc-Stefan Andres, ag text, Münster

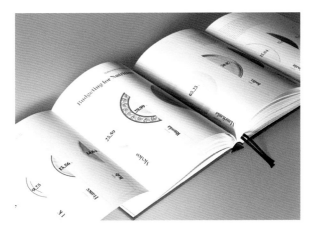

Wild Rose

[Book]

To celebrate its 20th anniversary, Greek skincare brand KORRES created the special "Wild Rose" edition as a tribute to its iconic ingredient. The edition stages a dramatic combination of older campaign images with contemporary ones, aiming to portray the timeless power of this important symbol, while taking the reader on a radiant journey into the heart of the brand. The aim of the design was to fascinate through an oversize format and an embossed linen-cover title. At the same time, subtle, unobtrusive typography and other typographic elements are kept low-key, thus heightening the effect of the picture.

Client
KORRES, Athens

Design
KORRES, Athens

Editor-in-Chief
George Anthoulakis, Athens

Editorial Design
STAGEDESIGNOFFICE, Athens

Desiqn Concept/Direction
Stavros Papagiannis, Athens

Graphic Design
Marianna Vouza, Athens

Production
ALPHABET SA, Athens

We Ride History

[Book]

To mark the 30th anniversary of the bicycle manufacturer Canyon, this internal publication was developed as a storybook that tells the company's history of success. Following the concept of "Every Canyon Tells a Story", it presents 150 curious and moving Canyon Crew stories representing the company's passion, team spirit and great vision. The individual stories are divided into seven chapters with titles such as "Conquering the Summit" or "Stage Jokes". The reduced design features a great deal of contrast to create an interesting framework for the anecdotes. The employee names are set in larger type to underscore the significance of everyone in the company.

Client
Canyon Bicycles GmbH, Koblenz

Design
KMS TEAM, Munich

Managing Partner
Knut Maierhofer

Managing Director
Patrick Märki

Art Direction
Jessica Krier

Graphic Design
Aurelian Hallhuber

Project Management
Kathrin Bach

→ Designer portrait on page 505

TAKKT AG – Added Value for Everyone

[Corporate Publishing]

The compactly designed 2016 sustainability report by the TAKKT Group carries the slogan "Added Value for Everyone" to demonstrate the company's strategy of establishing a sustainable balance between economic, environmental and social factors. Striking visual elements and informative graphics illustrate the key data, while a register in the form of rulers give readers a quick overview. A separate flyer listing the GRI G4 indicators can be found in a wallet on the last content page. The distinctive cover design sets out to convey that the company actively implements sustainability.

Client
TAKKT AG, Stuttgart

Design
Strichpunkt Design, Stuttgart/Berlin

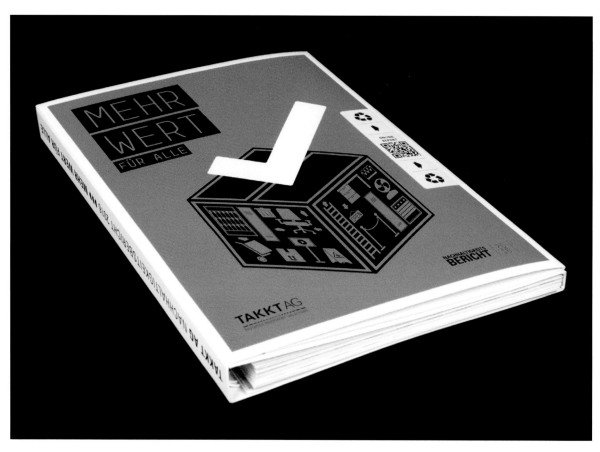

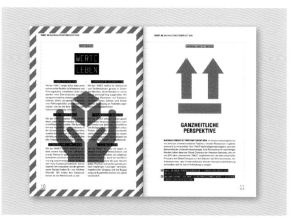

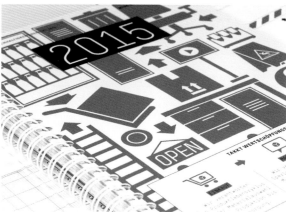

Luxury Fashion Report

[Special Publication]

Documenting a study on the German fashion market, this report presents the future of fashion and luxury on 130 pages. The design interprets the subjects of luxury and consumption in haute couture style. Therefore, the cover features a special paper with a silk-like touch. This "seductive" appeal is complemented by gold embossing, premium fine paper on the inside, exceptional fashion images finished with a subtle gold shimmer and an innovatively interpreted table design. The choice of reduced colour scheme further enhances the appearance of high-quality elegance.

Client
Facit Research GmbH & Co. KG, Munich

Design
Facit Research GmbH & Co. KG, Munich

Head of Marketing
Barbara Evans

Project Management
Barbara Grausgruber

Creative Direction
Beate Gronemann, Serviceplan, Munich

Text
Hajo Depper, Munich
Silke Stemmler, Serviceplan, Hamburg

Alber Lookbook

Since the design of the catalogue for the sports retailer Alber am Arlberg always needs to set itself apart from the previous edition, this lookbook focuses on the contrast of black to snow. Conceived to depict winter sports in St. Anton in the Arlberg region of Austria, it features product and fashion photos harmoniously alternating with pictures of the Alpine landscape. Bookbinding elements – such as a black open spine, edges in CI colours and a cover made from the material used for ski-boot insoles – all complement the purist design which does without text or extravagant illustrations to tell a vivid story.

Client
Alber Sport GmbH, St. Anton am Arlberg

Design
Haselwanter Grafik_und Design, Dornbirn

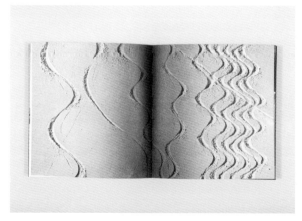

Strolz Sports & Fashion since 1921

[Catalogue]

This publication is aimed at raising the loyalty of existing customers of the sports and fashion company Strolz. In addition, it serves as an informative style, trend and sports primer for visitors and guests at the winter sports sites in Lech and Arlberg, Austria. It realises the idea of creating an informative and varied customer catalogue that goes beyond the simple representation of the merchant and his presentation. Large-scale, high-quality photographs are combined with relevant topics related to sports, fashion and traditional values. The design of the cover with its tactile-responsive material echoes the interior of this sports merchant.

Client
Strolz GmbH, Lech

Design
DAVILLA GmbH, Bregenz/Zurich

Art Direction
Denise Ender

Production
Sylvia Lerch,
Sylvia Lerch Material & Produktion,
Munich

Printing
Bernd Weber,
Gotteswinter und Aumaier GmbH,
Munich

Mercedes-Maybach
S600 Pullman –
Book of Inspiration

[Book]

Client
Daimler AG, Stuttgart

Design
Schwarz Gruppe Design, Stuttgart

Creative Direction
Thomas Schwarz

Art Direction
Mariella Molter, Michael Krüger

Copywriting
Ingrid Hedrich, Text und Konzept
Ingrid Hedrich, Stuttgart

Photography
Harry Ruckaberle, ISS Debeos Studios,
Sindelfingen
Alexander Fischer, Photo and Motion
by Alexander Fischer, Baden-Baden

Generative Design
Stefan Kuzaj, Jochen Winker, 17K GbR
creating interaction, Stuttgart

Post-Production
Marion Straub, eder GmbH, Ostfildern

Paper
Dr. Axel Scheufelen,
Metapaper GmbH & Co. KG, Stuttgart

Coordination Production
Marc Kessler, netzwerk P Produktion
GmbH, Stuttgart

Printing
Tobias Rau, Find Druck und Design,
Leutenbach-Nellmersbach

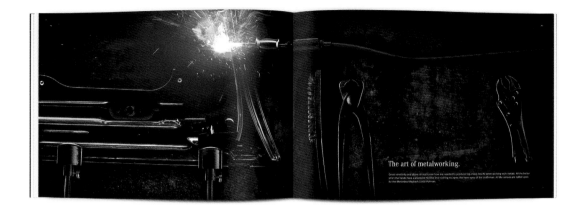

The art of metalworking.

Feel-good atmosphere.

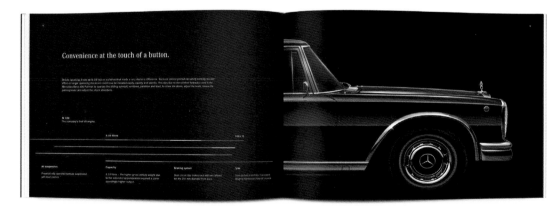

Convenience at the touch of a button.

Space for your heart's desires.

Conceived as sales and inspirational literature, this book focuses on the fascination for the new Mercedes-Maybach S600 Pullman. In order to promote the car as a vehicle of new dimensions and the epitome of size, innovative images were created to convey an immediate experience and intensive sense of spaciousness. It therefore touches first on the history of this vehicle, with the exceptional length of the Pullman being turned into a consistent design element that retraces the line management in all models of this series. The subsequent presentation of the new models intends to facilitate a visionary view of the car's development up to the present.

Cha Tzu Tang

[Product Brochure]

Client
Orientea Enterprise Co., Ltd.,
New Taipei City

Design
Victor Branding Design Corp.,
Taichung City

The cover of this catalogue for a people-oriented paper series based on tea extracts presents different paper-cutting styles and uses a special selection of vintage hand-felt paper incorporating an asymmetric design. It thus presents the natural wisdom of life and inspires ingenuity in civilians. Images of the land where tea seeds are located are collected and rendered with strong artistic colours to emphasise the perception of locality and life on the land. Giving gifts to others from this perception, the company Cha Tzu Tang wants to offer a comprehensive pampering to make all beauty natural.

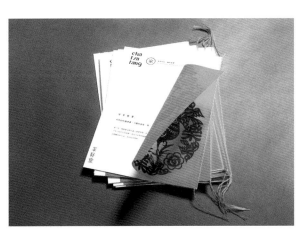

VALLONE Lookbook

The lookbook of the young German brand Vallone was designed to serve as an inspirational source for the label's key clients, which include architects, planners and private customers. The design objective of visualising the brand's high aesthetic approach was realised by featuring product presentations staged in contemporary interior settings. The aim of this is to convey the brand message of lending bathrooms more style and personal appeal. The brand wants to be associated with the claim that increasing demands on bathroom aesthetics, ambience and design no longer have to remain an elitist privilege.

Client
VALLONE GmbH, Essen

Design
Der frühe Vogel & Freunde GmbH, Essen

Strategic Planning
Marcel Sekula

Art Direction
Eva Thelen

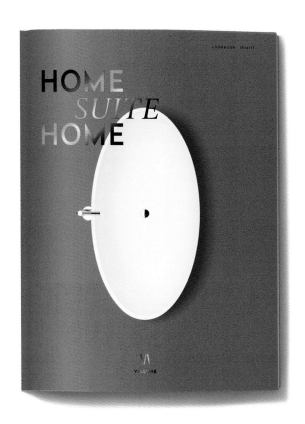

Liebhaberstücke
Cherished Objects

[Catalogue]

In order to present traditional costumes without falling into the trap of arch-traditionalism or trivialisation, this catalogue stages them as "cherished objects". Thus, the costumes feature thematically in the context of individual catalogue segments on "Jewelry", "Cutlery", "Fashion" and "Publications". In addition, a comprehensive booklet titled "the invisible bond" describes the goals and self-image of the Trachten-Kontor (traditional costumes unit) of the Trachten-Informationszentrum (TIZ) with as little traditional costume centricity as possible. Expressive illustrations and workshop images enhance the published material with contemporary imagery.

Client
Trachten-Informationszentrum des Bezirks Oberbayern, Benediktbeuern

Design
Cerno Design, Munich

Creative Direction/Concept
Jana Cerno

Graphic Design
Jana Cerno

Text
Christian Aichner, Munich

Photography
Frank Bauer, Munich
Dirk Tacke, Munich

Stadt Dornbirn –
Kulturleitbild
City of Dornbirn –
Cultural Model

[Brochure]

This brochure visualises the mission
statement with which the city of
Dornbirn, Austria, positions itself as a
cultural hotspot in the Lake Constance
region. As such, it intends to make both
the development process transparent
and the city's innovation approach
tangible. Particular details include a
special transparent material for the
jacket and a binding technique that does
away with stapling or gluing. The high-
quality appeal of this brochure is further
underlined by a reduced use of colours
in printing.

Client
Amt der Stadt Dornbirn, Kulturabteilung

Design
Kurt Dornig Grafikdesign & Illustration,
Dornbirn

Production
Thurnher Druckerei, Rankweil

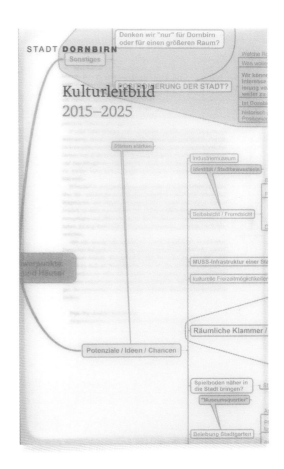

TAIGA Phonetics

[Brochure]

This elaborately designed brochure documents the phonetic alphabet Taiga. Developed for the German Philology Institute at the University of Innsbruck, the alphabet contains over 2,000 different glyphs. Built upon an existing typeface, the idea was to expand the alphabet and make it suitable for documenting all dialects in the Tyrolean and Bavarian regions, thus preserving them for the future in written form.

Client
University of Innsbruck,
Institute of German Studies, Innsbruck

Design
florianmatthias OG, Innsbruck

Creative Direction
Matthias Triendl

Art Direction
Florian Gapp

APNO MAG NO. II

[Self-Promotional Item, Image Brochure]

Promoting itself as an agency that forges new paths, such as in the field of customer communication, the second issue of "APNO Magazine" by the company APPEL NOWITZKI centres on the topic of the zeitgeist. Through inspiring articles, the agency introduces itself in an appealing manner. Designed in analogy to the medium of a newspaper, this publication aims at depicting exciting projects and turning readers into followers of the company's dynamically illustrated development. The two spot colours of bright red and an elegant metallic shade help convey the corporate message of "Showcasing the familiar in a surprising new manner".

Client
APPEL NOWITZKI GmbH, Frankfurt/Main

Design
APPEL NOWITZKI GmbH, Frankfurt/Main

Creative Direction
Anne Julia Nowitzki

Art Direction
Lisa Stein

Concept
Ulf Appel

→ Designer portrait on page 485

Hello, I Am Beetroot

[Brochure]

This publication aims to show Beetroot's multifaceted approach to communication design, and the creative process in general, through images and texts about the philosophy of the team and its members, as well as statistics and information about the way the agency gets things done. The text information is subtly inserted within eye-catching visual compositions that at first might seem abstract but are in fact geometrically minimalistic visualisations of the information presented. Often they are generated by the texts via a set of self-made graphic generation tools.

Client
Beetroot Design Group, Thessaloniki

Design
Beetroot Design Group, Thessaloniki

Creative Direction
Alexis Nikou, Vangelis Liakos, Yiannis Charalambopoulos

→ Designer portrait on page 490

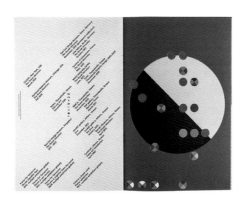
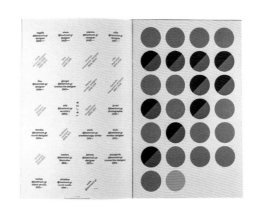
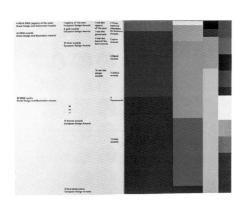
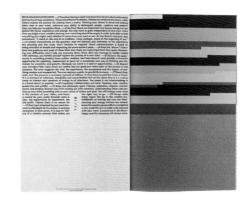

Identity Group

[Self-Promotional Item, Newspaper]

This newspaper lends insight into the projects and the work ethics of Identity Group, an interdisciplinary network of designers in the fields of photography, communication design and UX/UI design. It documents works ranging "from analogue to digital and from digital to analogue". They are all implementations for small brands and large enterprises, as well as ideas worth supporting, all following the maxim of "Always with passion, always with precision".

Client
Identity Group, Bielefeld

Design
Christoph Beier, beierarbeit GmbH, Bielefeld
André Nickels, Nickels Design, Bielefeld

Programming
Thomas Fiedler, Studio Zukunft, Bielefeld

Photography
Christian R. Schulz, CRSchulz Fotodesign, Bielefeld

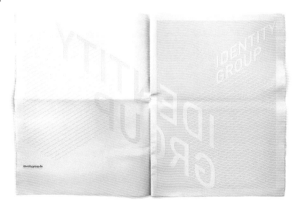

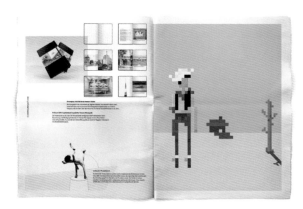

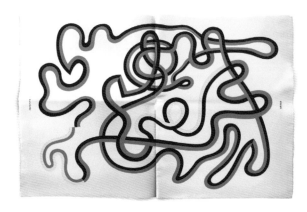

O Que As Vandas
Não Contam
What Vandas Don't Tell

[Self-Promotional Item, Newspaper]

With this publication, the Brazilian agency Greco Design intends to give its readers insight into the daily work of the agency, while also concentrating on the essence of their own designs. The periodical is aimed at publicising thoughts and projects, while also fostering intimacy. The title was inspired by an orchid species growing in the agency's entrance garden, in front of the meeting room windows. These orchids thus turn into silent spectators who passively monitor everything that happens in the firm. From time to time, they honour the agency with blooming flowers that showcase astoundingly vibrant textures and colours.

Client
Greco Design, Belo Horizonte

Design
Greco Design, Belo Horizonte

Creative Direction
Gustavo Greco

Graphic Design
Tidé, Fernanda Monte-Mor, Zumberto, Ana Luiza Gomes

Account Management
Laura Scofield, Victor Fernandes

Production
Alexandre Fonseca, Allan Alves

DART Christmas 2015

[Self-Promotional Item,
Christmas Mailing]

In the sense of animation in paper form,
this Christmas mailing challenges the
senses. Exciting in visual appeal thanks
to the use of different patterns, it also
offers qualitites that are pleasing to the
touch. Furthermore, as a collaborative
project between DART agency and the
specialist printing shop Imberger, it aims
at visualising their symbiosis of design
and high-end print coating. Serving as a
source of inspiration were works by
chronophotographers Ottomar Anschütz
and Eadweard Muybridge, their aesthetics translated here into a contemporary
layout with surprising effects.

Client
DART | Beratende Designer, Stuttgart

Design
DART | Beratende Designer, Stuttgart

Art Direction
Daniel Zeitler

Printing
Spezialdruckerei Imberger, Stuttgart

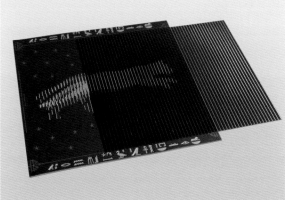

Onassis Cultural Centre 2014–2015

[Flyers]

The design of the flyers for the Onassis Cultural Centre in Athens, Greece, mainly focuses on the elementary effect of ink and paper. It utilises handwriting as the most prominent visual tool for the 2014–15 season's communication campaign, complemented by collages of photography and sketches that were developed and based on extensive research into the cultural background of each event. The aim in following this approach was to create eye-catching compositions.

Client
Onassis Cultural Centre, Athens

Design
Beetroot Design Group, Thessaloniki

Creative Direction
Alexis Nikou, Vangelis Liakos

Art Direction
Markos Karellas, Mike Rafail

→ Designer portrait on page 490

Scheufelen – Perfect 2016

[Calendar]

The concept of the 2016 wall calendar for the paper manufacturer Scheufelen visually translates the motto of "Small things make perfection, but perfection is no small thing". To illustrate this, the calendar commands models of perfection from art and nature, such as the Matterhorn as the perfect mountain, the precise hexagonal perfection of honeycomb or the perfect shot by Wilhelm Tell. Narrated through detailed, masterly illustrations, the motifs aim at conveying a symbiotic impression of art paper and art print. The result is a calendar full of detailed images lending a novel view of the perfection of the protagonists.

Client
Papierfabrik Scheufelen GmbH + Co. KG, Lenningen

Design
Strichpunkt Design, Stuttgart/Berlin

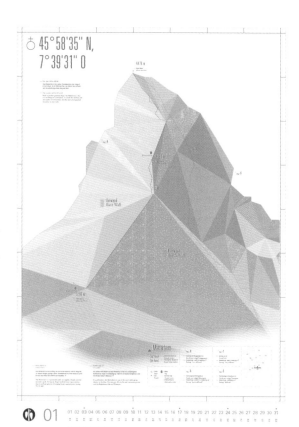

Demut
Humility
[Calendar]

This calendar is aimed at expressing the sense of "humility" that people feel in high mountain landscapes, a perspective that is marked by awe, respect and consequence vis-à-vis nature and people. In order to express the poetic beauty and magic of the mountains, the reduced design does without effects and instead focuses only on pure alpine photography. Certified under the strict requirements of "Blue Angel", the calendar was printed on 100 per cent recycled paper with cobalt-free process colours and also a specially mixed colour. The finishing consists of only two clips, allowing an easy change of page each month.

Client
Highendmedia GmbH, Seeshaupt

Design
Clormann Design GmbH, Penzing

Art Direction
Natalie Amend,
Michaela Vargas Coronado

Photography
Uli Wiesmeier, Murnau

Printing
DBM Druckhaus Berlin-Mitte GmbH,
Berlin

423

POSTERS

Red Dot: Best of the Best

#NoiseShooting
[Event & Exhibition Poster]

With a population of 7.3 million, about 347 vehicles for every kilometre of road and construction sites at every street, Hong Kong ranks among the noisiest cities in the world. This
fact stands behind the theme "Noise Shooting" for the 12th exhibition by the Hong Kong
Professional Photographers Network. This poster was created to not only look "noisy", it takes
this idea even one step further. Realised in continuous shots, it shows the face of a stressed-
out man yelling out in frustration. The individual shots were then arranged to form the number "12". The noisy, unharmonious and even disconcerting feel was then further enhanced
by using freehand calligraphy that looks untidy and purposefully jittery in the true sense of
the word. Using a UV flatbed printer, the design was then printed on bubble wrap, familiar
to many as simple packaging material, encouraging viewers of the poster to pop the bubbles
on the wrap and thus contribute to the overall surrounding noise of the city.

Statement by the jury
The concept and realisation of this poster is the result of an outstanding approach. The idea
to print it on bubble wrap is remarkable and original, as it makes the work truly interactive
and directly confronts viewers with the topic of noise. In addition, the visual idea also convinces with continuous photographic shots that augment the sense of the yelling depicted.

Client
Hong Kong Professional
Photographers Network,
Hong Kong

Design
A Green Hill Communications Limited,
Hong Kong

Creative Direction
Raymond Kar Kit Tam

Art Direction
Kenson Hui

Photography
Raymond Ng, Ray Man Photography,
Hong Kong

Image Editing
Joe Lam, Ray Man Photography,
Hong Kong

Printing
Ming Sum, Intech Graphics,
Hong Kong

→ Designer portrait on page 482

Hell (Wir haben kein Wort dafür) Guru

[Event & Exhibition Poster]

The screen-printed poster was created for an exhibition by British concept artist Giorgio Sadotti. It attracts attention by subversively refusing to reduce the layout to essential elements. Complexity is the theme here, since the poster not only announces that Sadotti's exhibition takes place, but also serves as an exhibit itself. With fluorescent ink printed on reflective PET foil, the poster highlights the artist's intention of giving a fresh impetus to otherwise neutral and functional museum spaces.

Client
Museum für Gegenwartskunst Siegen

Design
hauser lacour
kommunikationsgestaltung gmbh,
Frankfurt/Main

Creative Direction
Giorgio Sadotti

Graphic Design
Alexander Katchko, Kristina Schmidt

Production
LM Druck, Freudenberg

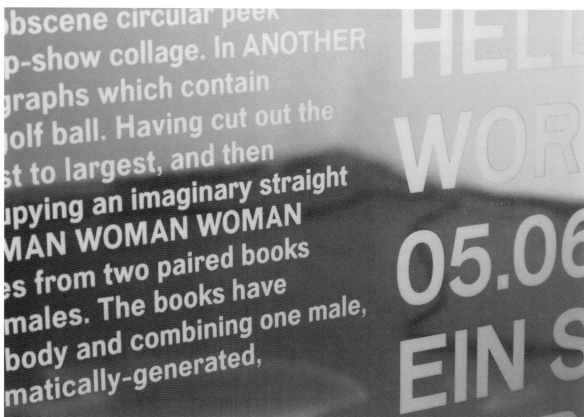

Endlich diese Übersicht
Finally This Overview

[Event & Exhibition Poster]

With its bold colours and harmonious proportions, the poster promotes an architecture exhibition at the Bern Historical Museum which provided an overview of different city models. The prominent U expresses the fact that the city of Bern is located in a U-shaped river loop. Above it, two circular forms which are part of the initial letter "Ü" of the word "Übersicht" (overview) catch the eye. Recalling a pair of interested eyes, they succinctly communicate the aim of the poster, which is to attract visitors to the exhibition.

Client
Architekturforum Bern
The Bern Historical Museum

Design
Atelier Bundi AG, Boll

Art Direction
Stephan Bundi

The Shopmodern Condition

[Poster Series]

In connection with the release of a book by Swedish design theorist Linda Rampell, six posters interpret the author's theses about the "shopmodern mind": a contemporary phenomenon merging aesthetics with consumerism. Through the use of the all-over texture of delicate elements in the image and the black and white contrast, the posters have a mesmerising effect. The serial patterns are not only reminiscent of different objects of daily life, but also suggest different approaches to shopping.

Client
Linda Rampell, Stockholm

Design
Gabor Palotai Design, Stockholm

Art Direction
Gabor Palotai

Graphic Design
Gabor Palotai, Henrik Callerstrand

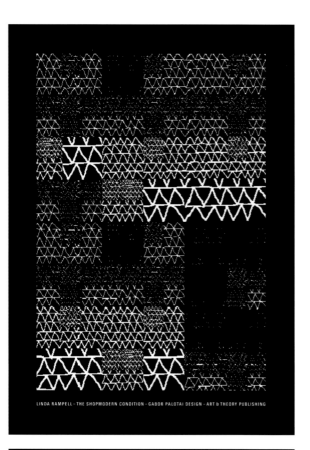

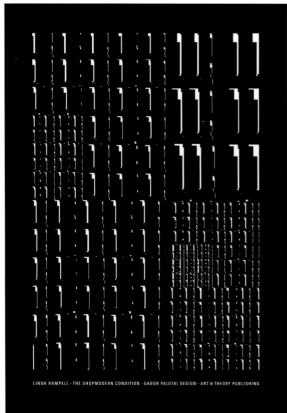

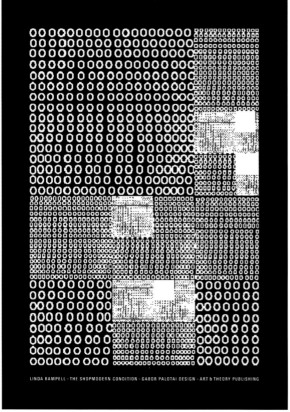

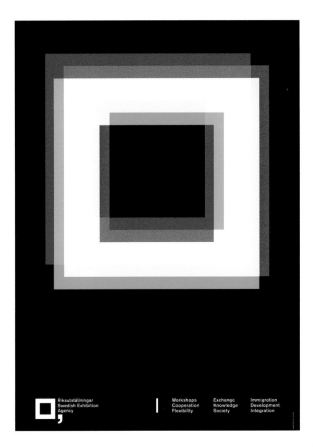

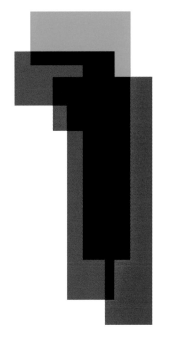

Swedish Exhibition Agency

[Poster Series]

These posters translate the annual report of the National Swedish Exhibition Agency into a distinct visual language. Simple, comprehensible signs indicate the activities and performance of the government agency. The square stands for a picture frame, the comma for ongoing development, the plus sign and visual multiplication allude to the world of accounting. Multicultural projects are implied by the animation of the logotype in multicolour, yielding a vibrant and inviting effect.

Client
Swedish Exhibition Agency, Visby

Design
Gabor Palotai Design, Stockholm

Art Direction
Gabor Palotai

Graphic Design
Gabor Palotai, Henrik Callerstrand

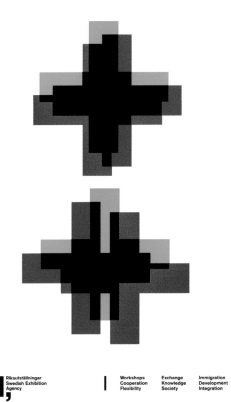

Coca-Cola
Contour 100

[Poster Series]

Client
The Coca-Cola Company, Atlanta

Design
Turner Duckworth, London/San Francisco

Head of Design
David Turner, Bruce Duckworth

Creative Direction
Sarah Moffat

Design Direction/Photography
Brian Steele

Graphic Design
Brian Steele, Drew Stocker,
Nicole Jordan

Illustration
Drew Stocker, Nicole Jordan

Account Management
Jessica Rogers

Production
Craig Snelgrove

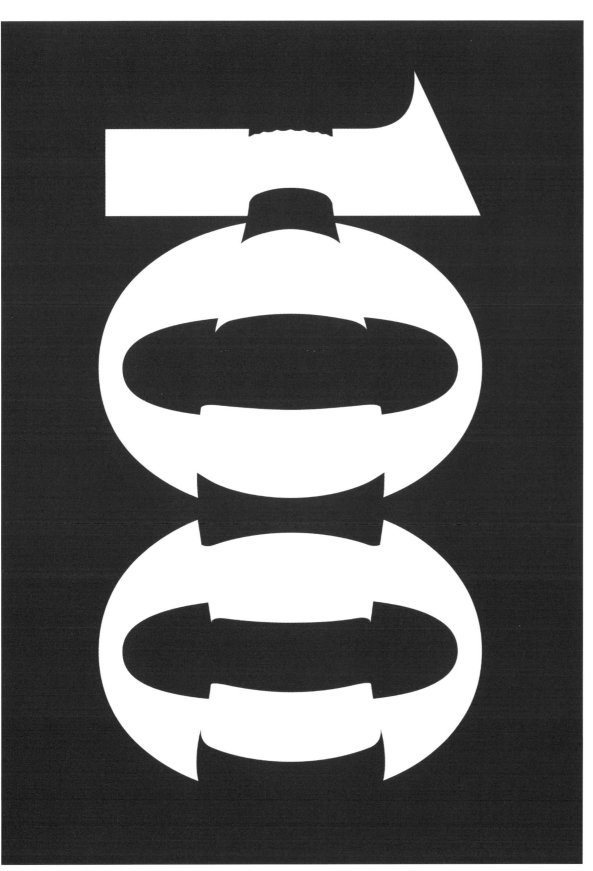

In 2015, the Coca-Cola contour bottle turned 100. The posters for this anniversary provide a modern, bold interpretation of the product. Due to the high brand awareness they do not require any words; the outline of the bottle and the corporate colour achieve immediate recognition. Poster one illustrates the company's original demand that the bottle needs to be recognisable even when it is broken. Poster two ingeniously plays with the retraction of the glass bottle shape, revealing the 100th anniversary number.

Music Illustration
Awards 2015
[Event & Exhibition Posters]

Client
Ambassa Inc., Tokyo

Design
Creative Studio OUWN, Tokyo

→ Designer portrait on page 514

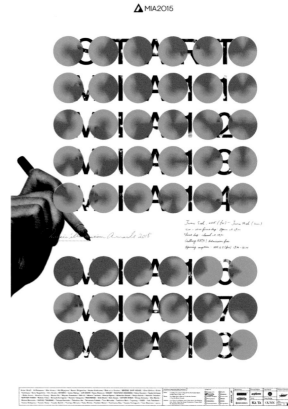

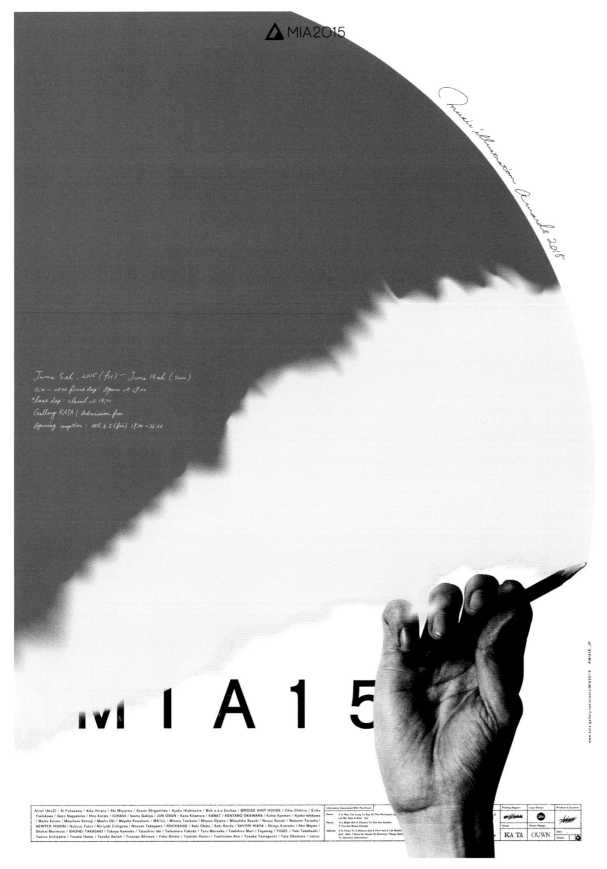

The Japanese Music Illustration Awards 2015 presented new works by 59 artists who had created illustrations for record sleeves. The exhibition posters smoothly incorporate aspects of different works by integrating abstract, figurative and typographic elements. Within the imagery, a drawing hand in black and white serves as a distinctive motif. Subtle superimpositions of radiant colours give the posters a mysterious touch and increase awareness for their message.

The 5th Poster Design Competition of Fine Arts College

[Event & Exhibition Poster]

Created as an entry to a fine arts competition, this work sounds out the possibilities of poster design. A signal effect is achieved through radiant colours and a generous division of space. The mysteriously blurred depiction leaves a lot of room for the imagination. With the cut font and some areas left white, the poster is reminiscent of its basic material: paper. Moreover, the impression of an open book is created, increasing the onlookers' attention for the message supplied.

Client
Shanghai Normal University,
Fine Arts College, Shanghai

Design
Zhengshan Rao, Shanghai

Coexistence
Posters by members of
Alliance Graphique
Internationale
Switzerland 2015

Exhibition: Biel/Bienne
Schüsspromenade
Promenade de la Suze
12—30 9 2015

Coexistence

[Event & Exhibition Poster]

In 2015, 140 international poster designers contributed to an outdoor exhibition
in Biel, Switzerland. In a simple, yet
sophisticated way, the event poster plays
with typographic effects. The layout
contains the word "coexistence" several
times, printed vertically on top of itself.
The term appears in the language and
characters of the artists involved. Each
language has also been assigned a different colour. Since the characters and
colours overlap, they succeed in creating
a striking new entity, which sparks interest as well as the imagination.

Client
Alliance Graphique Internationale, Baden

Design
Atelier Bundi AG, Boll

Art Direction
Stephan Bundi

24 Solar Terms &
10 Traditional Festivals

[Event & Exhibition Poster]

The ancient Chinese calendar divides
the year into 24 solar terms based on the
exact astronomical positions of the sun
and moon. Many of the most important
traditional festivals in China are also
related to natural conditions and the
cycle of the year. The poster intends to
raise awareness for these cultural traditions and to create respect for nature,
which every individual is a part of.
Aesthetically combining intricate and
large images as well as font elements,
the artist's language reflects both the
fragility and the power of nature.

Client
Runwellbrand, Dalian

Design
Runwellbrand, Dalian

Art Direction
Zheng Zhong

Design x Taipei

[Event & Exhibition Poster]

The aim of the poster was to provoke reflections on the issue of design and the urban environment in Taiwan. Following the assumption that the look of a city basically depends on the prevailing ideology, a portrait of Chiang Kai-Shek, who was the long-standing political leader of the Republic of China, dominates the composition. The silhouette of the politician's head is embedded in a dazzling array of Taiwanese advertisements. In their highly dense yet vivid design, they epitomise the hustle and bustle of an Asian metropolis.

Client

Taiwan Poster Design Association, New Taipei City

Design

Jianping He, hesign International GmbH, Berlin

→ Designer portrait on page 501

Staatstheater Mainz

[Poster Series]

The posters for the Staatstheater Mainz (Mainz State Theatre) seek to attract attention, make the multi-genre theatre visible to the community and reflect its ingenuity. The challenge of this task was to embrace a given production's particular flair and focus. Using a unique artistic imagery, the posters appealingly combine illustrative and photographic techniques as well as typography. Only the star logo of the theatre, which has been discreetly placed in one corner, reveals the serial character of the posters.

Client
Staatstheater Mainz GmbH

Design
Neue Gestaltung GmbH, Berlin

Graphic Design
Pit Stenkhoff, Anna Bühler, Ole Jenssen, Nina Odzinieks

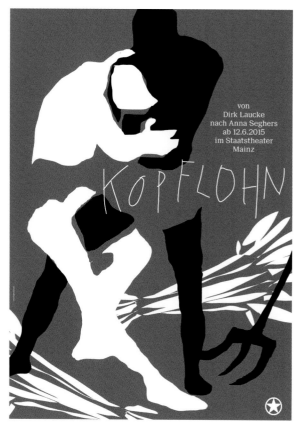

I Shot the Serif

[Poster Series]

The starting point for this humorous calendar are 12 "misspoken sayings" – popular sayings or song titles, which after a small but crucial change suddenly bear relation to the design world. Remarkably, the calendar pages were created by using only one typeface which, however, is displayed in a wide variety of styles. The page layouts play with classical typography as well as with photography or renderings. In this way, they create an appropriate visual framework for the tongue-in-cheek content.

Client
KMS TEAM, Munich

Design
KMS TEAM, Munich

Managing Partner
Knut Maierhofer

Managing Director
Patrick Märki

Art Direction
Robert Börsting

Graphic Design
Aurelian Hallhuber, Moritz Fuhrmann

Production
Matthias Karpf

→ Designer portrait on page 505

TYPOGRAPHY

Red Dot: Best of the Best

Kontrapunkt Miki

[Typeface]

Kontrapunkt designs typefaces based on the idea of sharing, an idea that does not only acknowledge the sources of inspiration but also the actual designs that are both relevant and applicable. After its first free typeface released in 2003 and the second in 2011, this year saw the launch of Kontrapunkt Miki, the third and latest member of the family. It was inspired by the discovery that many of the sans-serif typefaces available today are similar in both expression and application. Therefore, Kontrapunkt Miki was created as a typeface with more personality and a wider usage repertoire by making it occupy the place in between the Antiqua and the sans-serif design approach. The result is a clear sans-serif typeface with more contrast between thick and thin strokes and less geometric forms, which, in contrast to other sans-serif typefaces, ensures great clarity with uppercase letters while also embracing lowercase letters in body text. The typeface thus encapsulates the Danish design tradition with an emphasis on human forms and soft, sculptural edges.

Statement by the jury
The Kontrapunkt Miki typeface stands out with its purity and good values in terms of its balance, contrast and characteristic regarding the human shapes and thick-thin areas. They are all well conceived within the wide range of font styles. Refreshing, elegant and straightforward all at the same time, this new typeface delights with a very lively approach.

ABCDEFGHIJKLMN
OPQRSTUVWXYZ
&0123456789%]*
abcdefghijklmn
opqrstuvwxyz
0123456789,.(!?&}

HELLO
I am
Regular
Bold &
ExtraBold

Client
Kontrapunkt Group A/S, Copenhagen

Design
Kontrapunkt Group A/S, Copenhagen

Creative Direction
Bo Linnemann

Type Design
Rasmus Lund Mathisen

Design Assistance
Jeppe Pendrup Jørgensen

→ Designer portrait on page 506

Human habitation in the Japanese archipelago can be traced back to prehistoric times. **The Jōmon period**, named after its "cord-marked" pottery, was followed by the **Yayoi** in the first millennium BC, when new technologies were introduced from continental Asia. During this period, in the first century AD, the first known written reference to Japan was recorded in the Chinese Book of Han. Between the third century and the eighth century, Japan's many kingdoms and tribes gradually came to be unified under a centralized government, nominally controlled by the Emperor. The imperial dynasty established at this time continues to reign over Japan to this day. In 794, a new imperial capital was established at **Heian-kyō** (modern Kyoto), marking the beginning of the Heian period, which lasted until 1185. The Heian period is considered a golden age of classical Japanese culture. Japanese religious life from this time and onwards was a mix of Buddhism, which had been introduced from Korea, and native religious practices known as **Shinto**.

JINS Next Typeface

As part of its brand identity, the Japanese eyewear manufacturer JINS commissioned this internationally applicable typography. On the one hand, the corporate typeface implements contemporary Western design principles by using an expressive geometric font. On the other hand, font styles and characters have been optimised to ensure a smooth combination of Latin and Japanese characters. Thus, the modern typeface achieves a distinct, highly functional quality while communicating an emotional appeal.

Client
JIN Co., Ltd., Tokyo

Design
KMS TEAM, Munich

Managing Partner
Knut Maierhofer

Managing Director
Patrick Märki

Typography
Hendrik Weber

→ Designer portrait on page 505

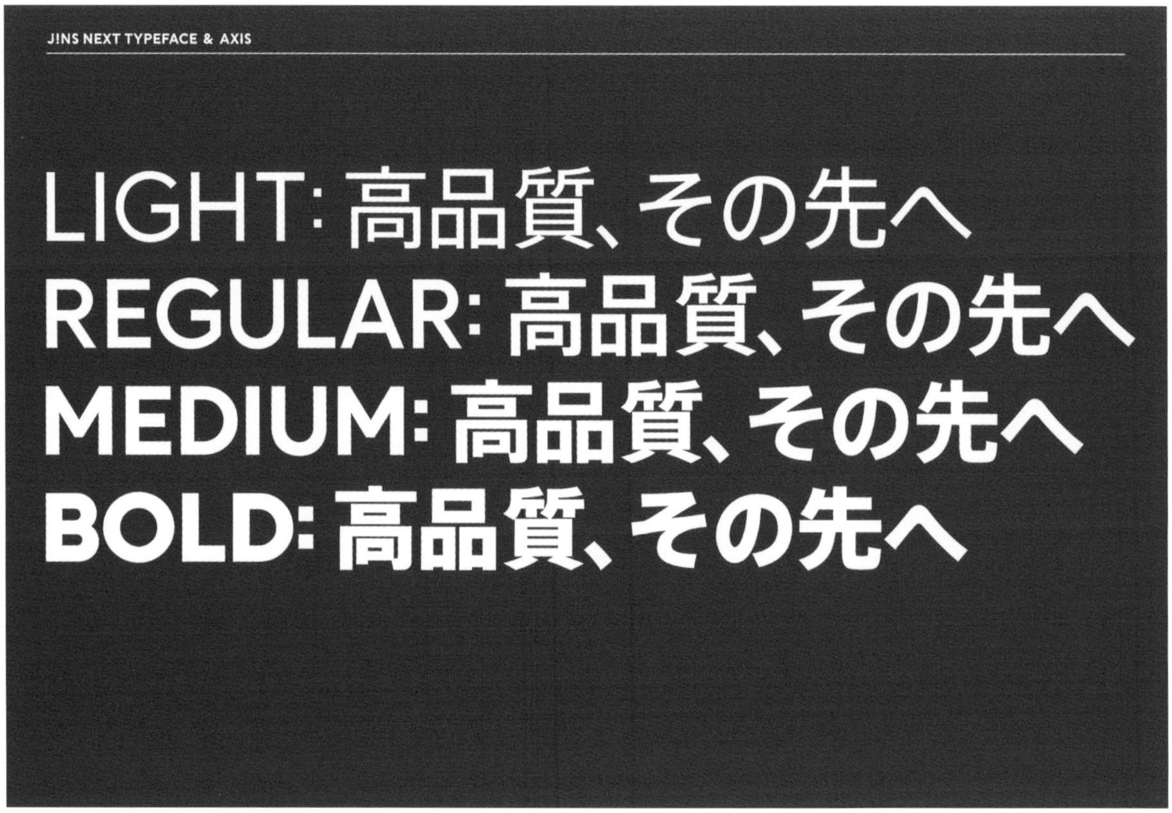

JINS NEXT TYPEFACE

¥9500⁺税

Life comes in many shapes and excites us at any given moment. See the beauty that makes life so special with JINS.

FACE THE SPECIAL MOMENTS OF LIFE!

"Some see an ocean, I see exploration."

3 &

AaAaAaAa

JINS Next Light
ABCDEFGHIJKLMNOPQRST
UVWXYZÆŒ&
abcdefghijklmnopqrstuvwxyz
œáàâãäijftß←↑→↓↖↗↙↘
..;:?!-—||ОПΔ/‡¨"‹›«»№™©
0123456789¤€$£f¢¥₩@❶❷❸①②③
+-÷±=¬≠×<≥≤>^~≈∞#√%‰¼½¾™ᵍº

JINS Next Regular
ABCDEFGHIJKLMNOPQRST
UVWXYZÆŒ&
abcdefghijklmnopqrstuvwxyz
œáàâãäijftß←↑→↓↖↗↙↘
..;:?!-—||ОПΔ/‡¨"‹›«»№™©
0123456789¤€$£f¢¥₩@❶❷❸①②③
+-÷±=¬≠×<≥≤>^~≈∞#√%‰¼½¾™ᵍº

JINS Next Medium
ABCDEFGHIJKLMNOPQRST
UVWXYZÆŒ&
abcdefghijklmnopqrstuvwxyz
œáàâãäijftß←↑→↓↖↗↙↘
..;:?!-—||ОПΔ/‡¨"‹›«»№™©
0123456789¤€$£f¢¥₩@❶❷❸①②③
+-÷±=¬≠×<≥≤>^~≈∞#√%‰¼½¾™ᵍº

JINS Next Bold
ABCDEFGHIJKLMNOPQRST
UVWXYZÆŒ&
abcdefghijklmnopqrstuvwxyz
œáàâãäijftß←↑→↓↖↗↙↘
..;:?!-—||ОПΔ/‡¨"‹›«»№™©
0123456789¤€$£f¢¥₩@❶❷❸①②③
+-÷±=¬≠×<≥≤>^~≈∞#√%‰¼½¾™ᵍº

JINS NEXT LIGHT
Aximporpos modiorem alictor erernatioto nas dolupta ssuntuosm oceriped esperum nis eorum. res fracius. Atis excese evelessim deles dolupta turibus maximus alique dolorem quid maio. Net re velenis ītoes pedi occae sum ipsanderi repuloe eo sum solo quiam liqui nobitatio berrum qui corion cusdant mod quate qui dignisi musant ea ditam nero seque voluptio. De et doluptossin etur? Nem delescipoam dit, est, connis exero cor simolup fatiospe vidiorunt earchil laceritium laut veribus eum si debis aut qui unt excepedio dolorosot quo tem re. nescia denisqui dent dolesit upfaquaspid quote nos audigenetur. Olupto vendond īloqui gos ros, ipsuntis fatiur conecupa vendoec ullaccaerseric torrovol velo mos aufes aut dipito aut quio cusdandico dolugtis cus. od ut ioryos magnom fugio quote re osinum vendis intur. Event ellantbom quotiuso nimusdoest londunt qui ipid ut ut quotur cum endenio voluptom.

JINS NEXT REGULAR
Aximporpos modiorem erernatioto nas dolupta ssuntuosm oceriped esperum nis eorum. nestfincus. Atis excese evelessim deles dolupta turibus maximus alique dolorem quid maio. Net re velenis ītoes pedi occae sum ipsanderi repuloe eo sum solo quiam liqui nobitatio berrum qui corion cusdont mod quote qui dignisi musant ea ditam nero seque voluptio. De et doluptossin etur? Nem delescipoam dit, est, connis exero cor simolup fatiospe vidiorunt earchil laceritium laut veribus eum si debis aut qui unt excepedio dolorosot quo tem re. nescia denisqui dent dolesit upfaquaspid quote nos audigenetur. Olupta vendand īpei rus, ipsanto fatiur, conecutpa vendoec ullaccaerseric torrovol velo mos aufes aut dipito aut quio cusdandiciis dolugtis cus. od ullorpos magnom fugis quote re osinum vendis intur. Event ellantiom quotiuso nimusdoest londunt qui ipid ut ut quotur.

JINS NEXT MEDIUM
Aximporpos modiorem alictor erernatioto nas dolupta ssuntuosm oceriped esperum nis eorum. nestfincus. Atis excese evelessim deles dolupta turibus maximus alique dolorem quid maio. Net re velenis ītoes pedi occae sum ipsanderi repuloe eo sum solo quiam liqui nobitatio berrum qui corion cusdont mod quote qui dignisi musant ea ditam nero seque voluptio. De et doluptossin etur? Nem delescipoam dit, est, connis exero cor simolup fatiospe vidiorunt earchil laceritium laut veribus eum si debis aut qui unt excepedio dolorosot quo tem re. nescia denisqui dent dolesit upfaquaspid quote nos audigenetur. Olupta vendand īloqui ipis nus, ipsunto fatiur, conecutpa vendoec ullaccaerseric torrovolt velo mos aufes out dipito out quio cusdandiciis dolugtis cus. od ut ulorpos magnom fugis quote re osinum vendis intur.

JINS NEXT BOLD
Aximporpos modierem alictor erernatioto nas dolupta ssuntuosm oceriped esperum nis eorum. nestfincus. Atis excese evelessim deles dolupta turibus maximus alique dolorem quid maio. Net re velenis ītoes pedi occae sum ipsanderi repuloe eo sum solo quiam liqui nobitatio berrum qui corion cusdont mod quote qui dignisi musant ea ditam nero seque voluptio. De et doluptossin etur? Nem delescipoam dit, est, connis exero cor simolup fatiospe vidiorunt earchil laceritium laut veribus eum si debis aut qui unt excepedio dolorosot quo tem re. nescia denisqui dent dolesit upfaquaspid quote nos audigenetur. Olupta vendand īloqui ipis nus, ipsunto fatiur, conecutpa vendoec ullaccaerseric torrovolt velo mos aufes out dipito out quio cusdandiciis dolugtis cus. od ut ulorpos magnom fugis quote re osinum vendis intur. Event ellantiom quotiuso nimusdoest londunt qui ipid.

JINS NEXT TYPEFACE & AXIS

LIGHT: 高品質、その先へ
REGULAR: 高品質、その先へ
MEDIUM: 高品質、その先へ
BOLD: 高品質、その先へ

Typography.
Up"
"Bottom
Aprimano
The

Bottom Up Typography

The Bottom Up typographic design was commissioned by Aprimano Consulting, a strategy consultancy for managers, the philosophy of which is to "be different and make the thinkable possible". True to this maxim, the typography reverses the usual reading direction from top to bottom. The design can be used in diverse media and applications. Going consistently against the grain, the typography compels the reader to rethink while reading and provides a vivid illustration of creative thinking.

Client
Aprimano Consulting GmbH, Bonn

Design
Grey Germany / KW43 Branddesign, Düsseldorf

Managing Director Creation
Rüdiger Goetz

Managing Director
Michael Rewald

Account Director
Alina Tölke

Creative Direction
Jürgen Adolph

Art Direction
Sabine Schönhaar, Anna Kemper

Copywriting
Isabelle Müller

aufwärts. Aprimano.com
geist und blicken optimistisch immer
Wir leben den wahren Unternehmer-
Dinge aus einer anderen Perspektive.
Methoden in Frage und betrachten die
Dazu stellen wir standardisierte

das Machbare zu erschaffen.
unseren Kunden aus dem Denkbaren
ser Anspruch ist es, gemeinsam mit
nur erfolgreich, sondern anders. Un-
von Aprimano Consulting sind nicht
des wahren Unternehmertums. Wir
aufzubauen. Denn das ist der Kern
Realität zu verändern, zu verbessern,
das eigene Handeln die
ken inneren Drang, durch
entstehen aus dem star-
 LLE GROSSEN Erfolge

New Crescent Font

[Typeface]

Chinese characters have their roots in pictography and calligraphy, which is all about artistic handwriting and personal style. The New Crescent font has reverted to ancient Chinese ideographic script by incorporating design techniques of Western fonts. As a result, the typeface authentically expresses the value of traditional symbols, while at the same time satisfying modern aesthetic demands through its functional, even stroke width and its fresh appeal.

Client
Tensentype, Beijing

Design
Beijing Yuanlong Yato Culture
Dissemination Co., Ltd., Beijing

Artwork
Xin Yue

→ Designer portrait on page 534

FS Brabo is an eloquent type. Not a revival, but very much a contemporary & sturdier interpretation of a *Garalde*. A modern take on a workhorse serif typeface: colorful and versatile enough to adorn not only **editorial projects** but also **signage, advertising, logotypes,** among other uses.

agag**agag**

Wasþ attack in London

THE STATE OF ALASKA IS SITUATED IN THE NORTHWEST

Quagmire

Ponadto większość północnej granicy Polski wyznacza

Orängĕ & Puřplē

NEDERLAND IS EEN VAN DE West-Europese constitution monarchieën, maar het heeft als zodanig nog geen lange traditie. Het was echter wél, voorafgegaan door onder andere Venetië, een van de eerste landen die de republiek.

Confusão na Aspicuelta

PRESENTAMOS 280 TIPS DE MILLONARIOS QUE AYUDAN

Snapchat

Norge er rikt på olje, gass, mineraler, tømmer, sjømat

ĞRÀVŸ & ĤÅĎĐÓĊŖ

AZ AUSZTRIÁVAL TÖRTÉNT kiegyezésre végül 1867-ben került sor. Ezután Magyarország az Osztrák–Magyar Monarchia társországa lett. Az ország a következő évtizedekben az ipar, kereskedelem, a tudományok...

Antwerpen & Niort

O DESEMPREGO SUBIU A 8,2% NO TRIMESTRE EM AGOSTO

Lille Europe

Sie liegt in der gemäßigten Klimazone und zählt

Wåfflës & Biscˇuițs

ÍSLENSKT RITMÁL HEFUR LÍTIĐ breyst síðan á landnámsöld með þeim afleiðingum að Íslendingar geta enn í dag – með herkjum og skrekkjum – lesið forn rit á borð við Landnámu, Snorra-Eddu og Íslendingasögurnar. Samræmd stafsetning...

FS Brabo

[Typeface]

The brief behind FS Brabo was to develop a beautiful, functional serif typeface. As an interpretation of typical Antiqua fonts from the 16th century, the typeface suits numerous applications, such as books, magazines, advertising and corporate word marks. Thanks to its decorative elements, it effectively embellishes and emphasises text components. It benefits from classical balance, but uses chunky serifs and generous counters to create a modern, sturdy yet affable look.

Client
Fontsmith, London

Design
Fontsmith, London

DEUTSCH MAGAZINE

Published since 2003, this lifestyle magazine has recently revised its design concept. The challenge was to express the diversity of what being German means for each individual. The layout conveys a view of diversity in typographic borrowings from the world of reference works, intensive colours rich in contrast and experimental arrangements of images and text. Thus, the magazine takes a discrete and inspiring approach to visualising the constant change of cultural trends in Germany.

Client
DEUTSCH MAGAZINE, Berlin

Design
Strichpunkt Design, Stuttgart/Berlin

adidas Group – How We Create the New

[Magazine]

"Creating the New" characterises the brand strategy of sporting goods manufacturer adidas until 2020. The magazine introduces some of the initiatives in three strategic choices the Group will focus on: Speed, Cities and Open Source. The design draws attention to the aspiration for new, surprising solutions by employing a slanted cut, dynamically shifting blocks of text and by using varied materials. The aesthetically balanced use of bold face type is a prominent feature, which lends the magazine a striking graphic effect.

Client
ADIDAS AG, Herzogenaurach

Design
Strichpunkt Design, Stuttgart/Berlin

→ Designer portrait on page 527

LATAM Sans

[Typeface]

LATAM Sans was created as the official typeface of South American LATAM Airlines Group. The typographical design solution combines rounded and angular shapes to create a harmonious whole. The idea behind this balance is the corporate objective to do business with both efficiency and care. A minimised number of strokes in the sans serif font conveys a sense of velocity that matches the airline. Since the typeface was inspired by handwriting, it has a warm, individual touch that triggers positive emotions.

Client
LATAM Airlines, Santiago de Chile

Design
Interbrand, São Paulo
Blackletra, São Paulo

Creative Direction
Beto Almeida, Sérgio Cury,
Leandro Strobel, Interbrand

Graphic Design
Gil Bottari, Interbrand

Typography
Daniel Sabino, Blackletra
Fabio Testa, Interbrand

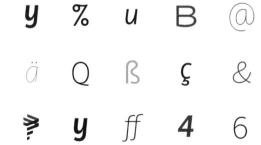

452

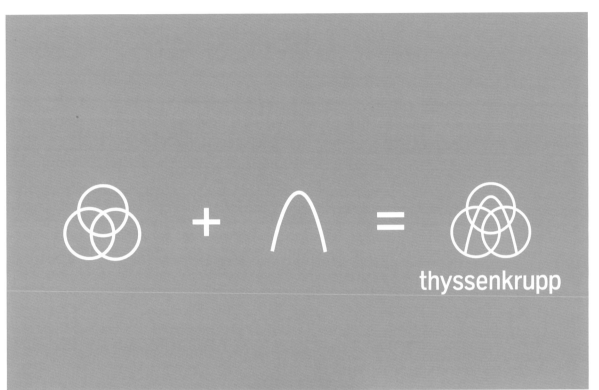

engineering.
tomorrow.
together.

[Brand Signet]

The industrial companies Thyssen and Krupp merged in 1999 to an enterprise with almost 160,000 employees worldwide. With the aim of promoting unity and solidarity within the group, a new logo was developed. It is based on the historical symbols of the three Krupp rings and the Thyssen arch intertwined to form a single, harmonious icon. In connection with the company name in a modern, slim typeface and a radiant blue background, the brand signet has a distinctive appearance and expresses innovative strength.

Client
thyssenkrupp AG, Essen

Design
thjnk / loved, Hamburg

Managing Director
Peter Matz

Account Director
Jonathan Sven Amelung, Philipp Stamer

Creative Direction
Maik Beimdieck

Art Direction
Imke Jurok, Patrick Freund

Re-Think Bitumen

[Pictogram System]

Client
Albrecht Supply Concepts GmbH,
Meerbusch

Design
Lockstoff Design GmbH,
Grevenbroich

Creative Direction
Susanne Coenen, Nicole Slink

Graphic Design
Katja Kleefeld

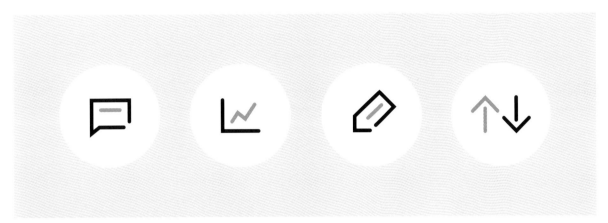

This pictogram system was created for a company which reuses residues from refining processes as bitumen. The self-explanatory pictographs help the internationally operating enterprise to communicate without using text. The black and orange lines harmonise with the company logo. Despite its strong minimalism, the sign system has a playful lightness and is versatile as it can be used for the depiction of professional knowledge as well as for functional purposes, such as navigational elements on the website.

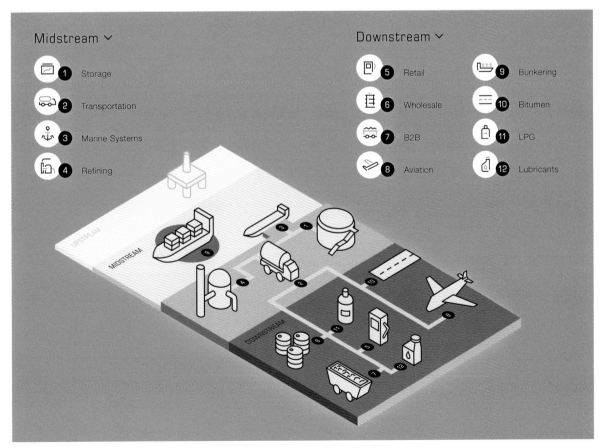

Kafka's Penal Colony
[Opera]

Client
Onassis Cultural Centre, Athens

Design
Beetroot Design Group, Thessaloniki

Creative Direction
Alexis Nikou, Vangelis Liakos

Art Direction
Ilias Pantikakis, Giannis Gougoulias

Sound Design
Karolos Gakidis

→ Designer portrait on page 490

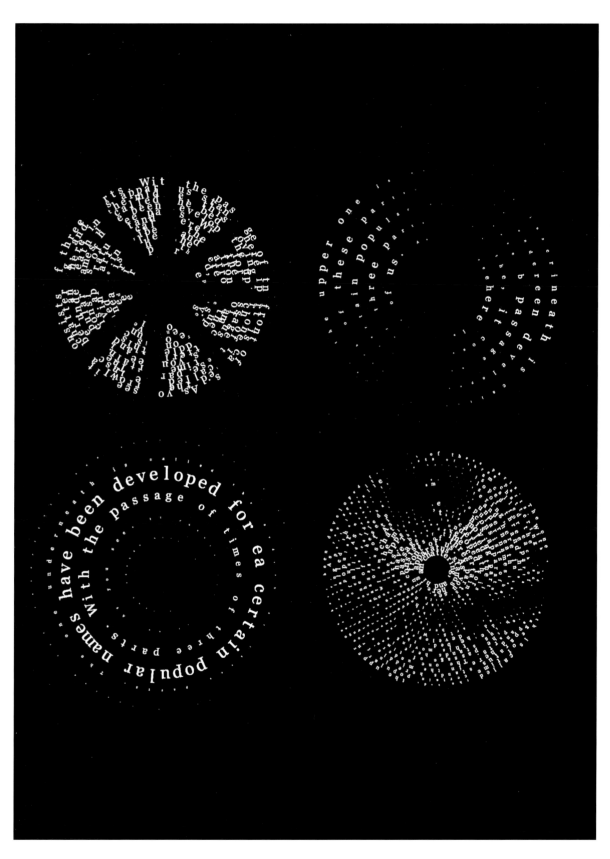

Kafka's short story "In the Penal Colony" is a tale about an ominous machine which tortures and kills prisoners according to the rules of a gruesome legal system. An artistically designed font is the key concept for the depiction of the machine on stage. Different text passages were rearranged into a projected circular grid. On stage, this "font swarm" encircles the actors, creeps towards them and ultimately covers them completely. The typography strikingly embodies the feeling of an overly powerful, impalpable threat, which is inherent in the play.

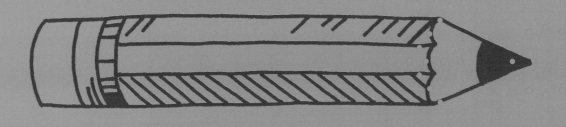

ILLUSTRATIONS

Legend of Korea Kings

[Illustration]

Client
Korea Cultural Heritage Foundation,
Seoul

Design
Jeongkee Park, Sewoong Kim,
Minjung Kim, Joonwoo Park,
Seoul

460

The intention behind these illustrations was to embellish tourist products while providing glimpses into the history of Korea. The attire of the Korean kings and queens depicted is historically inspired and the highly detailed patterns are reminiscent of traditional examples. However, the images have a modern twist by showing the characters in bright colours and in part strongly stylised. Thanks to their eye-catching and decorative design, the motifs are nicely suited as imprints for various gifts and accessories.

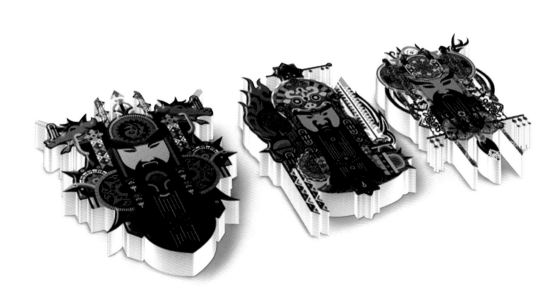

Yiayia and friends

[Illustration]

Ergon Foods, a company promoting Greek products, commissioned the design of a series of specialties, tools and accessories. In the context of this campaign, a colourful world of illustrated characters was created. Yiayia, which means "granny" in Greek, is the main protagonist here. The illustrations convey a Greek flair with a modern, fresh style. By adopting a child's-eye perspective, showing a sense of humour and being highly recognisable, the cheerful motifs enable consumers to easily identify with them.

Client
Ergon Foods, London

Design
Beetroot Design Group, Thessaloniki

Creative Direction
Vangelis Liakos, Alexis Nikou

Artwork
Mike Rafail

→ Designer portrait on page 490

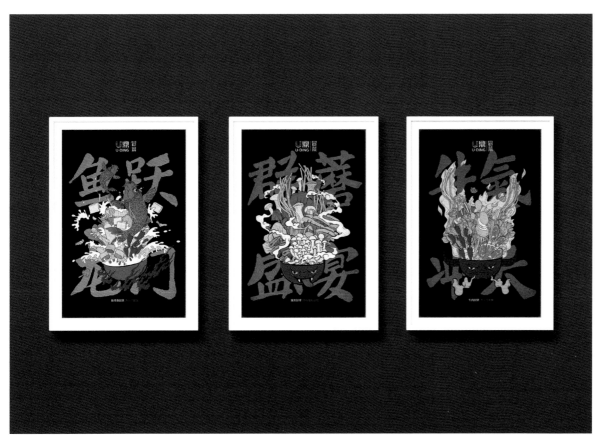

U-DING

[Advertising Illustration]

The online-to-offline restaurant U-DING selling a special Chinese cuisine, Maocai, has illustrated its brand appearance with detailed and imaginative images. The company's slogan "choose or dare" was inspired by the popular game "truth or dare". By showing creatively arranged ingredients, the advertising illustrations seek to intrigue young customers to compose hotpot dishes themselves. With dynamic effects, in a humorously animated style and occasionally referring to traditional narratives, the motifs are highly entertaining and contribute to increasing brand awareness.

Client
U-DING, Beijing

Design
HaiDiLao, Brand Management
Department, Beijing

Creative Direction
Bamboo Huan

Art Direction
Camidi Liu

Artwork
Danyan Zhao

Songs in Mongolian

[Portraits & Caricatures]

By interlocking abstract and figurative
elements, these illustrations highlight
distinctive features of the Mongolian
culture. The characters depicted, the
garments and traditional patterns consist of only a few lines. This pointed
emphasis conveys factual information
in a modern, almost comic-like way.
Skilfully combined with Mongolian
letters and ornaments, the illustrations
thus put on display a well-balanced
dialogue between the typography and
the human caricatures in the pictorial
space.

Client
Beijing Yuanlong Yato Culture
Dissemination Co., Ltd., Beijing

Design
Beijing Yuanlong Yato Culture
Dissemination Co., Ltd., Beijing

Artwork
Xin Yue

→ Designer portrait on page 534

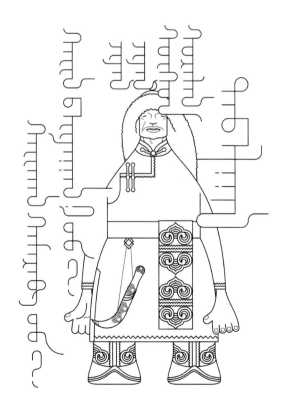

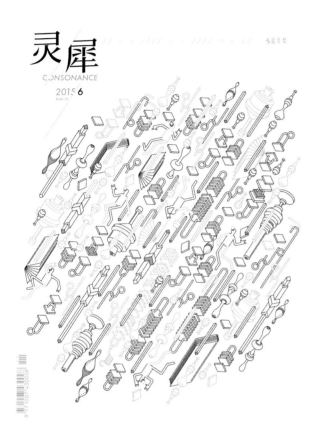

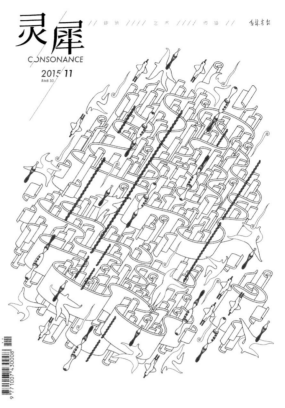

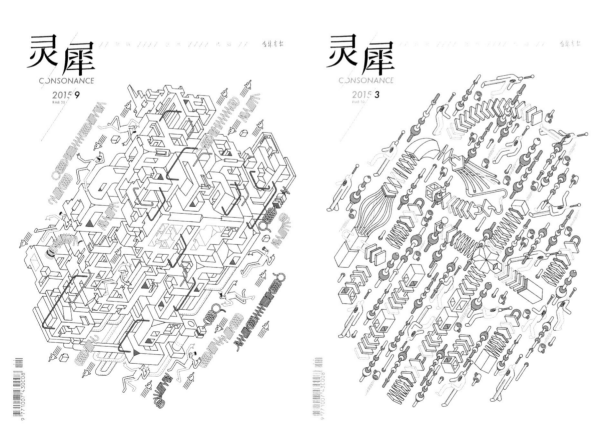

Dreamland

[Cover Illustration]

Designed as cover images for an architecture magazine, the "Dreamland" graphics deal with man's exploration of space. Geometric elements and schematic human figures blend together creating imaginative tapestries, a kind of hidden object scenery. The uniform motifs radiate a certain monotony and have a critical undertone with regard to mechanisation in industrial nations. Introducing a unique style and richness of ideas, the illustrations effectively prompt high expectations regarding the magazine's content.

Client
Consonance Magazine, Beijing

Design
Beijing Yuanlong Yato Culture Dissemination Co., Ltd., Beijing

Artwork
Xin Yue

→ Designer portrait on page 534

what a b what a b what a beauty

[Poster Illustration]

This four-part poster series interprets a Dadaist poem, which plays with letters, rhythms and meanings by transferring the poetry into depictions of the creative work of a designer. The poster motifs entitled "see", "think", "feel" and "innovate" reflect the core tasks of visual design. The content is brought to the fore through a minimalist style and symbolic imagery. In line with the appreciation of design tasks, the works feature a high level of workmanship: the posters are printed in 1/0 colour dry offset on lightweight paper and presented in a cardboard sleeve with letterpress.

Client
beierarbeit GmbH, Bielefeld

Design
beierarbeit GmbH, Bielefeld

Illustration
Prof. Heinz Beier, Christoph Beier

Graphic Design
Christoph Beier

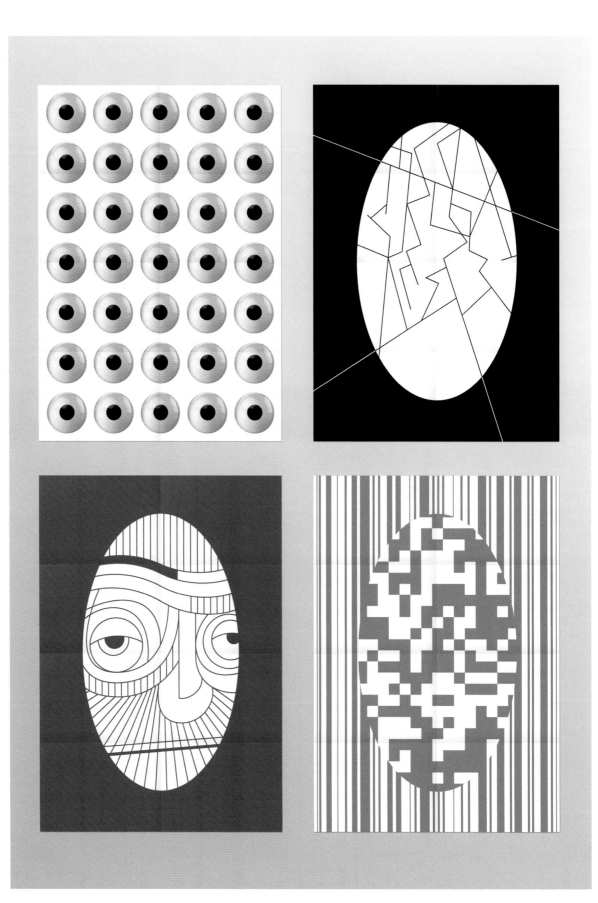

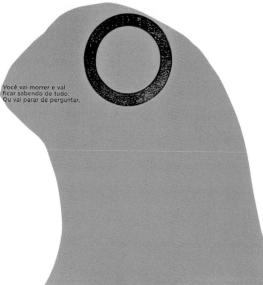

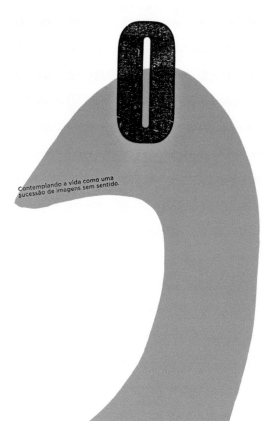

Pássaros

[Poster Illustration]

Designed for a vegan cultural event, the poster series stages highly simplified bird motifs. Their silhouette-like shapes are colour silkscreen prints; "eyes" and "beaks" were printed on top using letter-press. The animal characters are to attract observers while at the same time unsettling them with their ambiguity. A special intensity is attained by concentrating on the essential. Especially the almost painterly quality of the printed letter "O", for which wooden letterpress clichés were used, has been implemented in a striking way.

Client
Move Institute, São Paulo

Design
Casa Rex, São Paulo

Art Direction/Graphic Design
Gustavo Piqueira

#addyourcharacter

[Portraits & Caricatures]

This series of illustrations was created
to attract new staff for an advertising
agency. The basic idea of the campaign
was that job seekers are not only interested in their salary, their position or
major clients of a potential employer,
but most of all in their future colleagues.
Accordingly, the agency posted an illustration on Instagram every day, introducing a different staff member each
time. The entertaining portraits proved
to be very popular and properly fulfil
their purpose of conveying a pleasant
working atmosphere.

Client
deepblue networks AG, Hamburg

Design
deepblue networks AG, Hamburg

Creative Direction
Burkhard Müller, Oliver Drost

Artwork
Benedikt Bockshecker

Text
Stefan Anlauf

Motion Design
Thea Oppermann

Music/Sound Design
German Wahnsinn, Hamburg

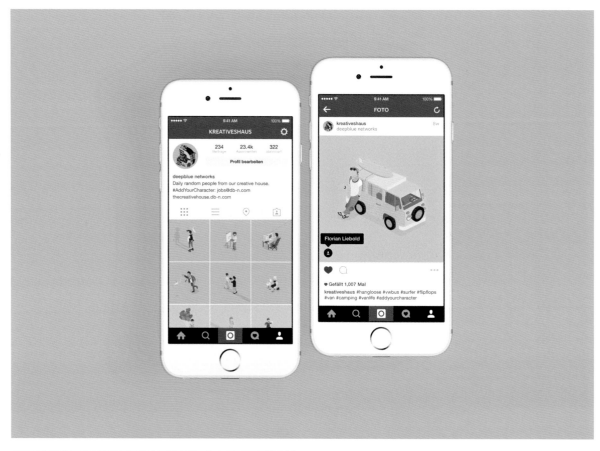

DFB Lap of Honour

[Illustration]

After Germany had won the FIFA World Cup in 2014, the German Football Association celebrated the victory with a tour of Germany called "Lap of Honour". The microsite accompanying the event featured a low-poly style of hexagons inspired by the pattern on the football. On the website, visitors were encouraged to create an individual vehicle choosing from two million variations in order to follow the world cup trophy on a digital fan parade. Thus, a virtual papercraft world, which had a clean but playful look, mutated into a lively experience.

Client
Deutscher Fußball-Bund e.V. (DFB), Frankfurt/Main

Design
Jung von Matt AG, Hamburg

Creative Direction
Fabian Roser, Michael Jonas

Art Direction
Boris Lisdat

Graphic Design
Robert Menzel

Concept
Karim Chughtai

Account Management
Markus Fuchtmann

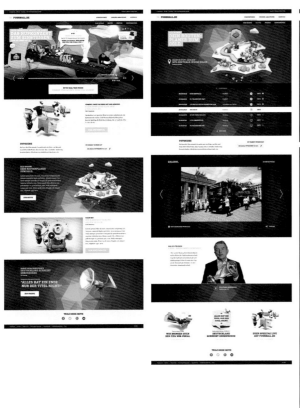
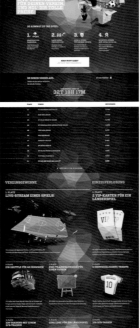
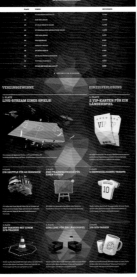

SOCIAL RESPONSIBILITY

Red Dot: Best of the Best

WhatsGerman

[Language-Learning App]

The WhatsGerman campaign aims at helping refugees arriving in Germany and who usually have to wait for an average of three months to take a German course, to learn the German language easier. The idea is based on the observation that the smartphone and the WhatsApp software are the most important tools for refugees to keep in contact among themselves and with people they had to leave behind. The ubiquitous use of smartphones and messengers thus inspired the development of the language course "WhatsGerman. Learning German on WhatsApp". Registering for the course is easy via the dedicated website, which gives visitors a choice between three courses that build upon each other. These courses were developed for WhatsApp together with language teachers. The lessons comprise text, emojis for illustration as well as videos demonstrating correct pronunciation. This offer was promoted using social media channels, postings in refugee accommodations and traditional PR.

Statement by the jury

WhatsGerman is a neat, straightforward and simple idea to provide refugees with what they need most, offering them the possibility and an easy access to learning basic German language skills. Alongside offering immediate help in language acquisition, WhatsGerman also conveys the positive message that these people are welcome and that Germany is in the process of finding solutions to help these people quickly and unbureaucratically.

Client
Plan.Net, Munich

Design
Plan.Net/Serviceplan, Munich

Chief Creative Officer
Alexander Schill (Global CCO),
Markus Maczey (CCO Plan.Net)

Executive Creative Direction
Michael Reill

Creative Direction
Bernd Nagenrauft

Art Direction
Andrea Prade

Copywriting
Friederike Fröhlich, Kathrin Vogl

→ Designer portrait on page 517

Maastrichtse Decolletés

[Fundraising Campaign]

The Cancer Research Fund Limburg initiated the campaign in 2015 in order to raise money for scientific research and new cancer treatments. It focused on breast cancer as the most common form of cancer. Shopkeepers were encouraged to support the project with special offers. The graphic realisation of the emotionally charged topic was based on tongue-in-cheek imagery: on posters, shop displays and Facebook pages, the advertised product appeared twice, thus forming a décolleté – a subtle yet instantly comprehensible reference to the goal of fundraising.

Client
Kankeronderzoekfonds Limburg, Maastricht

Design
Zuiderlicht, Maastricht

Concept
Peggy van Sebillen, Eline Dekker, Krista Lahaye, Bert van der Veur

Graphic Design
Bert van der Veur

Project Management
Krista Lahaye

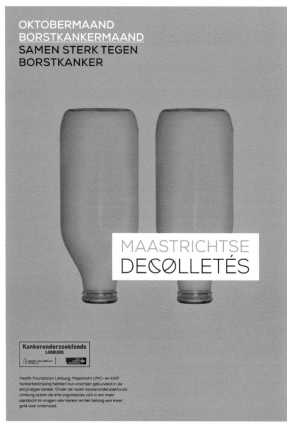

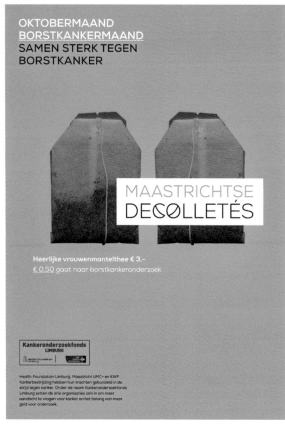

SHARE THE STORY | DONATION BASKET €0 | ATION BASKET €0

DONATE AND LET THE TRANSFORMATION BEGIN.

↓

New Baraka – Building a Home with 30,000 People

[Website]

Commissioned by an aid organisation, the microsite seeks to raise support for 30,000 slum inhabitants in Senegal's capital Dakar. The design skilfully uses storytelling: happy images, which appear like animated illustrations, as well as attentively developed audio and movement effects seek to convey the positive energy of everyone involved. Due to the site's clear structure, visitors can easily understand the project and then donate via mouse-click for building new houses or educational and care facilities.

Client
YOU Stiftung – Bildung für Kinder in Not, Düsseldorf

Design
denkwerk gmbh, Cologne

FoREST IN PEACE

[Branding]

In April 2014, the Korean ferry MV Sewol capsized in the Yellow Sea. 304 passengers, many of them high school students, were killed. After the disaster, a crowd-funding for a memorial forest was launched. Its catchy title contained both the object of the campaign and a blessing for the dead. The campaign's visual signet was a map which effectively combined the place of the catastrophe with the location of the planned forest project. The project achieved twice the funding goal, and a forest of extremely long-living ginkgo trees could be planted.

Client
Tree Planet, Seoul

Design
inspire/d, Seoul

Chief Executive Direction
Hyungsoo Kim, Tree Planet

Project Production
Sean Hepburn Ferrer, Honorary Chair of Audrey Hepburn Society, Florence

Project Direction
Mincheol Jeong, Tree Planet

Business Strategy Direction
Jaehyun Kim, Crevisse Partners, Seoul

Creative Direction/Brand Naming
Dongmin Kim, inspire/d

Art Direction
Boyoung Kim, inspire/d

Brand Design
Boyoung Kim, Yerim Kim, inspire/d

Project Planning
Hanna Lee, Tree Planet

Project Management
Jaeeun Lee, Tree Planet

Architecture
Sooin Yang, LIFETHINGS, Seoul

Photography
Jungwon Park, Studio ist, Seoul

Film Direction
Youngjin Jang, Vision Statement, Seoul

The 2 Euro T-Shirt – A Social Experiment

[Social Activation]

Would people still buy a 2-euro T-shirt if they knew how it was made? To answer this question, a T-shirt vending machine was built – but instead of simply dispensing a T-shirt, customers were prompted with a video showing under which miserable working conditions the T-shirt was produced. After watching the video, customers could choose whether they actually wanted to buy the T-shirt or donate the money instead. An overwhelming 90 per cent of the people using the vending machine decided to donate the money to the Fashion Revolution cause, rather than buy the 2-euro T-shirt – which sparked a discussion on social media. Reaching far beyond that single vending machine, a documentation of the experiment spawned more than 7.5 million online views, 250,000 social media shares and 440 million media impressions.

Client
Fashion Revolution, Berlin

Design
BBDO Berlin

Chief Creative Officer
Wolfgang Schneider

Executive Creative Direction
Jan Harbeck, Michael Schachtner

Art Direction/Script
Jessica Witt, Michail Paderin

Production
UNIT9, Berlin

→ Designer portrait on page 487

BETTER RE

[Branding]

Client
ENLIGHTEN, Seoul

Design
inspire/d, Seoul

Chief Executive Direction
Kiyong Shin, ENLIGHTEN

Business Strategy Direction
Jaehyun Kim, Crevisse Partners, Seoul

Creative Direction/Brand Naming
Dongmin Kim, inspire/d

Art Direction
Boyoung Kim, inspire/d

Brand Design
Boyoung Kim, Yerim Kim, inspire/d

Product Design
Kiyong Shin, Jeongsik Kim, ENLIGHTEN

Web UI/UX Planning
Jungyeon Sung, ENLIGHTEN

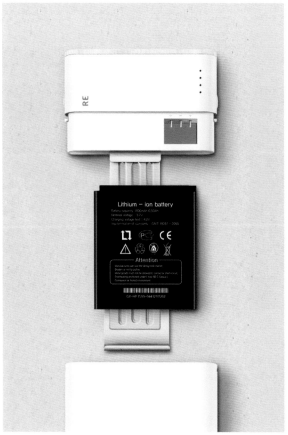

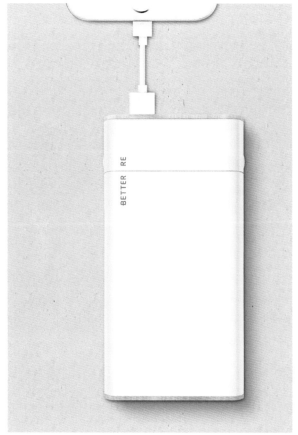

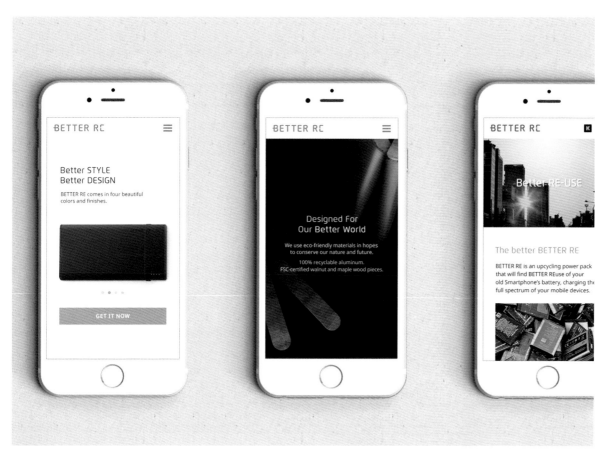

BETTER RE is a power pack that charges digital devices with upcycled smartphone batteries. The brand name plays with the pronunciation of "battery", the aim to be "better" and the abbreviation "re" standing for "recreating a better world". The typography of the logo also corresponds to the recycling concept: the second horizontal bar in the white letter "B" sticks out leftward, against the direction of reading, so that it appears as if it would fit into the grey indent of the letter "E" on the right. Thus, visually a circle is completed, which symbolises the sustainable approach of the brand.

DESIGNER PORTRAITS

A Green Hill
Raymond Kar Kit Tam
— Change is good, if it's for the better.

Red Dot: Best of the Best
→ Posters: page 426–427

Born in Hong Kong, Raymond Kar Kit Tam graduated in communication design from DesignFirst in 1991. This was soon followed by a succession of career milestones with Eric Chan Design Co. Ltd., Bates Graphix, BBDO and Ogilvy One. In 2009, Raymond Kar Kit Tam used his experience and talent to establish the small creative studio A Green Hill, working with a range of clients on integrated projects, stretching from brand identity to marketing campaign. Over the years, he has gained numerous awards, which include Red Dot, One Show, Graphis Competitions (Platinum Awards), HKDA Global Design Awards, and has had the honour of having his works selected in the Asia-Pacific Design Annual.

What is the best moment during a project phase?
When the client says yes to our proposal.

How do you attract attention?
Show people what they want to see, hear and know.

Is there a designer you would like to meet personally?
Stefan Sagmeister. I like his sense of humour, and I would like to find out more about his idea of "the power of time off".

What is your personal key to success?
My personal key to success is "WHY". Be curious, keep asking.

What are the main challenges you have to overcome in your work life?
Technology. It changes everything in the creative industry, every day.

Adhock Studio
Kasidist Sokantat
– If you do it right, it will last forever.
(Massimo Vignelli)

Red Dot: Best of the Best

Red Dot

Kasidist Sokantat graduated with a Bachelor of Communication Arts in advertising from Chulalongkorn University, Bangkok. He worked as graphic designer for TBWA\Thailand and J. Walter Thompson in Thailand for almost ten years. In 2011, he founded Adhock Studio, a multidisciplinary design studio, creating packaging design, branding, corporate identities and communication design with his dedication and motivation to improve the brands and businesses. The studio's clients include Kimberly-Clark, Unilever, Diageo, Beiersdorf, Danone, CIMB and many more.

What is the best moment during a project phase?
When the design is presented to the client and I can see the genuine appreciation of my work. From then on if the design ends up being used and leads to an increase in sales, then I know it was able to attract the consumers as well, which is an added bonus.

How do you convince clients?
Developing a great relationship with my clients is the key. I try to identify what problems they might have had in the past to see where to go from there.

Is there a designer you would like to meet personally?
I'm keeping up with Ken Lo from BLOW Hong Kong on Behance where all his works are published. He perfectly combines vivid colours with geometric shapes to create common objects.

What is your personal key to success?
Keep doing. Fail at it. Try again. Do better the second time.

allink
— A great brand needs a great story.

Red Dot
→ Brand Design: page 82–83

allink is one of the leading Swiss web and branding agencies. Since 2005, the team has been constantly growing while working with a broad range of clients: from traditional SMEs and thriving start-ups to some of Switzerland's largest companies in the retail market. The agency's approach is based on creating a unique brand story that reflects the very essence of a company, its values, beliefs and visions. During the design process, this brand story serves as a guideline, influencing both appearance and content of the brand. In this way, allink has helped an important number of clients to shape their brand identity and gain success in their respective markets.

What is the best moment during a project phase?
Usually, this moment happens a year after finishing a project: it's when we notice that our design has proved itself in everyday life, that our strategy is working well and that our creative output has been a success for the client.

How do you convince clients?
We know how to translate complex corporate strategies into strong, simple brand stories. To many of our clients, this process is an eye-opener as it helps them to sharpen their brand by focusing on their true strengths.

What are the main challenges you have to overcome in your work life?
The Internet has made it possible for design trends to spread like wildfire: every idea is immediately accessible worldwide. This is inspirational, but it can also be an obstacle in finding distinctive approaches.

APPEL NOWITZKI
Anne Julia Nowitzki, Ulf Appel
— Good design is good business.
(Thomas J. Watson, Jr.)

Red Dot
→ Publishing & Print Media: page 346
→ Publishing & Print Media: page 416

APPEL NOWITZKI is a Frankfurt-based office for strategic design and intelligent brand communication. Since 2013, the agency has been using a combination of strategy and design to help brands and companies to establish their identity or to develop it further and then to communicate it strongly. Empathy, appraisal, honesty and self-reflection are important values that the team foster in order to be successful and to delight people.

How do you attract attention?
Think big, sex sells and shout loud. This doesn't sound very intellectual, but unfortunately it works. It is not, of course, always the right thing to do. Sometimes a particular target group requires just the opposite for it to be a success. That's why we treat each case individually.

Is there a designer you would like to meet personally?
Anton Stankowski was a fantastic designer. He understood how to create highly concentrated symbols that became and remain timeless. A great role model!

What makes somebody a good designer?
A good designer is very sensitive – the ability to put himself or herself in someone else's shoes and broaden horizons.

What is your personal key to success?
Love what you do and do what you love. And learn to love what needs to be done.

Aune Creative
Helena Masalin
– No one can hit their target
with their eyes closed.
(Paulo Coelho)

Red Dot: Best of the Best
→ Packaging Design: page 112–113

Helena Masalin studied graphic design from 2004 to 2007 at the Pekka Halonen Academy in Finland during which, in 2006, she carried out an internship in Essedicom design agency in Florence. After graduation, she was a designer at TBWA\Helsinki from 2007 to 2009. In 2010, she lived for one year in Melbourne and worked as a designer for Optimo Designs agency. Moving back to Finland in 2011, she was inspired to set up her own company, now known as Aune Creative. For the last six years, Helena Masalin's clients have been both renowned, established Finnish brands as well as smaller, new companies.

What makes someone a good designer?
Being conscious about the environmental effects of design. There are choices that even graphic designers can make that have an effect. Mastering the art of listening and understanding the customer's needs, keeping in mind through out the process what you are doing and why.

Is there a designer you would like to meet personally?
Dieter Rams. Because he has always strived for things to be sustainable. And that 50 years ago!

What is your personal key to success?
Grit. Persistence. Never giving up.

What are the main challenges you have to overcome in your work life?
Leaving a so-called "safe job" and going on my own and therefore being my own toughest critic.

BBDO Berlin
Michael Schachtner,
Jessica Witt, Michail Paderin
— Simply having an idea isn't enough.

Red Dot: Grand Prix
→ Advertising: page 266–267

Red Dot
→ Social Responsibility: page 477

Michael Schachtner began his advertising career as an art director at Saatchi & Saatchi New York, where he won in his first year at Cannes Lions for Procter & Gamble's Tide. Other influential stops in his career were Y&R New York and BBH New York. Currently, he serves as executive creative director at BBDO Berlin.

Jessica Witt graduated from University of Western Australia with a degree in design communication and creative advertising. She began her career with an internship at BBDO Berlin and was hired soon after as an art director.

Michail Paderin, born in 1986, studied communication design at the University of Applied Sciences in Berlin and worked at DDB Tribal Berlin as a student assistant. After his graduation he started at BBDO Berlin.

What makes somebody a good designer?
Besides ambition, passion and talent, a good designer has the ability to observe, take note about problems and most importantly find a solution for them.

Is there a designer you would like to meet personally?
To meet George Lois would definitely be a highlight. Great work, great view on the world, and he has some great advice.

What is your personal key to success?
Don't take yourself too serious, surround yourself with great people from all creative fields and stay hungry.

BBDO Berlin
Samuel Weiß, Felix Boeck
— Moin, Moin!

Red Dot: Best of the Best
→ Advertising: page 274–275

Felix Boeck was born in Lüneburg in 1985 and studied graphic design at the Alsterdamm School of Visual Arts in Hamburg, whilst, at the same time, working as a 3D operator and creative retoucher in the Hamburg-based post-production alphadog. Subsequently, he moved to the agency Leagas Delaney as art director. There, he got to know his text partner Samuel Weiß, with whom he moved to BBDO Berlin in 2014. Since then, they have been responsible for smart.

What makes somebody a good designer?
The same skills as those of a good cabinetmaker: ambition, sweat, talent, dexterity and skin that can take a splinter or two.

What is the best moment during a project phase?
Definitely, the beginning and the end. By that, we mean the time when one sets off free and without any inhibitions; and the moment when despite the adversities you have somehow managed to cross the finishing line.

How do you convince clients?
By being completely convinced about an idea oneself. And if that is not the case with a smart haircut and a deep voice.

Is there a designer you would like to meet personally?
The manic British YouTuber and innovator Colin Furze. He's not a big name in the design world in the accepted sense of the word, but the way he transforms and peps up everyday objects is really gaga.

BBDO Berlin
Ricardo Wolff, Angelo Maia, David Missing, Michael Schachtner
– Why not?

Red Dot: Best of the Best
→ Advertising: page 272–273

Ricardo Wolff started his copywriting career at DDB Berlin after graduating from Miami Ad School in 2006. In 2007, he joined AlmapBBDO in Brazil to form the agency's first hybrid team. In 2013, he moved to BBDO Berlin as a creative director.
Angelo Maia, born in 1986, studied graphic design at Universidade Federal de Santa Catarina, Brazil. He worked as an art director in São Paulo at agencies such as Publicis and Moma, before joining BBDO Berlin.
David Missing worked for kempertrautmann (now thjnk) after finishing a course at Texterschmiede Hamburg. Subsequently, he moved to Jung von Matt/Spree, before he started at BBDO Berlin.
Michael Schachtner began his career as an art director at Saatchi & Saatchi New York, where he won in his first year at Cannes Lions for Procter & Gamble's Tide. After stops at Y&R New York and BBH New York, he joined BBDO Berlin serving as executive creative director.

What is the best moment during a project phase?
When the production finally begins and an idea turns into something real.

How do you convince clients?
The more you believe in an idea, the easier it is to sell it.

How do you attract attention?
By being stupid, but in a smart way.

How do you cope with competition?
We don't compete with people, we compete with their ideas.

Beetroot Design Group
– Beets are deadly serious.
(Tom Robbins)

Red Dot

Beetroot Design Group is a Thessaloniki-based communication design office and think tank, which has won many awards. It provides design services and solutions to a global clientele. The agency's creative mission is to uncover, develop and utilise the true essence of a brand, product or service and then develop and expand them so that they become recognised, appreciated and praised across the world. The team's interests vary from philosophy to politics, from ethics to aesthetics, from the personal to social issues. Its approach challenges norms, abolishes restrictions and champions a teamwork spirit. All of this is inspired by three components: skill, ability and proficiency.

What makes somebody a good designer?
Passion, vision and patience. We learn the skills and tools to do the job throughout our career.

What is the best moment during a project phase?
One of the best moments for us is when the implementation of a project begins and we see our idea taking physical form. Then, the excitement continues as we watch the reaction of the customer.

How do you attract attention?
Creativity and hard work always pay off. We strive for new concepts, which promote new ideas and are different. We initiate projects to satisfy our own creative appetite and we devour tons of ink every day.

What is your personal key to success?
Teamwork and companionship is everything.

BEMBEL–WITH–CARE
Benedikt Kuhn
— If you want to reach the source,
you have to swim against the current.

Red Dot
→ Packaging Design: page 143

Benedikt Kuhn, born in 1978, trained as a media designer in Heidelberg and simultaneously went into business as an independent graphic designer. Subsequently, he began to study communication design at Mannheim University of Applied Sciences and, in the course of his degree, created a campaign for his favourite drink, Apfelwein, the German equivalent of cider. The focus of the campaign was a melding of tradition and innovation, which led to the creation of the first Apfelwein in designer cans. This project experienced such immediate success that he founded the company and brand BEMBEL-WITH-CARE in 2007.

What makes somebody a good designer?
Passion, a disposition to experiment, and hard work.

How do you convince customers?
With authenticity.

How do you attract attention?
By deliberately being different.

How do you cope with competition?
Just let them get on with it.

Is there a designer you would like to meet personally?
Banksy. His art is right up my street. His genius keeps surprising me.

What is your personal key to success?
Being true to my principles and the right gut instinct.

BULLET Inc.
Aya Codama
— Rock 'n' Roll (in a positive way).

Red Dot
→ Packaging Design: page 139

Aya Codama was born in Osaka, Japan, in 1983. After studying graphic design at the Department of Design of Tokyo Zokei University, she joined AWATSUJI Design in 2007. In 2013, she left AWATSUJI Design and founded BULLET Inc. in Tokyo. Aya Codama engages in a wide range of graphic design, focusing on packaging design, but also including logo, website and book design projects. During her career, she has won a number of awards including iF Design Award, Red Dot Award, One Show (Gold), D&AD (Graphite) and Cannes Lions (Bronze).

What is the best moment during a project phase?
The moment when I'm struck by an idea that can achieve the objective. The subsequent steps of designing, printing trials, and advertising are there to turn that inspiration into reality.

How do you attract attention?
I think you have to be able to talk in an appealing way to the media and other stakeholders.

What is your personal key to success?
Above all, it is to truly feel good about what I design. What success really means to me is whether other people like my work.

What is your favourite communication project that is not one of your own?
When I was reading a magazine, I came across the striking bottle design of the mineral water Ty Nant. The bottle's shape resembled flowing water, which I found very appealing.

Cheil Germany
Jörn Welle, Roland Rudolf, Martin Wenzlawiak (Bacon Design), Daniel Gumbert
— Downward is the only way forward. (Dominick Cobb)

Red Dot: Best of the Best
→ Packaging Design: page 104–105

Jörn Welle, Roland Rudolf, Martin Wenzlawiak and Daniel Gumbert were born into a digital world. They therefore consider this technology to be something all-encompassing that can be used as a raw material to inform their creative work and produce networks: branded interactions that move products and brands, but above all people. Their clients include Samsung, Lufthansa, Deutsche Bahn, Deutsche Bank, paydirekt, Deutsche Telekom, Hankook, Jägermeister and many more.

What is the best moment during a project phase?
When everything comes together and one has this strange tingling sensation that the concept might really work.

How do you convince clients?
By listening, asking questions, with honesty.

How do you attract attention?
In design just like in daily life, surprisingly often through reticence.

Is there a designer you would like to meet personally?
Dieter Rams. Because there is a relatively big chance that we might run into him while shopping in the neighbourhood of our office.

What are the main challenges you have to overcome in your work life?
Achieving a consensus, living with it – and still not producing a result that ends up being mediocre.

Coreana Cosmetics Design Lab
— Art through nature.

Red Dot
→ Packaging Design: page 225

Coreana Cosmetics Co., Ltd. is one of the leading cosmetics companies in South Korea. It has been engaged in the manufacturing and distribution of natural cosmetics for over 28 years with the aim of creating beautiful products with nature's own ingredients. The company has a big dream, which is to share beauty and happiness with customers all over the world based on the motto of "Art through nature".

How do you attract attention?
Cosmetics are delighting consumer goods. We provide exceptional benefit to people and attract their attention by a delicate design form.

What is your personal key to success?
Above all, we always concentrate on a close contact with customers and ensuring there is a storytelling aspect to our design. In addition, we try to reflect our brand philosophy in the design.

What are the main challenges you have to overcome in your work life?
Communication skills, in other words, persuasive power is one of the most important aspects of competitiveness. A designer's ability to make unique product planning and implement the chosen plan is a key to creating a successful design product. A good product reflects the basic idea. Market analysis, brainstorming and convincing setting of direction are the basis of competitive design skill. The challenge is to maintain credible design skill and teamwork all the time.

Depot WPF
— In addition to being prominent, the project should create happiness.

Red Dot: Best of the Best
→ Brand Design: page 54–55
→ Brand Design: page 56–57

Red Dot
→ Packaging Design: page 192
→ Packaging Design: page 197

Depot WPF was founded in 1998 and has grown from a small packaging design studio turned to a 360-degree branding agency providing all possible branding services from market analysis to pre-press. It has more than 3,000 successful projects to its name, won prizes at most of the international awards (including Red Dot, Cannes Lions, One Show, Epica, Eurobest, etc.) and holds the first place in the branding category of the Russian creativity rating. It can boast a team of top specialists and supports the GLBA international branding alliance.

What makes somebody a good designer?
It's experience combined with creativity, curiosity and attention to detail.

What is the best moment during a project phase?
When you see your design on the shelves of a supermarket or in the city streets.

How do you cope with competition?
Working on any project, we try to exceed expectations, to do more or to do something else compared to what our competitors do. When we see that others are starting to copy our approach, we invent something new. That is how the industry develops.

What is your personal key to success?
There's no secret formula: everyone just needs to do his/her work a little better than the day before. Add a bit of magic to it – and there's the success!

Depot WPF
Alexey Andreev
— Come on! Go on! Move on!

Red Dot: Best of the Best

Red Dot

Alexey Andreev has been in the advertising industry since 1993. In 1998, he founded Depot WPF, which soon became one of the leading players in the branding industry in Russia. In 2009, he initiated the creation of the Russian Brand Consultancies Association and became its co-president. In addition, he is also an acting member of the Russian Academy of Advertising and the vice president of the Russian Association of Communication Agencies. He is furthermore curator and lecturer at the High School of Branding based in Moscow.

How do you attract attention?
We strongly believe that only great projects can attract attention to a branding agency. We understand that we are on the right path if we publish a project and find it both in the leading design or creative magazines and in the most authoritative business newspapers.

How do you convince clients?
Our guiding principle is personal responsibility. We offer solutions for which we have to be responsible, because we know how much mistakes can cost.

What are the main challenges you have to overcome in your work life?
Clients, for example, who try to rule the agency and invent the solution themselves, only using the agency as their hands. I just wonder: why do they hire one of the leading agencies in the country if they are certain they can do everything themselves? Thank God, the Russian market is developing rapidly and there are fewer and fewer such clients.

Feuerring GmbH
Beate Hoyer, Andreas Reichlin
— Surround yourself with beautiful
and authentic things whilst remaining
simple and true to yourself.

Red Dot: Best of the Best
→ Publishing & Print Media: page 342–343

Andreas Reichlin was born in Zug, Switzerland, in 1968. He carried out an apprenticeship as a wood sculptor and, besides other qualifications, studied at Lucerne University of Applied Sciences and Arts and the Académie de la Grande Chaumière in Paris. He has undertaken various study trips, participates in numerous exhibitions and his work can be seen in public areas. He runs an artist's studio in Immensee, Switzerland, and, together with Beate Hoyer, founded and runs the company Feuerring GmbH.
Beate Hoyer, born in Düsseldorf in 1965, is a specialist in international business. She founded the cultural association beflügelt in Immensee, graduated with a Bachelor of Science in applied psychology and is co-founder and director of the company Feuerring GmbH.

What is the best moment during a project phase?
When you see the implementation of the original idea for the first time and it exceeds your expectations. If the result is something new, then that is perfect!

What is your personal key to success?
Personal authenticity, a respectful attitude to people and sustainable thinking.

What are the main challenges you have to overcome in your work life?
We consider problems as a chance in as much that we move forward by tackling them.

Grey Germany/
KW43 Branddesign
Maruri Grey
— Only effective design is good design.

Red Dot: Grand Prix

→ Corporate Design: page 22–23

KW43 Branddesign is the corporate identity and corporate design specialist of the Grey group and a recognised expert for strategic brand design within Grey's interdisciplinary and holistic offer. As part of the international Grey network, Maruri Grey is established at the customer site in Ecuador and rates among the most awarded agencies in Latin America. By implementing an international cooperation of the two agencies, they succeeded to link German branding expertise with regional creativity and cultural insight.

What makes somebody a good designer?
A good designer has a definitive vision of how his work can change the perception of a defined target group – and a true interest in doing so.

How do you convince clients?
With in-depth knowledge of their individual situation, honest interest in their problem and rigorous dedication to the project.

How do you attract attention?
With a consistent track record in winning national awards, diligent PR work and a strong local presence.

How do you cope with competition?
The better the competition, the more it inspires and motivates us to improve.

What is your personal key to success?
Don't ever feel successful.

Sichuan Guge Dynasty Brand Design Consultant Co., Ltd.
Xia Ke
— Being original is the only real way.

Red Dot: Best of the Best

Red Dot

Xia Ke, the founder of Sichuan Guge Dynasty Brand Design Consultant Co., Ltd., won a Gold Award in the Pentawards 2015 worldwide packaging design competition, as the first Chinese Gold winner in the field of food. He has been rated as one of the top ten marketing experts of the Chinese food industry and is the executive director of China Packaging Federation, the chairman of the brand design and promotion branch of Sichuan Chamber of Commerce and a VIP artist of Artron Artist Net. Engaged in the industry for 20 years, he has made the development of almost one thousand brands and companies possible.

What is the best moment during a project phase?
It is the moment originality generates a unique idea, and the spirited conflict between different inspirations.

How do you attract attention?
I have been working in the industry for 20 years and have been focusing on one thing only. Persistence pays.

What are the main challenges you have to overcome in your work life?
It is to combine traditional Chinese culture with modern design, in a way that can be recognised by the market and fellow professional designers.

Which sectors or industries would you like to explore further in future?
I'd like to explore professional inventions and create a new industry.

Hang Hai, Meng Jie

Red Dot
→ Publishing & Print Media: page 378–379

Hang Hai, born in 1965, received his PhD in 2011. Currently, he is professor at the graphic design department in the School of Design of the China Central Academy of Fine Arts and also the deputy director of the art research centre for the Olympic Games. From 2004 to 2008, he worked for the Beijing Olympic & Paralympic Games and, from 2009 to 2011, for the Shenzhen 26th Summer Universiade as the creative director of the whole corporate identity including the medals and the wayfinding system.

Meng Jie, born in 1984, received her bachelor's degree from the digital media department in the School of Design of the China Central Academy of Fine Arts. She participated in the design of kit of parts, the image and look and the official poster for the Beijing 2008 Olympic Games and also in the design work for the Shenzhen 26th Summer Universiade. Since 2012, she has been a freelance designer.

What is your personal key to success?
We think it largely depends on chance. Besides, what is important is that, in our work, we devote all ourselves to doing what interests us and concentrate on perfecting all the details. We are never over-concerned about the result.

Is there a designer you would like to meet personally?
Dieter Rams. Because his designs have become not only classics, but also inspired the most extraordinary product design in this era. His ten principles of good design transcend time.

Jianping He
— Without hands-on practice,
design makes no sense.

Red Dot

Jianping He, born in China in 1973, works as a graphic designer, professor and publisher in Berlin. He studied graphic design at the China Academy of Art and fine arts at the Berlin University of the Arts and gained his PhD in cultural history at Free University of Berlin in 2011. He has been teaching at Berlin University of the Arts, as a guest professor at Hong Kong Polytechnic University and China Academy of Art. In 2002, he established his own design studio and publishing house, hesign, based in Berlin with a branch in Hangzhou. His works have won many international awards and are collected by numerous museums across the world. In addition, Jianping He acts as a judge at international design competitions and is a member of the Alliance Graphique Internationale.

What makes somebody a good designer?
Our personal determination and love for design.

What is the best moment during a project phase?
When I get creative ideas.

How do you cope with competition?
On the road of design, my biggest competitor is myself.

What is your favourite communication project that is not one of your own?
Recently, I noticed Michael Bierut's brand reconstruction project for MasterCard, and I greatly appreciate his design proposition.

Hoora Design
Huang-Yu Xu, Jing-Hui Wang
– Grasp the future!

Red Dot
→ Packaging Design: page 202

Hoora Design was established in 2008. With highly skilled designers, the studio offers customers various solution approaches and seeks to establish products by taking a fresh view. With the help of sensible marketing and rational measures, Hoora Design assists its clients in promptly adapting to market needs. By mastering future trends, the studio manages to create the biggest value for its clients. The origins for its design concepts come from the community in which it works and are based on natural trends which the studio magnifies. Leaving commercial and profit-related considerations aside, Hoora Design believes design itself to have a significant effect on people.

What makes somebody a good designer?
Being a good designer is being willing to see things from different angles. He or she must be objective and ignore the personal viewpoint. Every little detail can motivate creative thinking.

What is the best moment during a project phase?
The exploration stage is the best moment during the project phase. At this stage, we must search for information and gather data. It is the moment when we can see new things. This helps to think and see things differently.

How do you attract attention?
We have never thought about attracting other people's attention. The things we do demonstrate our good work ethic. We try our best to complete every project.

innisfree Design Team
Sunny Na
— Deliver healthy beauty acquired from nature's wisdom and embrace the consumer's willingness to conserve nature.

Red Dot: Best of the Best
→ Packaging Design: page 116–117

Sunny Na earned a master's degree in fashion styling at Istituto Marangoni in Milan and a bachelor's degree in fine arts at Ewha Womans University in South Korea. She is a product designer at innisfree, a Korean cosmetics brand only working with natural substances. The brand name "innisfree" means "an island that relaxes the skin". The aim is to provide healthy beauty for customers by using the natural benefits offered by the pure Jeju Island and to actualise an eco-friendly, green lifestyle that treats nature with respect.

How do you convince customers?
I focus on not only design itself, but also how to get across the concept of a product and its feature.

How do you attract attention?
I try to promote the authenticity of the brand with an outstanding product design concept.

How do you cope with competition?
I try to go deeper into the identity of our brand.

Is there a designer you would like to meet personally?
Alessandro Mendini. He is definitely my role model in design, because he works actively at his job regardless of whether the field is architecture or product design.

What is your personal key to success?
Designing what I want to do, not what I have to do.

Jäger & Jäger
Regina Jäger, Olaf Jäger
– The best is still to come.

Jäger & Jäger is an agency for brand identity and corporate communication. It was founded in 1997 by Regina Jäger and Olaf Jäger and since then has been serving companies and cultural institutions in Germany and abroad. In 2013, it was named European Design Agency of the Year.

Red Dot: Best of the Best
→ Annual Reports: page 302–303

Red Dot
→ Publishing & Print Media: page 382

What makes somebody a good designer?
The right combination of intellect, gut feeling and the determination to find the right solution for every project.

What is the best moment during a project phase?
When the fundamental idea has been developed out of the concept phase.

How do you attract attention?
By beating the drum. Honestly, making some noise is important; but such things are not always productive. Therefore, the way to draw attention must be appropriate to the brand. Attention can also be quiet, for example by creating subtle differences. This method normally lasts longer.

How do you cope with competition?
Attentively and calmly.

Is there a designer you would like to meet personally?
Somebody in whom personality, humanity and work are all attractive to the same degree. Kurt Weidemann was such a person. Conversations with him always helped us to move on.

KMS TEAM
— Strength resides in quality.

Red Dot

KMS TEAM is an international leading company specialising in brand strategy, design and communication. Founded by Knut Maierhofer in 1984, the award-winning brand agency today employs around 70 brand experts in the areas of strategy, branding, communications and interactive and since then has been a successful partner to brands, companies and people around the world. The basis for its way of thinking and working is "Tiefendesign" taking all strategic, design and personal aspects of brand development into consideration and linking them in an overarching process. In doing so clients are given a better understanding of their brands – an essential factor in their long-term success.

What makes somebody a good designer?
In addition to talent, there are three important factors: the unrelenting will to create something extraordinary, the courage to pursue new directions and the ability to thoroughly understand the requirements and connections that exist beyond the design.

How do you convince clients?
By inspiring them and by showing the potential of our concept.

How do you cope with competition?
Relaxed – we have seen over 30 years of healthy, continuous growth.

What is your personal key to success?
Persistence and sensibility, creativity and strategic thinking, a willingness to take risks and a sense of being grounded.

Kontrapunkt
Rasmus Lund Mathisen
— There is a typeface for everyone.

Red Dot: Best of the Best
→ Typography: page 444–445

Red Dot
→ Brand Design: page 80

Rasmus Lund Mathisen is today a type designer at Kontrapunkt having previously worked in the Netherlands and Sweden on both graphic and type design. His fascination for typography is evident from his graduation project at the Royal Danish Academy of Fine Arts. It focused on typefaces by sign painters in Copenhagen during the first part of the 20th century and earned him a master's degree. Rasmus Lund Mathisen has worked with a wide range of clients, among others Carlsberg, Novo Nordisk, VOGUE Magazine, the African design magazine OGOJIII, Danish Design Award and Danske Bank.

What makes somebody a good designer?
In the design field where everything changes all the time, trends come and go. You need to stay hungry to maintain your position in the sweet spot. A good designer never stops learning and never stops playing around.

What is the best moment during a project phase?
When the newly sharpened pencil meets the crisp white paper for the first time and the design process begins, that's the best moment.

How do you cope with competition?
Competition is everywhere. It makes everyone better and I gain great inspiration from looking at other designers' work.

What are the main challenges you have to overcome in your work life?
The limited design vocabulary around type design can sometimes be a challenge.

KOREFE
Christian Doering
– Everything that needs an explanation
is not worth the explanation.
(Voltaire)

Red Dot: Best of the Best
→ Packaging Design: page 120–121

Red Dot
→ Brand Design: page 71

Christian Doering has served as creative director and head of design since 2010 at KOREFE, the design and innovation arm of Kolle Rebbe, one of Germany's highly decorated communication agencies. His passion is brand development for, among others, the contemporary art project Maison Blessing or the electronic music scene, working together with record labels including Dial & Laid Records and BPitch Control as well as with the artists Ellen Allien and Pantha Du Prince. He is also a design consultant for the art magazine "Texte zur Kunst", a member of the Art Directors Club Germany and of the German Designer Club.

What makes somebody a good designer?
Design is about having a fantasy.

How do you convince clients?
Clients have to sense my passion to design and to the project.

How do you cope with competition?
You can learn from every designer you meet.

Is there a designer you would like to meet personally?
Yohji Yamamoto, because he is a genius and the master of black elegance.

What is your favourite communication project that is not one of your own?
Karl Lagerfeld's "Chanel Supermarket" at Grand Palais, Paris, 2014.

Lead82
Dániel Németh L., Zalán Péter Salát
— The strongest design element is the fantasy of readers and consumers. What is left out only intensifies what exists.

Red Dot: Best of the Best
→ Publishing & Print Media: page 340–341

Zalán Péter Salát, born in Budapest in 1972, taught himself book design and typography and subsequently learnt the basics of graphic design, photography and image editing as an apprentice with the best masters in the editorial offices of a Hungarian national daily. He founded Lead82, which is an open, creative team of Hungarian graphic designers who work in the spirit of slow design mainly for cultural and museum projects. Aside from art director Zalán Péter Salát, the team consists of Viktor Suszter, art director and graphic artist, and designer Dániel Németh L. Their designs have won international prizes on several occasions, including the German Design Award (Gold).

What makes somebody a good designer?
Less Behance and far more attention to yourself and to what is inside you. Wanting to make the best of yourself.

How do you convince clients?
With our openness and honesty, which are at a level unknown in today's corporate environment.

Is there a designer you would like to meet personally?
Irma Boom's sensitivity is palpable through her designs. If we met, the positive tension would be sensed. It is certain that we would get inspiration from her, which would be lasting. It would be a wonderful opportunity to ask her for advice.

Lenovo Design
— There is no such thing as good enough, everything can and will be made better.

Red Dot: Best of the Best
→ Packaging Design: page 122–123

Lenovo Design is an innovative design group that is made up of members with a variety of professions. In the past three decades, Lenovo Design has been responsible for optimising the product experience of the entire Lenovo product range, uplifting the brand image and providing Lenovo customers excellent, diverse and emotional services. As an important part of Lenovo Design, the Worldwide Brand Design Team includes dedicated designers who specialise in graphic design, photography as well as multimedia.

What makes somebody a good designer?
A good designer must be someone who is passionate about what he does, so that everything he does comes from dedication.

How do you convince customers?
By the use of work that has been created with passion to spark a reaction in people.

How do you attract attention?
By doing the opposite of what everyone else is doing, and by doing what you believe in.

How do you cope with competition?
Use competition as inspiration and motivation to do something better and different.

What is your personal key to success?
Define your own meaning of success, and believe in it.

LOOVVOOL
Hannes Unt
– Attention to detail makes all the difference.

Red Dot
→ Packaging Design: page 256–257

LOOVVOOL is a boutique design agency based in Hong Kong and Zurich, which develops concepts and brands for high-end lifestyle businesses. It was founded in 2004 by creative director Hannes Unt, who began his design career at the early age of 15 in Estonia's leading ad agency Division McCann. He has produced successful design and branding solutions for many clients from all over the world, in various industries including hospitality, yachting, lifestyle, interiors, photography, retail and real estate. LOOVVOOL's works have claimed recognition at international design competitions such as Red Dot Award, HKDA Global Design Awards, World Luxury Award, European Design Awards and REBRAND Awards.

What makes somebody a good designer?
First, you have to be a good listener in order to identify and pinpoint core problems that you're going to solve. You also need to be business savvy to get a better sense of what your client really needs. You always have to be curious. The desire to do great work is paramount.

How do you convince clients?
You have to get on the same wavelength as the client and build trust, otherwise it's not possible to do meaningful work.

What are the main challenges you have to overcome in your work life?
Sometimes the work life can take over your whole life, so one of the main challenges is in finding a good balance and not forgetting about the other important things in life.

MILCH+HONIG designkultur
Christina Sofie John,
Rafael Bernardo Dietzel
— See the world with the heart,
so the eye falls in love.

Red Dot: Grand Prix
→ Publishing & Print Media: page 336–337

Red Dot
→ Publishing & Print Media: page 347

Christina Sofie John is a qualified communication designer. She studied at the Georg Simon Ohm University of Applied Sciences in Nuremberg and, after some time spent in Shanghai and London, worked at Ebmeyer & Ebmeyer and lucie-p in Munich. From 2013 to 2014, she was a lecturer in typography at the University of Applied Sciences in Munich. In 2009, together with Rafael Bernardo Dietzel, she founded the creative agency MILCH+HONIG designkultur. Rafael Bernardo Dietzel is also a qualified communication designer. He studied at the HfG Gmünd and the Royal Academy of Art The Hague. Subsequently, he worked as a designer at the agencies Linientreu and Martin et Karczinski. He was also a lecturer in typography at the University of Applied Sciences in Munich and the HfG Gmünd. Currently, together with Christina Sofie John, he is a director of MILCH+HONIG designkultur.

What makes somebody a good designer?
Reinvent yourself over and over again and surprise people with design and concepts. Have the courage to try something new and now and again upset people with it.

How do you convince clients?
By being enthusiastic ourselves about a project. Key for us is relevant content and surprising design.

What are the main challenges you have to overcome in your work life?
The decision "OK, we'll leave it as it is".

MUTABOR Design
Sven Ritterhoff
— Design is complex – keep it simple.

Red Dot: Best of the Best
→ Corporate Design: page 26–27

Since 2013, Sven Ritterhoff, creative director and associated partner at MUTABOR Design, has been overseeing interdisciplinary design projects for brands such as Audi, VW, MINI, bulthaup, rotring, Deutsche Stimmklinik or Beisser. He began work as a copywriter for BBDO Düsseldorf in 1999, but moved to Leagas Delaney Hamburg in 2000. From 2001 on, he spent two years working for Lo Breier at the P. agency in Hamburg. He has won numerous awards and has been a member of the Art Directors Club since 2013. He is also active in design juries and regularly speaks at design conferences and lectures at various universities.

What makes somebody a good designer?
In addition to all the artisanal and technical skills that are the bedrock of all design work, what characterises a good designer is his or her intuition for an idea. Not everyone is lucky enough to be able repeatedly to seek out a good idea, to translate it for media and to fight for it at all times.

How do you convince clients?
It may sound trivial, but firstly, by listening carefully, then with good work. That's how you create trust: the perfect breeding ground for good design – and good collaboration.

What are the main challenges you have to overcome in your work life?
The main challenge to realising a design in a meaningful way is often a mix of a lack of courage, time, trust and yes, even money.

MUTABOR Design
Carolin Stiller, Barbara Madl
— Better a good horoscope than a bad motto.

Red Dot: Best of the Best
→ Corporate Design: page 24–25

Carolin Stiller graduated in communication design in 2013 and subsequently carried out internships in Munich and Berlin. In 2014, she
started at MUTABOR Design in Hamburg where she is working as a
designer.
Barbara Madl graduated in communication design from U5 Academy
in Munich in 2013. She carried out internships at Serviceplan in
Munich and MUTABOR Design in Hamburg where she is now working
as a senior designer.

What makes somebody a good designer?
Modesty and good intuition.

What is the best moment during a project phase?
The feeling you get when everything is going according to plan and
the lunchtimes.

How do you convince clients?
With perseverance.

How do you cope with competition?
Often competition produces very good stuff and therefore gives you
inspiration and incentive. It encourages you regularly to reflect on
what you are doing and to question things.

**What are the main challenges you have to overcome in your
work life?**
Timid clients.

OUWN
Atsushi Ishiguro

— OUWN goes beyond advertising and explores cutting-edge designs that incorporate art and other media. We are constantly pursuing new designs.

Red Dot
→ Posters: page 434–435

Atsushi Ishiguro worked at MR_DESIGN in Tokyo, an agency headed by Kenjiro Sano. In 2013, he founded his own design company OUWN. His recent works received accolades, for example the Frappuccino 2015 campaign for Starbucks and the NEW FIND campaign for Roppongi Hills, a large-scale Japanese shopping facility. He was the only Japanese participant in the Notebook#2 project, in which up-and-coming designers from various countries took part. In his work, he uses a wide range of creative skills that span art, design and other media.

What makes somebody a good designer?
I think that a good designer is almost like a physician. He works closely with the client to redefine the issues, share information and smoothly bring the process to a solution. A designer should also be someone who constantly gets people smiling.

What is the best moment during a project phase?
That would be when the final product is neither of a greater nor lesser quality than I envisioned, but exactly as intended and it reaches its full potential. Then, when clients and others see it, they smile or are surprised – these expressions of delight are the best for me.

How do you convince clients?
I put much emphasis on detailed conversations with clients and get them to decide after listening to what I've had to say. I like discussion. The works we produce and propose have meaning and ideas behind them, so provided our message is on the mark, it usually will be conveyed to the other party.

Pearlfisher
Karen Welman
– Your brain doesn't know the difference between imagination and reality, therefore imagination can become reality.

Red Dot
→ Packaging Design: page 208

Karen Welman studied design at Epsom School of Art and then went on to learn the real business with Michael Peters Group. She is one of the founding partners of Pearlfisher, an agency that prides itself on creative excellence and still being independent. It has four studios around the world, London, New York, Copenhagen and San Francisco. The agency designs for Challenger & Iconic brands, creating and expressing truth and longing in every brief. Karen Welman has won many awards for her work in international competitions and was also named one of the top ten global female inventors some years ago.

What makes somebody a good designer?
Ideas and attention to detail.

What is the best moment during a project phase?
Coming up with that eureka moment for an idea.

How do you convince clients?
The ideas should sell themselves.

How do you cope with competition?
Don't compete, solve the problems and do what is right for the brand.

Is there a designer you would like to meet personally?
Sir Paul Smith, again and again because he continuously strives for excellence.

Pearlfisher
Wagamama Team
– We're a strategic design agency, building desirable Challenger & Iconic brands.

Red Dot
→ Packaging Design: page 185

Based in London, New York, Copenhagen and San Francisco, Pearlfisher is an independent creative agency that combines a single philosophy and unique structure to bring its collective talent and expertise to every brand. For 25 years, the agency has been forming partnerships with clients all around the world, harnessing change, expressing meaning and making an impact through strategic brand design.

What is the best moment during a project phase?
The moment when ideas start to become real and tangible; when the team and client see mock-ups and concepts coming to life.

How do you convince clients?
By showing and not telling. The right clients don't need convincing of a great idea.

How do you attract attention?
By doing great work that makes a tangible, creative impact and delivers a commercial return on investment. By being true to our principles and working in partnership with our clients.

How do you cope with competition?
By being positive about what competition means. Competition is good – it keeps our energy levels high, our thinking focused and our work fresh, lucid and bold.

What is your personal key to success?
A hunger to be innovative and solve problems.

Plan.Net/Serviceplan
Kathrin Vogl, Andrea Prade, Friederike Fröhlich
– Get shit done!

Red Dot: Best of the Best
→ Social Responsibility: page 472–473

Kathrin Vogl, Andrea Prade and Friederike Fröhlich have been working as a team at Plan.Net Campaign in Munich for around two years. The integration of innovative ideas into their daily work means for them successful digital communication.

What makes somebody a good designer?
Design should not only be good-looking, but should also bring additional benefits.

What is the best moment during a project phase?
When you notice that an idea works and everything falls automatically into place.

How do you attract attention?
Not necessarily by making a lot of noise, but rather by unusual solutions that intrigue people.

How do you cope with competition?
Basically, it doesn't do any harm to look around a bit, but that should inspire you rather than restrict you.

Is there a designer you would like to meet personally?
Jessica Walsh, because she is courageous and unconventional.

What is your personal key to success?
Be relaxed, have fun and don't make things too complicated.

Maria Ponomareva
– Design skill is like a muscle:
keeping it in good shape requires
regular training.

Red Dot
→ Packaging Design: page 216

Maria Ponomareva graduated in visual arts from the Nizhny Novgorod State Pedagogical University and received a degree in visual communication from the British Higher School of Art & Design in Moscow. During her more than ten years of experience in communication design, she has worked in leading Russian branding agencies and currently lives and works in New York as a designer and art director. She has won numerous awards in renowned competitions such as Cannes Lions, Red Dot Award, Golden Drum, Pentawards, Ad Stars and was awarded the title of Student of the Year 2011 by the Art Directors Club Russia.

What makes somebody a good designer?
In addition to all the essential professional skills, a good designer should be socially conscious and morally responsible. Good design should never lend itself to a low-quality product.

What is the best moment during a project phase?
For an FMCG (Fast-Moving Consumer Goods) designer, there's nothing like the feeling of seeing a product you designed on store shelves or in other people's shopping baskets.

How do you attract attention?
I've been fortunate enough to have won a few international awards, which inherently get some notice. Another method is to pitch work to popular design blogs. If all else fails, there's always the old "wear panties on your head to an opening" routine.

Pravda A/S
Vibeke Krag Rasmussen
— Always seek magic.

Red Dot: Best of the Best
→ Annual Reports: page 306–307

Vibeke Krag Rasmussen, born in 1980, studied industrial design at Konstfack in Stockholm and holds a master's degree in architecture from Aarhus School of Architecture. After graduating in 2008, she worked for five years as senior concept designer at Hatch & Bloom. Since 2013, she has developed creative concepts and designs as an art director at the Danish business-to-business agency Pravda. She is also the owner of Will and Wall, an online shop with graphic art prints.

What is the best moment during a project phase?
I actually like the fact that a project has different phases. It challenges my ideas and shapes them for the real world. And I love how working with different projects at the same time makes my job versatile.

How do you convince clients?
I don't! The ideas do. However, it's important to ensure that the clients take ownership of the ideas so that they start to convince themselves.

How do you attract attention?
I'm not a very extrovert character, but when it comes to my work, I kind of put the boldness into it. In other words, I prefer to let my work do the talking.

What are the main challenges you have to overcome in your work life?
Structure. Budgets. Deadlines.

Proad Identity
Jennifer Tsai
— Design needs soul; a brand must have culture; a human being should have style.

Jennifer Tsai, an expert in the field of branding, is founder and president of Proad Identity in Taipei and Shanghai. The agency does work for top companies such as TWTC, Lite-On and NOVA and has won many awards in renowned competitions. Jennifer Tsai is also vice president of the Royal Balibay International Centre, director of the Taiwan Graphic Design Association and a jury member in various international design competitions. In order to provide clients better international competitiveness and services, she and five colleagues from different countries have together created the co-work alliance Global Design Source (GDS).

What makes somebody a good designer?
Keep thinking, keep discovering, and keep doing design.

What is the best moment during a project phase?
When the clients tell me that my designs help them to create branding value.

How do you convince clients?
I tell them: if good design can win awards, then it can also make for good sales.

How do you attract attention?
With elegant design and a convincing viewpoint.

What is your personal key to success?
I don't understand why, but my brain is full of ideas and I know that if I don't keep designing and disseminating ideas, I will explode.

Rong
Li Sun
— Good design is driven by detailed observation of normal daily life.

Li Sun holds a master's degree from Rhode Island School of Design and is currently the design director of the design and consulting company Rong.

What makes somebody a good designer?
A good observer who can reach the core of normal things.

What is the best moment during a project phase?
The moment when you are struggling with the concept, but you know the answer is close.

How do you convince clients?
Put yourself in their shoes.

How do you attract attention?
Speak less, but when you do, only about the essentials.

Is there a designer you would like to meet personally?
The Japanese artist Oki Sato and his brand Nendo. He is the model I look up to.

What is your personal key to success?
Trust your instinct and pursue it with no hesitation.

Rose de Claire, design.
Albert Seyser
— Yesterday is gone. Tomorrow is unknown. What counts, is today.

Red Dot: Best of the Best
→ Publishing & Print Media: page 338–339

Albert Seyser, born in Linz, Austria, in 1956, studied design, theology, philosophy and psychology. After participating in an international scholarship in Brussels, he founded, together with his wife Babeth Neiers, the design agency Rose de Claire in Luxembourg in 1987. The agency shaped the corporate identity of many important Luxembourg institutions and, in 1999, the visual identity of the Luxembourg Government and all its ministries.

What makes somebody a good designer?
Enthusiasm, self-confidence and the willingness to take a risk.

What is the best moment during a project phase?
When everyone involved senses that the project is developing its own momentum.

How do you convince clients?
By openness, creativity and the ability to find a solution.

How do you cope with competition?
When you are happy with yourself, you possess neither envy nor arrogance.

What is your favourite communication project that is not one of your own?
The English King James Bible often found in a hotel room. Its typography and aesthetic properties are outstanding.

Serviceplan
Julius Steffens, Philipp Stute
— Make it happen.

Red Dot: Best of the Best
→ Advertising: page 270–271

Julius Steffens (art) and Philipp Stute (text) are the creative directors of the content section of Serviceplan in Berlin. They have worked together since 2009 and, during this time, have developed campaigns for a variety of clients including the German TV stations ARD and ZDF, the Deutsches Historisches Museum (German Historical Museum) and the Deutscher Anwaltverein (German Bar Association).

What makes somebody a good designer?
He identifies the problem before finding the solution. A good designer does not see his work as an end in itself.

How do you convince clients?
With good ideas and comprehensible arguments. The last time round, a strawberry tart was useful.

How do you cope with competition?
Competition is extremely important to know one's own position. Nothing spurs you on more than a really good campaign that unfortunately was not done by you.

Is there a designer you would like to meet personally?
Kurt Weidemann, if he was still alive. His opinions on typefaces and corporate design still impress us.

What are the main challenges you have to overcome in your work life?
The three fatal blows: it doesn't work, it exists already, I don't like it.

Zi Huai Shen
— To devote myself to create high degree of fabulousness.

Red Dot
→ Brand Design: page 90–91
→ Packaging Design: page 228–229

Zi Huai Shen, born in Taiwan in 1985, graduated from the Department and Graduate School of Visual Communication Design of Kun Shan University and currently is creative director of SUMP DESIGN. Working for clients, including One 2 Tea House, Carrieme, Byozyme, Sugar & Spice and Royal Tea, he has been honoured e.g. with Huacan Award, SHDC 50/100 Cutting-Edge Exhibition 2012, Taiwan Visual Design Award 2010 and Golden Pin Design Award 2009. In addition, many of his works can be seen in design publications such as Brand Issue No. 23, TOP GRAPHIC DESIGN, Outstanding Chinese Character Design Works Invitation Exhibition 2013 and Asia-Pacific Design No. 9 & No. 11.

How do you convince clients?
I utilise the power of strategy and visual skills to persuade my clients.

What is your personal key to success?
I am enthusiastic about design and handle everything with positive action and attitude.

What are the main challenges you have to overcome in your work life?
It is hard to afford much importance to the quality of life since I pay so much attention to my design career. I plan to overcome the conflict between work and private life and would like to devise a perfect time management plan for both my work and daily life.

Skybox Design Agency
Remco Knol
— It is thorough design which truly defines and elevates brands.

Red Dot
→ Packaging Design: page 170–171

From 1990 to 1993, Remco Knol studied photography at the Grafisch Lyceum Amsterdam, followed by design and concept until 1997. Afterwards, he began to work at FHV BBDO, first as a junior designer and then as a designer and design director. Since 2009, he has been creative director at Skybox Design Agency.

What makes somebody a good designer?
A good designer works both pragmatically and thoroughly. He or she should be able to identify with a brand or at least the values of a brand while keeping in mind his or her own perception regarding shape and content.

What is the best moment during a project phase?
The most defining moments are the best, whether we are discussing things within the team to push things to a higher level, or whether we are presenting the project to a client and feel its enthusiasm.

How do you convince clients?
Essential to any project is a common foundation, which we need to be able to start working. Once this is clear for both the client and for us, it allows us to present a persuasive concept. Convincing the client is hardly needed once the starting point is clear.

What is your personal key to success?
An open vision when it comes to clients and a high standard when it comes to the quality of design in general.

Spazio Di Paolo
Mario Di Paolo
– The best ideas are those
which inspire others.

Red Dot: Best of the Best
→ Packaging Design: page 102–103

Red Dot
→ Packaging Design: page 135

Mario Di Paolo, a designer and photographer, is founder and CEO of the communication and marketing company Spazio Di Paolo, which specialises in food and beverage. He has received many awards at prestigious design competitions from across the world for his marketing strategies and for the originality of his packaging designs. Spazio Di Paolo has been recognised as one of the most influential companies within the communication sphere according to the "Who's Who in Wine" guide from the magazine "Civiltà del bere".

How do you convince clients?
My work is characterised by marketing research and knowledge of the product itself. This allows me to create packagings that depict the essence of the product using images, signs and a link to the product's origins. I think that is convincing when my clients start projects with me.

Is there a designer you would like to meet personally?
If I could go back in time, I would definitely like to have met Alvar Aalto because of his functional harmony and his artistic sensitivity.

What is your personal key to success?
The influence I receive from contemporary art. Since I was a child, I have lived in close proximity to some of the greatest contemporary artists in the world. Then as now, I have worked for them.

Strichpunkt Design
Tobias Nusser, Agnetha Wohlert, Christian Schwentke
— The future belongs to the brave.

Red Dot: Best of the Best
→ Annual Reports: page 304–305

Red Dot
→ Typography: page 451

Tobias Nusser studied communication design at HfG Gmünd. Subsequently, he worked for Jung von Matt/Neckar. He moved to Strichpunkt Design in 2007 where, today, he is creative director and manager of the agency's Berlin office.
Agnetha Wohlert studied communication design at the University of Applied Sciences and Arts in Dortmund. Since then, she has been working for Strichpunkt Design in Berlin where, today, she is the head of design in the areas of corporate communication, branding and packaging.
Christian Schwentke studied communication design at HTWG Konstanz and obtained a master's degree in editorial design at Burg Giebichenstein University of Art and Design Halle. In 2015, he started at Strichpunkt Design as junior art director in Berlin.

What makes somebody a good designer?
Empathy. In design, it is always a matter of prompting a reaction from the other person. The ability to interpret ideas and expectations skilfully or consciously to break away from them. You can only do that if you can understand how other people feel.

What is the best moment during a project phase?
When the idea says "hello".

How do you convince clients?
By being very close to our clients right from the start. If you develop ideas in a project and everyone is part of the process, people don't need convincing.

Styleplus Design
— We tend to work with clients who have products and services we use or would use ourselves. (Stefan Sagmeister)

Red Dot
→ Packaging Design: page 161

Styleplus Design is a team based in Taipei, consisting of creatives from various expertise in design and art. Putting great emphasis on solving cultural and societal problems through their creations, they want to "make a difference" and see "style" as the essential "plus". By connecting identity, creativity, marketing, production, digital and aesthetics, the studio offers a total solution for clients and the community.

What makes somebody a good designer?
Open-mindedness and attention to detail.

How do you convince clients?
The best tools to convincing clients are experience and professionalism.

How do you attract attention?
By intelligent and minimalist designs.

How do you cope with competition?
With mutual respect followed by immense amounts of research and analysis.

What is your personal key to success?
The definition of success is to work hard.

What are the main challenges you have to overcome in your work life?
Balancing between logic and feelings.

The SAEM International
— Put sincerity in all things.

The beauty heritage brand "the SAEM" was officially launched in 2011. In 2013, the brand identity was relaunched because of the implementation of the SAEM's new mission of "Global Eco" and a natural and sustainable design. In 2014, the SAEM began to develop the overseas market in earnest and, since then, has been steadily developing and researching its design and new materials that are ecological.

What makes somebody a good designer?
When a designer solves the needs of society by approaching them in a creative way and by having a critical mind and the ability to grasp a trend.

How do you attract attention?
We aim to design in such a way that satisfies our customers' emotional needs. We design a product in accordance with the brand philosophy and in a manner that excites a customer's emotion.

How do you cope with competition?
There comes a moment when a product has no future due to increased competition. We then make the best use of accumulated data to analyse the consumption and market trends and change the whole game by introducing a new product.

Which sectors or industries would you like to explore further in future?
We would like to introduce emotional products from other categories and suggest the business model that leads to their success in the market.

TigerPan Packaging Design Lab.
Tiger Pan
— In me the tiger sniffs the rose.
(Siegfried Sassoon)

Tiger Pan is a passionate and influential product packaging designer in China who designs products with an appealing commercial value. He has won more than 50 design awards in various categories, including Red Dot Award and Pentawards, and is often invited to lecture on and curate within the design world. He has been appointed as visiting professor to several universities in China.

How do you convince clients?
I always openly share my ideas and thoughts with clients to build a consensus in a shared spirit of open dialogue. Communication has to be engaging, authoritative and persuasive.

How do you attract attention?
The theory of attraction comes from differentiation. Our experience tells us not to do the traditional market and customer analysis, nor to analyse the pros and cons of the previous version of a product at an early design stage. These rules may become barriers of innovation and inspiration. Instead, designers should follow their intuition to create a vision reflecting their unique understanding of the product.

Is there a designer you would like to meet personally?
I would love to meet Marc Newson. I would like to discuss with him the difference in aesthetics between East and West and the influence in art and design.

Vetica Group, Taiwan Branch
— Transforming business strategies into brand values through precision and simplicity.

Red Dot: Best of the Best
→ Packaging Design: page 108–109

Vetica's Taiwan Branch is the Swiss group's first base outside their mother country. It was established in the summer of 2006 and is located in the transportation hub and cultural centre of Taipei City. Vetica has witnessed Taiwan's recent economic development and transformation into a global design city. The Taiwan Branch is the Asian operations headquarters with a subsidiary in Hong Kong. The design team is striving to be the best partner for Asian enterprises by providing them with guidance on how to achieve the goal of building global brands and successful products and service solutions.

What makes somebody a good designer?
An open mind and a positive attitude to teamwork spirit with the ability to think ahead.

How do you attract attention?
By active listening and sharing thoughts to achieve the very best result.

How do you cope with competition?
Competition exists. It helps to encourage better thinking and solutions. We are our biggest rival – how to improve and transcend each project.

What is your personal key to success?
Humility, setting high and reachable goals, consistent learning and hard work.

Alexander von Lengerke
— Make challenging contents comprehensible to a wide audience.

Red Dot
→ Publishing & Print Media: page 388

Alexander von Lengerke was born in 1970 and studied practical theology before qualifying as a graphic designer at the Architectural Association School of Architecture in London. Subsequently, he studied graphic and media design at the London College of Communication. He then worked in design agencies in Berlin and Düsseldorf before becoming freelance. Since then, he has lived in Cologne and specialises in the fields of corporate, communication and book design for medium-sized companies in particular charitable organisations.

What makes somebody a good designer?
The ability to make even complex subjects understandable and attractive to all target groups, while at the same time reflecting the true content.

What is the best moment during a project phase?
When the content and the conceptual ideas come together in such a way that they create something big.

Is there a designer you would like to meet personally?
Saul Bass (very much) and Kyle Cooper because of their posters and film-title sequences and Erik Spiekermann because of his typography.

What is your personal key to success?
Well, I'd say it is "1 per cent inspiration and 99 per cent sweat" (Thomas Edison). I started very small and built myself up with patience and perseverance.

WIN CREATING IMAGES
Cathrin Jo Ann Wind, Luc Bütz
— Packaging that makes the world happier.

Red Dot
→ Packaging Design: page 238

Cathrin Jo Ann Wind and Luc Bütz founded the agency in 1997. Under the umbrella of WIN Creating Images, the WIN Group also comprises WINcommunication and WINdesign GmbH and is active in the market as a packaging design agency run by its owners. Its headquarters are in Aachen and it has further offices in Cologne, Munich and Berlin. WIN employs 100 creatives and strategists and offers strategic packaging design, consistent brand management and an exceptional image strength. dm-drogerie markt, Lindt & Sprüngli, Emmi, Merz Consumer Care, Teekanne and Rewe Group are among its portfolio of international clients.

What is the best moment during a project phase?
When goose bumps convinces you that the idea is something special.

How do you convince clients?
In that, the joint projects are successful in the marketplace.

What is your personal key to success?
Only the best designers work for us.

Beijing Yuanlong Yato Culture Dissemination Co., Ltd.
Xin Yue
— Time for space.

Red Dot

Xin Yue, born in China in 1957, studied at the Central Academy of Arts and Design in Beijing. Since 2004, he has been director, vice president and art director of Beijing Yuanlong Yato Culture Dissemination Co., Ltd. Furthermore, he serves as a visiting professor at Tsinghua University Academy of Arts & Design, Central Academy of Fine Arts, Beijing Institute of Fashion Technology and Daejeon University. His major works include visual identification systems for China Mobile, China Post, China Southern Airlines, Beijing Capital Museum and the National Library of China. As part of the eight-member panel responsible for designing the official posters for the Beijing 2008 Olympic Games, Xin Yue was involved in the selection and revision of the posters.

What makes somebody a good designer?
A good designer needs to be talented, work hard, stay focused and be wise.

What is the best moment during a project phase?
When you can design throughout the full lifecycle of a project. The endless possibility that emerges from this process is essential to a design success.

How do you convince clients?
I don't often try to convince them. I hope they are convinced by the design.

How do you attract attention?
If my works attract attention, I hope that the attention is a result of my observations, meditation and expression.

534

Shenzhen Yuto Packaging Technology Co., Ltd.
Chen Ying Song
− Do the right thing, do the best.

Red Dot

Chen Ying Song has been engaged in design for more than ten years and, in his work, aims to interpret the spirit of traditional Chinese culture in a modern visual language. He focuses on visual communication design services, with emphasis on brand strategy and based on the use of visual design to produce a communication between the brand and the consumer. His constantly developing work in packaging design interprets the core values of the products and has won many important international design awards, including iF Design Award, Mobius Awards, WorldStar Awards and Pentawards.

How do you attract attention?
With unusual, creative features and forms of expression. Of course, the idea must be in line with customers' brand culture.

Is there a designer you would like to meet personally?
The Japanese designer Kenya Hara. I like his design, because it is very concise and full of oriental Zen rhythm.

What is your personal key to success?
Focus and never give up. Discover the different creative features and ways to express forms. Naturally, they are based on the understanding of brand culture.

What are the main challenges you have to overcome in your work life?
To accept the challenges of a new industry that we are not familiar with and has never been tried out.

Shenzhen Yuto Packaging Technology Co., Ltd.
Wan Yue Ding
— If you keep walking, how far is the farthest?

Red Dot
→ Packaging Design: page 138

Wan Yue Ding is a packaging designer. Initially, she studied painting and later majored in design. Currently, she works at Shenzhen Yuto Packaging Technology Co., Ltd.

What makes somebody a good designer?
Firstly, a good designer needs to be full of passion, be it for life or work. Secondly, have a pair of eyes that recognise beauty. Finally, possessing rich cultural heritage allows designers better to interpret the work they do.

How do you attract attention?
I like to use rich colours to attract the attention of others.

How do you cope with competition?
In my mind, it is just learning from others rather than competition. There is no fixed reason for success.

Is there a designer you would like to meet personally?
I would really like to meet the Japanese artist Yayoi Kusama.

What are the main challenges you have to overcome in your work life?
Laziness is something I have to overcome.

Which sectors or industries would you like to explore further in future?
The packaging industry was my choice from the very beginning; and also the industry I will continue to explore in the future.

zinnobergruen
Tobias Schwarzer, Bärbel Muhlack
— Good design is good.

Red Dot: Best of the Best
→ Publishing & Print Media: page 344–345

Tobias Schwarzer studied architecture at the University of Applied Sciences Stuttgart and subsequently at the Kunstakademie Düsseldorf. He then worked with diverse design and architecture agencies. Bärbel Muhlack graduated in visual communication from the University of Applied Sciences Düsseldorf and, after that, worked in well-known design agencies where she was responsible for projects ranging from complex corporate designs to books and packaging design. In 2001, Tobias Schwarzer and Bärbel Muhlack founded the design agency zinnobergruen and, since then, have been working for publishing houses, service providers and industrial companies in almost every field of communication activity.

What makes somebody a good designer?
Conceptual strength accompanied by a feeling for good design.

How do you convince clients?
With innovative concepts and by always coming up with new ideas.

How do you attract attention?
Get away from the mainstream and dare to do something new.

What are the main challenges you have to overcome in your work life?
The implementation of an idea – and at the same time to satisfy your own expectations.